GERMAN
MYSTICAL WRITINGS

The German Library: Volume 5

Volkmar Sander, General Editor

GERMAN
MYSTICAL WRITINGS

Edited by Karen J. Campbell

Foreword by Carol Zaleski

CONTINUUM • NEW YORK

1991
The Continuum Publishing Company
370 Lexington Avenue, New York, NY 10017

The German Library
is published in cooperation with Deutsches Haus,
New York University.
This volume has been supported by a grant
from the Marie Baier Foundation.

Printed in the United States of America
Typesetting output: TEXSource, Houston

Library of Congress Cataloging-in-Publication Data
German mystical writings / edited by Karen J. Campbell ; foreword by
Carol Zaleski.
    p.   cm. — (The German library ; v. 5)
    ISBN 0-8264-0347-6. — ISBN 0-8246-0348-4 (pbk.)
    1. Mysticism—Early works to 1800. 2. Religious literature,
German. I. Campbell, Karen J. II. Series
BV5080.G38   1991
248.2'2—dc20   91-15124
                                                            CIP

Acknowledgments will be found on page 269,
which constitutes an extension of the copyright page.

Contents

HEINRICH SEUSE

JOHANNES TAULER

ANONYMOUS

JACOB BOEHME

ANGELUS SILESIUS (JOHANNES SCHEFFLER)

Foreword

The present volume is a timely addition to The German Library. Here the reader will become acquainted with the most remarkable flowering of mystical speculation and expression in the Christian West. Even in translation, the works from which Karen Campbell has made her judicious selection display extraordinary cultural vitality as well as deep insight into the structures and rhythms of spiritual life. The literature represented here has only begun to be fully appreciated in our day; it deserves to be still better known by all who take an interest in religion and culture.

The authors included in this volume are cultural and religious innovators of the first rank, who struggled against the constraints of the language and traditions from which they drew so richly. Some of them came into conflict with religious authorities, and have therefore come to be celebrated as religious rebels in many recent popular writings on mysticism. Yet the German mystics were never merely outsiders; as Karen Campbell indicates in her historical introduction, they were in every way part of the culture and tradition to which they belonged. Their relationship to the norms of Christian orthodoxy, like their relationship to the conventions of German language and literature, was marked by creative tension. It was in their very effort to be profoundly faithful to tradition, and to penetrate to its core, that they produced their most challenging ideas. The reader will therefore discover in these selections many signs of that radical fidelity to which no facile understanding of the mystics as rebels or heretics can do justice.

What does mysticism mean for the Christian tradition? Fundamentally, it means sharing in the life of the Spirit, living out of the graces conferred by baptism, by which the *imago Dei* in human nature is restored. As Hildegard of Bingen puts it, "the One who had created humanity in the divine image and likeness wished to draw us back to God" (p. 15). To be drawn back to God is the vocation of all human beings, not just of an elite group of religious specialists. The desire to return and be reordered by love is implanted in each of us; and if that "holy longing" (to use Hildegard's expression) is suppressed, both the human personality and the human community are bound to suffer fragmentation and discord.

In this sense, the mystical impulse in Christianity is understood to be but a deepening of the ordinary life of faith, as lived within a community of faith, nourished by common prayer and sacraments.

The readings included here present a mystical tradition that is far from being privatistic or quietistic. For Hildegard, the summit of perfection is not a flight of the alone to the Alone, but rather a corporate blessedness, in which "our soul will thereafter be a temple of the Holy Spirit in the community of true faith" (p. 31). For Eckhart, contemplative experience is suited "for those good and perfect persons only, who have so absorbed the essence of virtue that virtue emanates from them without their trying to make it do so" (p. 96); and again, "what we plant in the soil of contemplation we shall reap in the harvest of action" (p. 103). For Tauler, Eckhart's disciple, mysticism is an integrated path of "loving ascent to God" and loving descent to serve humanity (p. 187).

Almost universally, the mystics warn against excessive concern with private experiences, altered states of consciousness, raptures, and visions. Some mystics reject visions altogether, on the premise that the highest stage of contemplative experience transcends all images. Others point out, as a matter of practical discernment, that visionaries are especially vulnerable to being tricked by their own nervous systems or by demonic influences. For a vision or locution to be deemed valid, it must be received as a pure gift, rather than claimed as one's own attainment; and it must bear fruit in a conversion of morals, thus bringing the mystic back into the community of faith.

In his "Talks of Instruction," a series of lessons on discernment delivered to Dominican students, Meister Eckhart cautions, "We ought to get over amusing ourselves with such raptures for the sake of that better love, and to accomplish through loving service what men most need, spiritually, socially, or physically.... if a person were in such a rapturous state as St. Paul once entered, and he knew of a sick man who wanted a cup of soup, it would be far better to withdraw from the rapture for love's sake and serve him who is in need" (p. 79). Here the mystical path is presented as a purification of the will, rather than as an enticement of the spiritual senses. The practical side of this path (one might say, its ordinariness) is evident, too, as Meister Eckhart outlines a way of working in the world, watchful, free from compulsive attachment to the task at hand, always prepared "to find God as much in one thing as in another" (p. 76). From this standpoint, the distance between mysticism and ordinary faith (provided it is a vital faith) seems small.

Yet there is another strain in the Christian literature of Northern Europe, especially since the Reformation, which would contrast the way of the mystics to the way of faith. "Mysticism is not content to wait for God's revelation," writes the master ironist Søren Kierkegaard, who sees in mysticism a fundamentally pagan impulse to attain identity with God. "Mysticism is esoteric atheism," declares the great Swiss theologian Karl Barth, for whom mysticism, like all "natural theology," arrogantly substitutes human for divine initiative.

What concerns Kierkegaard and Barth and the "dialectical" or "neo-orthodox" theologians whom they have inspired, is the risk that mystical confidence in the essential knowability of God might render faith in the revealed word of God no longer necessary nor even intelligible. This risk is most clearly present in those mystical works that reflect Platonic influence. The Platonizing Christian mystics tend to speak of God as at once wholly transcendent and immediately accessible to the purified intellect. God is beyond all; yet God can be known. To know God, and to return to one's own divine origins, one has only to leave behind the realm of the senses, change, temporality, and imagination, and ascend to an intellective union with the one divine reality.

This Platonic model of ecstatic ascent readily finds its way into the Christian spiritual tradition not only for reasons of historical influence, but also because it so effectively and poignantly evokes actual mystical experience. What works as a dramatic and narrative model, however, may not fit the needs of theology. Translated into metaphysics or theology, the model of ecstatic contemplative ascent poses a threat not just to a stodgy and defensive orthodoxy, but to the whole tradition's deepest commitment to its own experience of finding God revealed in creation, in history, in Christ incarnate, in the sacraments, and in the eternally self-communicating love of the Trinity. The problem is therefore a real one; yet the neo-orthodox solution is unnecessarily extreme. In polemical fashion, they caricature mysticism as a self-propelled, privatistic, pseudo-gnostic effort to merge with the Godhead; they then attribute everything attractive about the way of the mystics to the path of faith. Partly as a result of the misunderstandings created by this polemic over mysticism versus faith, the classics of Christian mystical literature have suffered on the one hand from neglect by serious religious thinkers, and on the other hand from naive popularization by those who disdain the ordinary mysticism that is central to the life of faith. Similar misunderstandings have arisen in other religious traditions, leading some scholars to place exaggerated emphasis on the conflict between mysticism and law in Jewish and Islamic traditions, or between self-power and Other-power practices in East Asian Buddhism. In each of these cases, the misunderstanding can be traced to an effort to extract mysticisms from the faith traditions in which they are embedded.

Mysticism of Being and Mysticism of Love

Underlying every form of Christian mysticism is a twofold attitude of awe and intimacy, with deep roots in the Biblical tradition. In accord with the religion of Israel, the mystics of the Church insist that "all flesh is grass; God alone endures." In the paradoxes, numinous silences, and iconoclastic sayings that abound in the literature of Christian mysticism, one hears a reverberation of prophetic warnings against idolatry. Yet the same God, of whom it is said "no one shall see him and live," is the God who wishes to be known through the medium of prophetic revelation and prayerful encounter. The same God who utterly transcends all creatures is intimately present to all creatures through the power of God's being and God's self-communicative love. It is on God's revealed promises that the mystics stake their claim; and no school of Christian (or Jewish or Islamic) mysticism has flourished that did not seek to balance the principle of divine transcendence with the promise of divine immanence.

It is common for scholars of Western mysticism to speak of two recurrent types: the "mysticism of being" (*Wesensmystik*) and the "mysticism of love" or "bridal mysticism" (*Brautmystik*). Historically, the two types have developed alongside each other, and both tendencies are therefore richly represented here.

The mysticism of being (typified by the writings included here from Eckhart and Tauler, but also found in the other selections) maps a path of ascent toward union with God — an audacious idea, were it not for the belief that God indeed wishes to be known.

As Eckhart puts it, we possess at the very core of our being a silent sanctuary where the divine word is eternally spoken, the divine being fully present. Here we are already at one with God. In order to experience this oneness, however, it is necessary first to withdraw one's attention from outward things; abstain from memories, images, concepts, ideas (even ideas about God); suspend all voluntary efforts (even virtuous efforts); and allow the divine energies to work upon us. To become who we were meant to be, to restore the *imago Dei* within to its intended luster, we must strip away all that is not God.

The practice of detached engagement in everyday life is therefore far more than a specialized ascetic discipline or (to use a contemporary idiom) a technique for stress reduction; when perfected, it mirrors God's own detached engagement in the world, and cultivates that state of receptivity that alone permits the soul to experience the eternal birth of the divine word within. For this reason, Eckhart places "disinterest" (*Abgeschiedenheit*) at the summit of the hierarchy of contemplative virtues.

In the mysticism of love, or *Brautmystik*, the divine–human encounter is more intensely personal, affective, Christocentric, and visionary or imagistic. At the summit of the hierarchy of contemplative virtues, one finds not disinterest, but ardent longing. Mechthild of Magdeburg, who combines the nuptial imagery of *Brautmystik* with the ascensional language of *Wesensmystik*, speaks not only of the soul's longing to return to God, but also of God's burning desire for the soul (p. 37). To become who we were meant to be, to restore the *imago Dei* within to its intended brilliance, we must cling to God with all our might, remembering God's graciousness without forgetting God's otherness. As Mechthild writes (echoing the eighth-century Sufi saint Rabi'ah), "She would that He might send her to Hell, if only He might be loved above all measure by all creatures" (p. 36).

The mysticism of being and the mysticism of love are not separate schools but historically intertwined paths, compatible in principle though varying in theme. The excerpts from Jacob Boehme and Angelus Silesius show how it is possible to combine the "way of negation" (typical of the mysticism of being) with an ardent and visionary Christocentric mysticism. Both the apophatic mysticism of being and the Christocentric mysticism of love travel by way of darkness into the light of divine presence, by way of nothingness into the fullness of divine being, by way of death into eternal life. Both tell us that to begin this journey toward a deathless state, it is necessary first of all to die. Not just the body, but the soul itself must die "even down to its roots," as Eckhart tells us (p. 126). Dying to the self, one may be reborn to a wider life against which death cannot prevail.

Traditional Christian theology insists that the deathless state is not a simple birthright, but a gift from the Cross; hence in the writings of profound and sensitive theologians like Karl Barth and Hans Urs von Balthasar, "natural" mysticisms are suspect. Yet the mystics of the Church tell us that this gift from the Cross is the very life of the soul, rather than something extrinsic and alien to it. How understandable, then, that they should find kindred spirits among the mystics of all other religious traditions; and how apt, too, that the discoveries they made in religious life have so greatly enriched the cultural, literary, and linguistic heritage of Germany, its European neighbors, and, ultimately, the whole human family.

CAROL ZALESKI

Introduction

What is the nature of mystical experience and, by extension, of mystical writing? Since popular understanding of the term has recently suffered through its overuse, it may be useful to clarify what it is we mean by "mystical" before coming to consider the place of such writing in a German, and specifically Christian, literary context. For help on such matters, there can be few authorities to rival Meister Eckhart as he speaks to us in his sermons. Consider the lessons he draws in one of these. "God gives to all things alike, and as they proceed from God they are alike," he affirms here. "Angels, men, and creatures all flow out of God in whom their prime origin is." Not only are these creatures *like* God, continues Eckhart, but

> [i]n this likeness or identity God takes such delight that He pours His whole nature and being into it. His pleasure is as great, to take a simile, as that of a horse, let loose to run over a green heath where the ground is level and smooth, to gallop as a horse will, as fast as he can over the greensward — for this is a horse's pleasure and expresses his nature. It is so with God. It is His pleasure and rapture to discover identity, because He can always put his whole nature into it — for He is this identity itself.

Or, to sum things up: "He teaches that we are to be identical with Him" (pp. 133, 134–35 in this volume).

The mystic, we might say, is the person who has heeded this teaching and sought to respond in kind, taking as his ultimate goal that same identification with God which is God's identification with him. This is the experience conventionally known as *unio mystica*. Likened by Meister Eckhart to the rapture of a running horse, its definition has been refined in our own century by the celebrated psychologist of religion William James. According to James, the identifying characteristics of a mystical (as opposed to simply a "religious") experience are ineffability, transiency, and a distinctive "noetic" quality — i.e., the impression conveyed, to the human participant, of a dimension of supernal knowledge otherwise inaccessible by human means.[1] It is this highly personal and finally elusive experience that mystical writing, then, attempts to document: either directly, by recreating the event of mystical union itself; or indirectly, by recommending particular avenues of approach to it, or by testifying to its after-effects.

The texts brought together in this volume attest to the efforts of German mystics to communicate this essentially incommunicable experience through some five hundred years of literary history. Taken together, they comprise a kind of mystical harvest selected from that extended period — the Middle Ages to the Baroque — which was most conducive to the production of esoteric religious writing in Germany. This is a harvest as notable for its richness and formal variety as it is for the recurrence within it of a few key themes and images continually striving for creative reexpression. To appreciate the first point, it is only necessary to glance at the range of literary types included here — among them dialogues and visions, sermons, songs, and epigrams — as well as at the cast of authors represented: men and women, Roman Catholics and Protestants, monastics and laymen. (Relevant information on individual authors or selections is given in the short introductions preceding each section of the book.) But to appreciate the second point properly requires at least a rudimentary sense of the foundations of Western European mysticism as a whole, and of its eventual development in two generally distinct but ultimately complementary metaphorical directions: that of so-called "speculative" or "intellectual mysticism" and that of "love mysticism." The first of these is abstract, rigorous, dispassionate; the second, affective, anthropomorphic, erotically charged. Within the German tradition, the former is most closely identified with the thought of Meister Eckhart, the latter with the writing of Mechthild of Magdeburg. A

---

1. See William James's discussion of "Mysticism" in *The Varieties of Religious Experience: A Study in Human Nature* (New York: New American Library, 1958), 292–328.

few broad historical observations must suffice here to suggest the matrix from which both emerged.[2] The original theater for the pursuit of mystical activity in the West was the Mediterranean. It was here, in the first several centuries of the common era, that a synthesis was effected between Classical and Judeo-Christian ideas (largely through the efforts of the Neoplatonists) that had major implications for the theory and practice of the contemplative life (especially in the context of monasticism). If there is one central idea that we can draw out of these developments, it is that Christian mystical practice arose, and justified itself, as a response to the basic human problem of the creature's separation from God, its source. While in Biblical terms this separation was always formulated in terms of the Fall, its correlative in Platonic philosophy was the notion of the soul's descent from the stars to the earth (cf. the *Timaeus*); it was part of the Neoplatonic project to bring these two ideas into mutual relation. The Christian mystic, in effect, sought a means of "returning home," by spiritually traversing the vast hierarchy that now separated him from God and by renewing, through *unio mystica*, that sense of identification with Him that also afforded a premonition of the afterlife.

In the elaboration of these Neoplatonic ideas and their application to the Christian life, three figures emerge as particularly important in this early period: Plotinus (third century), the preeminent representative of Neoplatonism itself; St. Augustine (fourth–fifth centuries), the greatest of the Church Fathers; and Pseudo-Dionysius (probably early sixth century), the philosopher who spuriously identified himself as Dionysius the Areopagite, a contemporary of the apostle Paul. If Plotinus emphasized the possibility of a spiritual reunion with God in the first place, then it was St. Augustine who was most influential in recommending how it might best be achieved — through the cultivation of inner experience in a life centered around Christian contemplation (*vita contemplativa*), pursued in an attitude of deliberate humility. The main contribution of Pseudo-Dionysius to this evolving tradition, his negative theology, was, in turn, basically rhetorical in its thrust. He proposed that God, being essentially ineffable, is only apprehensible through negation, i.e., we can only say

---

2. A more detailed treatment of the relevant developments is offered by Walter Holden Capps and Wendy M. Wright in their excellent introduction to *Silent Fire: An Invitation to Western Mysticism* (San Francisco: Harper & Row, 1978).

what He is *not*. This was an idea widely embraced by later mystics, who applied it also to their own (ineffable) experience of *unio mystica*.

More or less contemporary with the development of these ideas, the growth of monasticism from its origins in the Egyptian desert (under St. Anthony and Pachomius: third and fourth centuries) was providing a practical framework for their application. John Cassian (fourth–fifth centuries) was responsible for importing this tradition to Europe; St. Benedict (fifth–sixth centuries) for formalizing the famous Rule that stabilized it there, thanks in no small part to the efforts of Pope Gregory the Great after him (latter sixth century). It was in the context of monastic *reform* over five centuries later, however, that the first great European mystic stepped onto the stage in the person of Bernard of Clairvaux (late eleventh–twelfth centuries). The most prominent member of the newly founded Cistercian order, he is significant not only because he ushered in the tradition of mystical writing on the European mainland but because he stressed the emotional dimension of *unio mystica* in his teaching, returning allegorically to the Song of Songs to liken the principals in mystical union, the mystic (or individual soul) and God, to the Bride and Bridegroom presented there. This allegorical recourse to the Song of Songs became a virtual staple of European love mysticism in his wake — a metaphorical approach often favored by religious women (who were in any case educated to view themselves as "Brides of Christ") but not entirely confined to them, as the writings of, e.g., Heinrich Seuse and Jacob Boehme readily illustrate.

Nor was the emphasis on the affective dimension of religious experience uniform even among women writers. Hildegard of Bingen (1098–1179), the first of the authors included in this volume, was a contemporary and associate of Bernard who stands apart from the other representatives of the German tradition on two counts. First, because she wrote in Latin, while the later writers expressed themselves in the less traditional medium of the vernacular (although Meister Eckhart, notably, used both). Second, while she is routinely classified as a "mystic" like they are, her actual subject matter is not so much personal and experiential as it is impersonal and visionary. Afforded through her revelations insights into the construction and meaning of the universe, she recounts, in her *Book of Divine Works*, the contents of these visions in sober, measured language and then offers simple "translations" of their allegorical meaning for the benefit of her audience.

In both her style and overall objective, then, Hildegard differs markedly from the next writer represented here, Mechthild of Magdeburg (c. 1207–82), whose celebrated work, *The Flowing Light of the Godhead*, ranks as the first major mystical tract of the medieval German vernacular. A Beguine, Mechthild turned instinctively to a quasi-autobiographical format and to the figurative tradition of love mysticism to communicate the intensity of the mystical experience she sustained (sporadically) over the course of many years. While her style is colored on the one hand by the secular love-song (*Minnesang*) conventions of her age (a feature it shares with the somewhat later work of Heinrich Seuse), it is distinguished also by an ecstatic quality that surfaces again in the writing of such later European mystics as Catherine of Siena (fourteenth century) and Teresa of Avila (sixteenth century) — women who, like Mechthild, were predisposed to ill health but nonetheless strongly attracted to a regimen of rigorous asceticism. (A similar ecstatic tendency can be observed in some of the compositions of Jacob Boehme, whose sickliness, perhaps not coincidentally, was a major limiting factor in his life.) Foregoing all "creaturely" blandishments in order to prepare herself for her heavenly Bridegroom, Mechthild's Bride in effect makes a virtue of her suffering — a suffering which achieves a kind of apotheosis in the peak moments of her mystical experience.

A somewhat calmer rapture sounds from the writing of Meister Eckhart (c. 1260–1327/28), the most famous of all the German mystics and the most influential. A Dominican who, unlike Hildegard and Mechthild, was extensively educated (in the Scholastic tradition), he favored sermons and "talks of instruction" as a means of imparting his religious insights to his circle of followers. Like Mechthild, he sought to transcend the "creaturely" in order to achieve mystical union, but unlike her, he avoided anthropomorphic representation of the Deity. His emphasis was on promoting the readiness of the individual soul for its hoped-for union with the Godhead, which was itself imagined as being beyond all qualification, consistent with Neoplatonic premises and particularly the legacy of Pseudo-Dionysius. (The term "Godhead" itself is typically preferred by mystics to "God," implying as it does a greater level of abstraction.) The actual event of *unio mystica* Eckhart often likened to the birth of Christ into the innermost preserve of the soul, a metaphor also taken up by Johannes Tauler (c. 1300–1361), who was, along with his fellow Dominican Heinrich Seuse (c. 1295–1366), Eckhart's most important disciple in the flowering of fourteenth-century mysticism. (Since their writings, along with the anonymous selections "Granum Sinapis" and "Theologia Germanica," echo Eckhartian ideas, they will not be described here separately.) As the principal proponent of intellectual or speculative mysticism in Germany, Meister Eckhart succeeded in revitalizing the Neoplatonic legacy in such a way as to temper its innate tendency toward abstraction with an emphasis on practical application. With allowances made for the paradoxical language in which they are often couched, the most memorable of his sermons often read like thoughtful pages in a surprisingly down-to-earth instruction manual on how to be a mystic.

As representatives of a slightly later age — the German Baroque — the work of the two final authors included here must be set in relation not only to the Classical background sketched out above but also to another influence that made itself felt most dramatically in Europe during the Renaissance: Hermeticism, or the tradition that formed the metaphysical basis of alchemy. Both Jacob Boehme (1575–1624), the Protestant shoemaker and visionary, and Angelus Silesius (1624–77), the Protestant-born Catholic priest, were raised in a quarter of Europe — Silesia — that was particularly receptive to the ideas of Paracelsus, the great Swiss alchemist, and to that intellectual current which has been designated "esoteric alchemy."[3] This was a tradition that had grown up as a philosophical extension of alchemy as it is usually understood (i.e., "exoteric alchemy"): the transmutation of gold (or silver) from baser elements. To further this concrete objective of winning gold, a kind of spiritual rationale for the whole enterprise had evolved over the course of time which equated success in the laboratory with divine favor. Within this esoteric tradition, analogies were developed between the process of physical transmutation (of metals) and the process of *spiritual* transformation, whereby imperfect souls could be redeemed and ennobled. A critical symbolic link was established between the *lapis*

---

3. The useful distinction between esoteric and exoteric alchemy is observed by Eric John Holmyard in his book *Alchemy* (Baltimore: Penguin, 1968).

philosophorum or philosophers' stone, the sought-after catalyst of the transmutation process (also known as the "Tincture" or "Elixir"), and Jesus Christ, the agent of spiritual transformation (cf. his characterization in Matthew 21:42 and elsewhere in the New Testament as the "stone" or "cornerstone"). In the work of both Boehme and Silesius, the alchemical terminology sometimes adopted must be understood accordingly.

Of these two writers, it is Boehme who was the more original and whose contributions to the mystical tradition have been the more enduring. A virtual autodidact, he produced a succession of writings that are remarkable both for their variety and for the theosophical worldview they advance, however idiosyncratically. Basic to Boehme's thinking is the notion of an all-inclusive Godhead, one incorporating into itself both "wrath-fire" and "love-light," and of the unfolding of human events in terms of the dynamic interaction of these contraries. The general compatibility of his assumptions with the central tenets of Kabbalah — that form of Jewish mysticism that reached its apex in thirteenth-century Spain — has often been noted. Although no direct line of influence can be traced back from Boehme to Jewish tradition, some sort of indirect connection appears likely, perhaps through the mediating influence of Hermetic philosophy.

As all of the foregoing may suggest, to read each of these authors with attention to historical context is to dispel the myth that mystical writing (and mystical experience itself) is somehow ultimately unconnected to mundane realities or that it floats irretrievably in some otherworldly sphere. To the contrary: perhaps despite their own best efforts to distance themselves from their immediate circumstances, the special concerns and psychological priorities of individual mystics speak clearly enough from their writings, particularly in their chosen metaphors. The historian of language Hans Eggers, for example, has noted how frequently the medieval mystics — virtually all of them born into the aristocracy — gravitate to the adjective *edel* (noble) as an epithet of choice.[4] But the relationship does not only work in one direction, of course, since the literary productions of all these writers coalesced into a tradition that itself took on a

---

4. See Hans Eggers's chapter "Die Sprache der Gottsuche und der Gotter-kenntnis" in *Deutsche Sprachgeschichte*, Vol. 2: *Das Mittelhochdeutsche* (Reinbek bei Hamburg: Rowohlt, 1965), 175–211, here 192.

particular importance within the greater German literary tradition and exerted influence beyond it as well. The principal literary innovations usually cited in connection with early German mysticism are that it paved the way for autobiographical writing, with its emphasis on a first-person confessional style, and that it provided the first real literary forum for women in Germany. At least as significant were the linguistic innovations it brought with it. The list of neologisms employed by mystics in an effort to communicate the ineffable *unio mystica* is truly impressive; terms like *învluz* (influence), *unsprechelîch* (ineffable), and *isticheit* ("is-ness") were either coined by them directly or taken over and popularized from a German Scholastic vocabulary that had been generated to provide vernacular equivalents for Latin terms and was itself of recent vintage. It is noteworthy that the most original figures of the entire German tradition — Mechthild, Meister Eckhart, and Jacob Boehme — were also the most daring in their use of language, as each was brought up against its limits. Not coincidentally, to occupy a liminal place linguistically was also to operate at the limits of orthodox belief, as the persistent problems of each with religious authorities all too clearly illustrate.

But the significance of early German mysticism does not exhaust itself in these innovations. Well after the first great religious impulses of German mysticism had waned and the historical events that had helped set them in motion had receded (e.g., the plague and general unrest of the fourteenth century; the Thirty Years' War of the early seventeenth), the ideas that informed this tradition continued to exert their influence in contexts both religious and secular. In a religious sense, it is to seventeenth- and eighteenth-century Pietism we would look next in tracing the course of inward-directed religiosity in German history, and beyond that — via a somewhat different route — to Rudolf Steiner and his founding of the Anthroposophical movement in the early part of this century. In more secular terms, the legacy of mystical (and particularly Boehmean) ideas can be documented in the work of numerous Romantics (e.g., Novalis, E. T. A. Hoffmann, and the painter Philipp Otto Runge), as well as more recent authors like Hugo von Hofmannsthal ("The Letter of Lord Chandos"), and Hermann Hesse (*Siddhartha*). A recent major exhibition in American art museums has even documented the unexpected relevance of Meister Eckhart, Boehme, and others to a whole generation of modern abstract artists, including Kandinsky and Klee.[5]

The legacy of this mystical literary tradition, then — comprising, after the writings of the German Reformation, the most important religious corpus of the German language — is a vital and enduring one. For this reason, as well as for their intrinsic merits, the texts collected here amply repay the attention we bring to them.

K. J. C.

A Note on Scriptural Citations and Footnotes

Chapter and verse of Scriptural citations appearing throughout correspond to the New Revised Standard Version as presented in *The New Oxford Annotated Bible with the Apocrypha.*

Footnotes accompanying individual selections include some retained in their wording or sense from the original translators or editors. Where these extend beyond simple glosses of the text or where they provide conjectural material, attribution to the original commentator is given parenthetically.

---

5. Relevant materials have been compiled by Maurice Tuchman et al. in *The Spiritual in Art: Abstract Painting 1890–1985,* the volume that appeared to accompany the exhibition first held at the Los Angeles County Museum of Art from November 23, 1986, to March 8, 1987 (New York: Abbeville Press, 1986).

GERMAN
MYSTICAL WRITINGS

Hildegard of Bingen

Hildegard of Bingen (1098–1179)* was one of the most accomplished figures of her own age or any other. Born the tenth child of noble parents in Bermersheim (Rhenish Hesse), she was sent away at the age of eight to be educated at the Benedictine cloister at Disibodenberg. She took her vows there some years later and, in 1136, was chosen abbess of the community. In 1151 she moved her charges to a convent which she had had constructed on the Rupertsberg near Bingen. It was from this base of operations that she acquired an increasingly high profile — as committed campaigner for monastic reform, correspondent of numerous European heads of state, author of medical treatises, and composer of hymns and sequences. It was primarily as a visionary, however, that she gained her greatest following, beginning at the age of forty-two to write down (in Latin) the revelations to which she had been subject since childhood. In addition to *The Book of Divine Works* (*Liber divinorum operum:* 1163–73/74), excerpted here, her best-known work is *Know the Ways* (*Scivias:* 1141–51). Although Hildegard is usually identified as the first of the great German mystics, her concern was not with conveying the experience of *unio mystica* as such but with presenting, in language often evocative of the Book of Revelation, her visions of a cosmic order. Despite the limitations of her education, she confidently claimed authority for these visions, and the Church concurred, in 1147/48 officially pronouncing them to be of divine origin.

---

*The present English text by Robert Cunningham is based on Heinrich Schipperges's German translation of Hildegard's medieval Latin text. In a few sections it retains Schipperges's bracketed *summaries* of original material he deemed too repetitious to (re-)translate.

From The Book of Divine Works

Foreword

And it occurred in the sixth year, after I had been troubled for five years with marvelous and true visions. In these visions a true view of the everlasting light had shown me — a totally uneducated human being — the diversity of many ways of life.

It was the beginning of the first year of the present visions that this took place; and I was in my fifty-sixth year. Then I had a vision so deep and overpowering that I trembled over my whole body and began to fall ill because of my bodily weakness. For seven years I wrote about this vision but could scarcely complete the task.

It was in the year 1163 of the Incarnation of our Lord, when the oppression of the See of Rome under Henry, the Roman emperor, was not yet ended.* A voice from heaven resounded, saying to me:

O wretched creature and daughter of much toil, even though you have been thoroughly seared, so to speak, by countless grave sufferings of the body, the depth of the mysteries of God has completely permeated you. Transmit for the benefit of humanity an accurate account of what you see with your inner eye and what you hear with the inner ear of your soul. As a result, human beings should learn how to know their Creator and should no longer refuse to adore God worthily and reverently. Therefore, write this down — not as your heart is inclined but rather as My testimony wishes. For I am without any beginning or end of life. This vision has not been contrived by you, nor has it been conceived by any other human

*The actual principals in this struggle were the Emperor Friedrich Barbarossa (r. 1152–90) and Pope Alexander III (r. 1159–81).

being. Instead, I have established all of it from before the be-ginning of the world. And just as I knew the human species even before its creation, I also saw in advance everything that humanity would need.

I — wretched and fragile creature that I am — began then to write with a trembling hand, even though I was shaken by countless illnesses. In this connection I had confidence in the testimony of that man* whom — as I mentioned in my earlier visions — I had sought out and visited in secret. And I also had confidence in that girl† whom I have already named in my earlier visions. While I set about my task of writing, I looked up again to the true and living light as to what I should write down. For everything I had written in my earlier visions and came to know later I saw under [the influence of] heavenly mysteries while my body was fully awake and while I was in my right mind. I saw it with the inner eye of my spirit and grasped it with my inner ear. In this connection I was never in a condition similar to sleep, nor was I ever in a state of spiritual rapture, as I have already emphasized in connection with my earlier visions. In addition, I did not explain anything in testimony of the truth that I might have derived from the realm of human sentiments, but rather only what I have received from the heavenly mysteries.

And once again I heard a voice from heaven instructing me. And it said, *"Write down what I tell you!"*

First Vision: On the Origin of Life‡

Vision One: 1

And I saw within the mystery of God, in the midst of the south-ern breezes, a wondrously beautiful image. It had a human form, and its countenance was of such beauty and radiance that I could have more easily gazed at the sun than at that face. A broad golden

---

*The monk Volmar, Hildegard's secretary.

†The nun Richardis of Stade, one of Hildegard's assistants.

‡As will be clear to the reader, Hildegard's imagery in the following draws heavily on the Book of Revelation.

ring circled its head. In this ring above the head there appeared a second countenance, like that of an elderly man, its chin and beard resting on the crown of the first head. On both sides of the figure a wing grew out of the shoulders. The wings rose above the abovementioned ring and were joined there. At the topmost part of the right wing's curve appeared an eagle's head. Its eyes were like fire, and in them the brilliance of angels streamed forth as in a mirror. On the topmost part of the left wing's curve was a human head, which shone like the gleaming of the stars. Both faces were turned toward the East. From the shoulders of the figure a wing extended to its knees. The figure was wrapped in a garment that shone like the sun. Its hands carried a lamb, which shone like a brilliant day. The figure's feet trod upon a monster of dreadful appearance, poisonous and black, and a serpent which had fastened its teeth onto the monster's right ear. Its body was wound obliquely across the monster's head; its tail extended on the left side as far as the feet.

Vision One: 2*

I, the highest and fiery power, have kindled every spark of life, and I emit nothing that is deadly. I decide on all reality. With My lofty wings I fly above the globe: With wisdom I have rightly put the universe in order. I, the fiery life of divine essence, am aflame beyond the beauty of the meadows. I gleam in the waters, and I burn in the sun, moon and stars. With every breeze, as with invisible life that contains everything, I awaken everything to life. The air lives by turning green and being in bloom. The waters flow as if they were alive. The sun lives in its light, and the moon is enkindled, after its disappearance, once again by the light of the sun so that the moon is again revived. The stars, too, give a clear light with their beaming. I have established pillars that bear the entire globe as well as the power of the winds which, once again, have subordinate wings — so to speak, weaker winds — which through their gentle power resist the mighty winds so that they do not become dangerous. In the same way, too, the body envelops

*The figure speaks as follows.

the soul and maintains it so that the soul does not blow away. For just as the breath of the soul strengthens and fortifies the body so that it does not disappear, the more powerful winds, too, revive the surrounding winds so that they can provide their appropriate service.

And thus I remain hidden in every kind of reality as a fiery power. Everything burns because of Me in such a way as our breath constantly moves us, like the wind-tossed flame in a fire. All of this lives in its essence, and there is no death in it. For I am life. I am also Reason, which bears within itself the breath of the resounding Word, through which the whole of creation is made. I breathe life into everything so that nothing is mortal in respect to its species. For I am life.

I am life, whole and entire — not struck from stones, not blooming out of twigs, not rooted in a man's power to beget children. Rather all life has its roots in me. Reason is the root, the resounding Word blooms out of it.

Since God is Reason, how could it be that God, who causes all divine actions to come to fruition through human beings, is not active? God created men and women in the divine image and likeness, and marked each of these creatures according to a fixed standard in human beings. From eternity it was in the mind of God to wish to create humanity, God's own handi- work. And when God completed this action, God gave over to act with it just as God had formed the divine handiwork, humanity.

And thus I serve by helping. For all life lights up out of Me. I am life that remains ever the same, without beginning and without end. For this life is God, who is always in motion and constantly in action, and yet this life is manifest in a threefold power. For eternity is called the "Father," the Word is called the "Son," and the breath that binds both of them together is called the "Holy Spirit." And God has likewise marked humanity; in human beings there are body, soul, and reason. The fact that I am aglow above the beauty of earthly realms has the following meaning: The Earth is the material out of which God forms human beings. The fact that I am illuminated in the water signifies the soul, which permeates the entire body just as water flows through the entire Earth.

The fact that I am afire in the sun and moon signifies reason; for the stars are countless words of reason. And the fact that I awaken the universe with a breath of air as with the invisible life that contains everything, has the following significance: Through air and wind whatever is growing toward maturity is enlivened and supported, and in no way does it diverge from its inner being.

Vision One: 3

And again I heard a voice from heaven saying to me:

God, who created everything, has formed humanity according to the divine image and likeness, and marked in human beings both the higher and the lower creatures. God loved humanity so much that God designated for it the place from which the fallen angel was ejected, intending for human beings all the splendor and honor which that angel lost along with his bliss. The countenance you are gazing at is an indication of this fact.

For what you see as a marvelously beautiful figure in God's mystery and in the midst of southern breezes — a figure similar to a human being — signifies the Love of our heavenly Father. It is Love — in the power of the everlasting Godhead, full of exquisite beauty, marvelous in its mysterious gifts. Love appears in a human form because God's Son, when He put on flesh, redeemed our lost humanity in the service of Love. On this account the countenance is of such beauty and splendor that you can more easily gaze at the sun than at it. For the abundance of Love gleams and shines in the sublime lightning flash of its gifts in such a way that it surpasses every insight of human understanding by which we can otherwise know in our soul the most varied things. As a result, none of us can grasp this abundance with our minds. But this fact will be shown here in an allegory so that we can know in faith what we cannot see with our outward eyes.

Vision One: 4

Another golden ring surrounds the head of this appearance, for the Catholic faith, which has spread throughout the entire globe, began out of the most brilliant glow of the first dawn.

Only faith grasps in deepest reverence the abundance of this love, which exceeds all understanding: the fact that God through the Incarnation of the divine Son redeemed humanity and strengthened it through the inspiration of the Holy Spirit. Thus the one God is known in the Trinity — God who was God in the Godhead eternally and without any beginning. In this circular image you see above the head also another head, which is like that of an elderly man. This signifies that the overpowering loving-kindness of the Godhead, which is without beginning and end, hastens to the aid of believers. Its chin and beard rest on the crown of the first countenance. In God's total design and providence the climax of the highest love was that God's Son in His humanity led the lost human race back to the heavenly kingdom.

Vision One: 5

A wing emerges from each side of the figure's neck. Both wings rise above the ring and are joined there because the love of God and the love of our neighbor — if they proceed through the divine power of love in the unity of faith and embrace this faith with the greatest longing — cannot be separated as long as the holy Godhead conceals the immeasurable splendor of its glory from human beings and as long as human beings abide in the shadow of death. For they are bereft of the heavenly garment they lost through Adam.

Vision One: 6

On the topmost part of the right wing's curve you can see the head of an eagle with fiery eyes. In those eyes a choir of angels shines as in a mirror: When people subject themselves to God on the height of triumphant subservience and overcome Satan, they will advance and enjoy the bliss of divine protection. And if they are inflamed by the Holy Spirit and lift up their hearts and turn their eyes to God, the blessed spirits will appear within them in total brightness and carry up to God the surrender of those individuals' hearts. For spiritual people, who in the devotion of their hearts often gaze at God like the angels, are marked with an eagle. Therefore, the blessed spirits who constantly gaze at God rejoice in the good deeds of the just. They display these deeds to God by their own being. And thus they persist in praising God and never cease to do so, for they can never exhaust the divine fullness. For who could ever count the immeasurable works God accomplishes in the power of divine omnipotence? No one! The brilliance of many reflections in a mirror is characteristic of the angels. Within this brilliance the angels gaze at God. For no one acts and has such power as God, and no one is like the Deity. For God is not subject to such a thing as time.

Vision One: 7

Everything God has done was done by the Deity before the beginning of time in the divine present. In the pure and holy Godhead all visible and invisible things shine before all eternity without a temporal moment and without the elapse of time, just as trees and other bodily things are reflected in adjacent waters without being within them in a bodily fashion, even though their outlines may appear in this mirror. When God said, "Let it be done!" things were enclosed at once within their forms, just as the divine providence had seen them in an incorporeal way before time was. Just as everything in front of a mirror shines within that mirror, all the works of the holy Godhead shine within it in a timeless way. For how should God exist without having prior knowledge of the divine works? And each divine work, once it has been enclosed within its body, is complete in the function that is appropriate for it. For the holy Godhead knew in advance how it would assist that work, serving it with knowledge and comprehension. As a ray of light lets us distinguish the form of a creature, God's pure providence sees the forms of creation even before they are enclosed within their bodies. This is because everything God wished to create, even before this work had a body, shone in the divine foreknowledge and according to the divine likeness, just as we can see the rays of the sun before we see the sun itself. And just as the sun's rays indicate the sun, the angels reveal God by their hymns of praise. And just as the sun cannot exist without its light, the Godhead could not be if it were not for the angels' praise. God's providence went before while the divine work came afterward. If this providence had not gone before, the work would not have appeared. In the same way, we cannot recognize someone from his or her bodily appearance unless we can see that person's face. But if we see the face, we will praise also the whole form of that individual. This is the way that God's providence and work are within us human beings.

Vision One: 8

At that time an immeasurably large choir of angels sought to make something of themselves. For when they beheld their remarkable glory and their beauty shining in all its dazzling fullness, they forgot about their Maker. They had not even begun to praise God when they thought that all by themselves the splendor of their glory was so great that no one could resist them. Thus they wanted to overshadow God's splendor. But when they saw that they could never exhaust God's wondrous mysteries, they turned away from the Deity, full of disgust. Those who were supposed to celebrate God's praise said in their self-deception that because of their dazzling splendor they should select another God. On this account they plunged downward into darkness, reduced to such a state of impotence that they can only affect a creature when the Creator lets them do so. For God adorned the first of all the angels, Lucifer, with so much of the beauty granted to all creation that the whole heavenly host of angels was illuminated by Lucifer. But now that he has turned toward contradiction, Lucifer has become uglier than ugliness itself. For by the might of anger the holy Godhead flung Lucifer down to the place deprived of all light.

Vision One: 9

Shining like the starry light, a human face appears above the top of the curve of the left wing. This means that those among us who take up the defense of our Creator are at the pinnacle of victorious humility since we humbly suppress the earthly things that, so to speak, attack us from the left. Such persons have a human face. For they have begun to live according to the dignity human nature has taught them and not like animals. Therefore, they make known their good intentions through the just deeds of their hearts, and they shine in the brightest splendor.

Vision One: 10

When God said, "Let there be light," the light of the spirit arose. This refers to the angels. Intended are both the angels who remained true to God and those who fell into the outermost regions of darkness without light. This happened because the fallen angels chose not to realize that the true light that shone forth in eternity before the origin of everything was God, since they wanted to bring about something similar to God, even though the existence of such a being was an impossibility. At that time God caused another form of life to arise — a form the Deity clothed with a body.

This refers to humanity. God gave to us human beings the place and honor of the fallen angels so that we might complete God's glory, which is something those angels had refused to do. By this "human face" are marked those who are devoted to the world according to the deeds of the body. Yet according to their spiritual attitude they constantly serve God and do not forget, in the midst of all their worldly obligations, what belongs to the spirit in their service of God. Their faces are turned to the east because both the clergy and the laity in their longing to serve God and to preserve their souls for life should return toward the place where the holy conversion arises and the fountain of bliss is found.

Vision One: 11

From each shoulder of this figure a wing extends down to the knees, because the Son of God has attracted and kept, through the power of His love, the just and sinners. Since the just have lived correctly, He carries them on His shoulders, while He carries sinners on His knees because He has called them back from the path of error. He makes all of them partners in a higher community. In the same way someone wishing to carry a burden holds it partly on his knees and partly on his shoulder. In knowledgeable love we are led, soul and body, to the fullness of salvation, even though we often fail to maintain the proper attitude of constancy. Thus we are instructed to an incomparable extent in heavenly and spiritual things as the gifts of the Holy Spirit flow through us from above with a wealth of purity and holiness. In earthly affairs, too, these gifts educate us to the advantage of our bodily needs, yet in quite a different way. Nevertheless, we know ourselves to be weak and frail and mortal in these matters, even though we have been strengthened by so many gifts of grace.

Vision One: 12

The figure wears a garment that shines with the brilliance of the sun. This is a sign of the Son of God who in His love has assumed a human body unstained by sin and beautiful as the sun. Just as the sun shines sublimely over all creation at such a height that no one can encroach upon it, so no one can grasp the Incarnation of the Son of God in its essence — except through faith. In its hand the figure carries a lamb as brilliant as the light of day. For love has revealed in the deeds of the Son of God the gentleness of a true faith that outshines everything else — as this love chose martyrs, confessors, and penitents from the ranks of publicans and sinners, as it converted atheists into righteous believers, and turned Saul into Paul, so that all of them could fly into the harmony of heaven. Thus love has perfected its achievement, bit by bit yet clearly and definitely, so that no weakness may remain, and so that all fullness may be attained. We human beings cannot create anything like it. For when we are active with our limited possibilities, we can scarcely bear to end what we are doing so that it can be inspected by others. For we are aware that the little bird that emerges from the egg and as yet has no wings does not try to fly right away. After its wings have grown, the bird will fly because it sees that flying is appropriate for it.

Vision One: 13

The figure treads upon both a frightful monster of a poisonously dark hue and a serpent. For true love, which follows in the footsteps of the Son of God, tramples upon all injustice that is convoluted by the countless vices of dissension. Injustice is also dreadful in its very nature, poisonous in its temptations, and black in its abandonment. In addition, love destroys thus the old serpent lying in wait for believers. For the Son of God has destroyed this serpent by the cross. Indeed, the serpent has fastened its jaws to the monster's ear and coiled itself about the monster's head and body in such a way as to reach its feet. This symbolizes Satan who at times conceals his deceptions as a kind of kindness. He fastens his jaws in strife and, after this beginning, briskly trots out a whole family of vices. Finally, he openly displays the perversity of open conflict that he has previously concealed. For the serpent is more cunning than all the other reptiles and destroys as much as it can by acting with the utmost speed. This is what is indicated by the various hues of the serpent's hide. Satan acted in this same fashion. Realizing his own beauty, he aimed at being like his Creator. This is the very same advice he whispered into Adam's ear, so to speak, through the serpent's mouth. And Satan will not cease to do so until the Day of Judgment, as is shown by his tail.

But love is at work in the circles of eternity, without reference to time, like heat within a fire. In the divine providence God foresaw all creatures that were created in the fullness of divine love in such a way that humanity did not lack among them for refreshment or service. For God bound them to humanity the way a flame is bound to fire. Yet God created the first angel along with the fullness of beauty, as described above. When that angel looked at himself, he felt hatred for his lord and sought to rule all by himself. But God cast him down into the bog of the abyss. From this time onwards, that mutineer has gone about insinuating his evil counsel. And we human beings are in agreement with him.

Vision One: 14

When God created humanity, the Deity clothed us with a heavenly garment so that we would shine in great splendor. But Satan saw the woman and realized that she would be the mother who would bear in her womb a world of great possibilities. By the same cunning through which he had fallen away from God, Satan managed to get the better of God, so to speak, by bringing about an agreement between himself and this divine work, that is, between himself and the human species. Since the woman felt that she had become different through her enjoyment of the apple, she gave it also to her husband. Thus both of them lost their heavenly garment.

Vision One: 15

Since God quickly asked, "Adam, where are you?" this indicated that the One who had created humanity in the divine image and likeness wished to draw us back to God. When Adam was sent into exile, God covered the man's nakedness by an act of gracious cooperation. In place of his luminous garment, Adam was given a sheepskin, and God substituted for Paradise a place of exile. God bound the woman to the man by an oath of loyalty that should never be broken. Indeed, they were in agreement with each other, like the body and soul God has joined together in unity. Hence, anyone who destroys this bond of fealty and persists in doing so without repentance will be expelled to Babylon, a place full of chaos and drought. That land lies fallow, deprived of both the green beauty of life and God's blessing. The divine vengeance will befall such an individual up to the last generation of blood relationship that may result from his or her hot blood. For a sin of this nature will affect the very last human being.

Vision One: 16

Just as Adam is the begetter of the entire human race, spiritual people lead the way by means of the Son of God, who was made flesh in the body of a virgin. Such people will be fecund, just as by means of an angel God promised Abraham that his seed would be as numerous as the stars of heaven. For Scripture states: " 'Look up to heaven and count the stars if you can. Such will be your descendants,' He told him. Abram put a faith in Yahweh, who counted this as making him justified" (Genesis 15:5–6). This is to be understood as addressed to you who pray to God, and sincerely honor God, look at God's mysteries, and see the reward of those who can shine before God day and night — to the extent that this is possible for those encumbered with the burden of their bodies. For as long as we enjoy the things of the flesh, we can never fully grasp the things of the spirit. But by means of true signs, a message will be given to anyone who makes an effort to honor God with an exceedingly ardent heart. In this way the seed of your heart will be multiplied and placed in a clear light because you have sown on good soil that which has been watered with the grace of the Holy Spirit. Before the highest God this seed will ascend and shine in the blissful power of its virtue, just as a multitude of stars gleams in heaven. Therefore, whoever shows devout faith in the divine promise by clinging to the height of a true faith in God, by scorning earthly things, and by revering heavenly things, will be counted as righteous among the children of God. He or she has loved truth, and nothing false has been found in that person's heart.

Vision One: 17

For God knew that Abraham's mind was free of the serpent's deception because Abraham's actions did not harm anyone else. Therefore, God chose from Abraham's stock the dormant Earth that had within itself not a jot of the taste whereby the old serpent had deceived the first woman. And the Earth, which was foreshadowed by Aaron's staff, was the Virgin Mary. In her great humility she was the king's enclosed bridal chamber. For when she received the message from the throne that the king wished to dwell within her secret womb, she looked at the Earth of which she was made and spoke of herself as God's handmaiden. The woman who had been deceived [Eve] did not do so, and she was the one who desired something that she should not have possessed. Abraham's obedience — the obedience through which God tested Abraham by showing him the ram caught in the thornbush — was a prefigurement of the Blessed Virgin's obedience. She, too, believed the messenger of God and wished matters to be as he had stated. On this account God's Son took on the garment of flesh within her, as was prefigured by the ram in the thornbush. When God promised Abraham offspring as numerous as the stars of heaven, God foresaw that in the offspring the fullness of the heavenly community would be completed. Since Abraham was full of confidence in God and believed all these things, Abraham will be called the father of all who inherit the Kingdom of Heaven.

Let all who fear and love God open up their hearts, in complete devotion, to these words. Let them understand that such words are being proclaimed for the salvation of our body and soul — not by a human voice but rather by Myself, the One who am.*

Seventh Vision: Preparation for Christ

Vision Seven: 1

Then I saw in the eastern corner, right at the beginning of the east, a piece of marble that lay there like a mighty mountain — very tall and all of a block. Only one doorway was cut into it, and it was like the doorway of a great city. A radiance as bright as that of the sun overflowed all the marble block, but did not extend beyond it. Figures of human beings, including children, youths, and old people, extended from this rock to the eastern edge and in a southerly direction. These people were like stars behind a cloud. Their voices penetrated far to the west, like a storm raging in a foam-covered sea. From on high a radiance overflowed them, outshining every beauty possible to human imagination. This radiance permeated the whole vision with a radiance that was quickly withdrawn.

Near the eastern border stood two other figures, which were close to each other. The first had the head and torso of a leopard and human eyes, but its hands were like the claws of a bear. I was unable to distinguish any other features of this figure. It was clothed in a

---

*Here and elsewhere, the explicator's voice assumes divine authority.

stony garment that permitted no motion. It had its head reversed so that the figure faced the north.

The second figure, which was adjacent, had the face and hands of a human being. Its hands were clasped, showing claws like those of a hawk. It was clothed in a wooden gown that was white from its top to the navel. Underneath, the gown was reddish in color as far as the loins. From the loins to the knees the gown was gray while it was colorful in an unruly manner from the knees to the soles of the feet. Across its hips the figure carried a sword. It stood there without any motion, and its face was turned to the west.

Consequently I beheld everywhere in the southern region a crowd of persons fluttering in the breezes like a cloud. Some had golden crowns, others flourished palm branches in their hands, and still others held flutes, zithers, or brass instruments. And the music of these instruments resounded like a delightful resonance in the clouds.

Vision Seven: 3

"My heart is stirred by a noble theme: I address my poem to the king" (Psalm 45:1). This verse is to be understood in the following way: I, the Father of all, reveal openly and in the sight of all creatures that the power of My heart has brought forth the true Word, which is a noble theme: I begot My Son by whom everything has been created exceedingly well. Hence, I the One who does not change, reveal My deeds to the One who will rule over the entire Earth. All the deeds I have created since the very beginning are known to My Son.

In its power Wisdom indicated the true Word by announcing that the true Word by which everything has been created is the Word become flesh and full of wondrous deeds. Wisdom has presented it [the Word] as the king of future kingdoms and the right seed sprung from an intact kingdom of the Earth, unsullied by human generation. By the inspiration of the Holy Spirit old men and women and young people came to know this Wisdom — all those who have spoken through many signs of this offspring, the Word of God, through the inspiration of the Holy Spirit.

God created the [first] man from the Earth and changed him into flesh and blood. But God took the woman from the man, and she remained flesh from flesh, which had not been changed into something else. But both knew from this spirit of Wisdom that through the inspiration of the Holy Spirit a woman would bear the Son of God, just as a blossom grows out of the gentle air. Aaron's rod also indicates this. Taken from a tree, it indicates the Virgin Mary. The male has been taken out of her in such a way that she could never be disturbed by the lust of sexual union. Instead, by the loving fire of the Holy Spirit she bore that unique man. But God surrounded that man with all creation so that every creature that has come from Him might rejoice that all His voices listen to Him. The prophets said that a woman should give birth by an act of love and should enter into life, like a branch sprouting from the tree of Jesse. And all attributed this virgin birth to the king, who is the Son of God.

Since this woman protected the Son of God, those who saw and listened to Him in His own form loved Him more than if they had not seen Him. For they could not fully recognize what they saw in the shadow. And thus this task was given to the prophets because they announced like a shadow in the resonance of a shadow. Nevertheless, all these things have been arranged later among humans because the sound of Wisdom has explained them out of the hidden mysteries of the Godhead.

Vision Seven: 4

The two adjacent figures in the east have the following significance: At the dawn of justice (to which an allusion is made by means of Abel), God introduced two different moral systems for humanity. These systems are closely related to each other in time, despite many variations. The first figure indicates the period before the Flood, which was without any law at all; the second, the period after the Flood, which was under the law.

[The figure of the leopard signifies the strong and primitive nature of the human species in its natural savagery and its diabolical depravity. The iron garment is a symbol of the harshness and the weight of its sins. The figure has turned its gaze to the north because the people of this primitive period did not wish to turn away from evil toward goodness, even though their conscience showed them the infamous aspect of their doings. The figure's human arms and bear claws, however, indicate that those people, in their contradictory behavior, had not yet subjected themselves to the disciplined order of a human way of life.]

When God created Heaven and Earth, God divided the Earth up in such a way that part of it was unchanging while another part was subject to change. Out of the changeable matter God formed humanity. Therefore, when we are awake and when we are asleep, we are subject to changeability. In the waking state we can see with the light of our eyes, depending on the position of the sun. But if we cannot see with the light of our eyes, we are like one whose soul is darkened as if by the night.

Vision Seven: 5

And God placed humanity on an Earth full of life. The Earth was not supposed to be lighted by the orbit of the sun's rays. Instead, it was supposed to be flooded by the living light of eternity. Meanwhile, humanity transgressed against God's command and was thrown back into the changeableness of our earthly condition. But the first man had begotten two sons: The first son offered sacrifices to God while the other slew his brother, thus becoming guilty of his death. For the second son murdered the one offering sacrifices to God and heeding God's voice! As a result of this bloody deed a mighty lamentation went up.

During the first stage of creation, humanity had so much power and ability that it could overpower even the strongest animals. People played with the animals and rejoiced in them. The animals respected human beings, tamed their own savagery, and became subject to humanity without altering their animal nature. But human beings changed the fair condition of their reason and mated with the animals. If something was born of this union that resembled more a human being than an animal, they hated and scorned it. But if the creature was more like an animal than a human being, they embraced it in a kiss of love.

In addition, the humans of this period displayed an ambivalent attitude, just as the leopard and the bear can exhibit the habits either of human beings or of animals. Such people did not have the dazzlingly fair wings of reason on which they might soar upward in true faith and hope to God.

Because of the above-mentioned transgression their wings were stunted. This sin had been suggested to them by the old serpent in order to destroy the honor of their reason, which the serpent persecuted with a great hatred. The Devil said, in fact, to himself: "What has the One on high done now! Such a deed is more in accord with my plan than God's. On this account I shall overcome God through the divine creation...."

Vision Seven: 6

But after the Earth was filled with such a perverse people, I — the One who am — could no longer endure this criminal wickedness. I resolved to destroy by water all human beings, except for a few men and women who knew Me....

By water and fire God accomplished divine judgment on men and women. Since God had formed them from these elements, humanity is hard pressed by both of them. And just as God penetrates the whole Earth with the moistness of water and shapes and strengthens the Earth with blazing heat, God thoroughly moistens men and women with the humors of the divine body and strengthens them with the blazing heat of the soul. But human beings, who had heeded God after the Flood in order to renew their species, became inflamed with the fear of God because they were afraid of the judgment they had already experienced. And they began to bring gifts as sacrifices to God.

Vision Seven: 7

From this time forward we human beings — generation after generation — have declined in power with respect to those who lived before the Flood. And as the Earth changed, our altered powers were weakened because we followed the old deceiver who had exchanged his former splendor for the baseness of the serpent. Yet the serpent seeks to deceive those it wishes to deceive and to flee from those it wishes to flee from. This is how the old enemy behaves: He destroys his victim skillfully with the fatal poison of treachery. But he quickly flees from those who overcome him. This is because the Devil will retreat from such individuals just as he himself was cast out of heaven.

That period resulted in such a flowering of our fear of God that we could withstand the old serpent. It could no longer go about with its treacherous advice to us to forget God, as it had done before the Flood. For after that event God created new Earth and new people. And God placed the rainbow above the clouds as a sign. Never again should the waters drown the entire Earth and the human race with it. . . .

Vision Seven: 8

The second figure, which has the face and clasped hands of a human being, as well as the feet of a hawk, indicates the period after the Flood when the life of human beings was subject to the Law.

[The wooden garment symbolizes the Law of the Old Covenant. The colors point to the time of Moses, Abraham, and the Babylonian captivity, and finally to the coming of the Son of Man. The figure is here motionless because as yet people feel no inclination toward spiritual insight.]

But the fiery dragon felt a mighty hatred for all who had been spared by the waters. Gnashing its teeth, it said to itself:

"I shall dedicate all my skills, I shall stamp and sift them so that I can destroy by other impediments those who were not drowned in the Flood. Thus I shall once again make them subject to myself!"

Vision Seven: 9

And thus the period of history after the Flood extends from Noah until the Incarnation of My Son, who converts to spiritual insight all who believe in Him. With Him began another era, which did not lead to life according to the flesh but according to the spirit.

For in Noah I have revealed many signs of wonder. And just as in Adam I was mindful of the whole human race, I predicted in Noah the age that was to come. From his tribe came the strong and active prophets who faithfully announced with a skillful tongue what they saw in the Holy Spirit. This message was that God would send into the world the divine Word, which was in God before there was time. And this Word became flesh so that the whole world was amazed. Their fluent tongues spread this wonder rapidly across the world by affirming that the fairest child of our species would come into the world.

Thus Reason speaks first of all and then accomplishes its deed according to its statement. For if that statement had not been made, the deed could not have taken place. For God expressed the world and humanity by the Word. This Word, which is without beginning, achieved a specific deed as a result of which the world put on its garment. Thus if we should sin and then recognize God, God could draw us again to the divine with this garment. For if the Word had not adopted this garment, we human beings could not be saved, just as a fallen angel could not be rescued. But what would it mean if God were not able to rescue that angel from his failure in case the angel would only regretfully recognize God? Just as it pleased almighty God to create the human species, God was also pleased to redeem anyone who has trust in the divine.

For this reason God secretly caused Wisdom to emerge from the divine Spirit. Wisdom was sent forth under a shadow until God had completed the divine work. Before this achievement, however, God announced it with advance signs. For in Noah God displayed the ark; to Abraham circumcision was given; to Moses the Law was taught so that the restlessness of passion, which rages like a serpent's tongue, might be confused by Wisdom. And just as the Devil had betrayed human beings by means of animals, he was to be crushed by animal sacrifices at rites in honor of God prior to the coming of the Saint of all saints....

[Three signs came in haste before the Son of God: the sacrifice of animals, the circumcision of the first-born children, and the Law. And just as the plough prepares the Earth, the chosen people have been prepared by Scripture, which they could not fully understand at the time. The Son of God first of all revealed to believers all the mysteries of His coming and His rapture.]

Vision Seven: 10

The spirit of believers spreads as swiftly as the clouds. The longing of the soul by which blissful persons seek God's work in order to carry it out — that longing can never be put to rest. Thus streams that originate in the sea never cease to flow. And because that holy longing, which is the source of all good, is rooted to such a degree in those persons, God adorns them with the heavenly host. For such persons cling to God in such a way that they cannot be separated from God.

God's order of creation foresaw from the beginning that we were to be renewed in our spiritual life. And if God permitted animals to be bound, slaughtered, and burnt under the Law so that their blood might flow, this was a sign that those persons who hasten like clouds and look up to the divine would be tortured and killed and then offered up for the love of God. Since such persons nurse in this way at the breast of virtue by avoiding lust and other vices, they already bear in their hands the palm of victory. Indeed, they shed their blood before they might have the misfortune to fall out of the net of justice through the faithless acts.

In this way they are crucified in two ways: by fighting against their body and by shedding their blood in accord with God's command. Hence, they resemble the angels who constantly stand before God. But persons who carry out their tasks in life by teaching others according to the command of almighty God resound, so to speak, on flutes of sanctity. For by the voice of reason they chant justice right into the hearts of men and women. Thus says the Word, and that sound resounds once more. The Word is heard by means of sound, and it is also disseminated so that it can be heard. Just as a flute can strengthen the human voice, the teacher's voice can be strengthened among other human beings through the fear and love of God. Thus that voice can bring believers together and drive off unbelievers.

[Other people persist in the virginity and glorification of the angels. Like eagles they look up to God. They are like the dawn and live with the simplicity of a dove. They are the ones who play upon the zither. Still others make use of the wind instruments by serving humbly upon the Earth and thus opening themselves up for Heaven. And so they are joined to the hymns of praise of the angels who overcame arrogance.]

And we human beings have our existence like a deed carried out by the right side of almighty God — a deed of God's right hand. We shall complete the choir of the fallen angels. And thus we serve also to defend the good angels. God has great joy in these two systems of order: the angels' order of creation and that of human beings. God has joy in the angels' hymn of praise and in the holy deeds of human beings. By them God has accomplished in accord with the divine will everything foreseen from all eternity. But angels are constant before God's countenance while human beings are inconstant. Therefore, our actions so often fail while nothing is lacking in the angels' hymn of praise.

Heaven and Earth concern God so because they were created by God for the divine honor. But because we humans are mortal, the divine revelations, which at times were made known to the prophets and sages, have often been veiled as if by a shadow. But if in days to come we will be relieved of our inconstancy and become unchangeable, we shall behold through our understanding God's splendor and may be permitted to abide forever with God. This has been declared by My servant David in accord with My will.

Vision Seven: 11

"I sing for joy in the shadow of Your wings; my soul clings close to You, Your right hand supports me" (Psalm 63:7–8). This passage should mean and be interpreted in the following way: Under Your protection and shield, O God, I shall rejoice if I am freed of the burden of sin. My soul will long to come to You with good deeds. This loud sighing snatches me up to You and calls me to the might of Your strength so that I may be unafraid before my enemies. For I am an instrument that You have made because You held me in Your plan before the origin of time. For You have created me such that creation is at my disposal.

And since you have created me in this way, You have given me also the gift of acting in accord with You. For it was You who made me. Hence I am yours. You have clad Yourself with spotless flesh, as it is fitting for You as the Creator, and thus You have stretched the hem of Your garment. With a song of praise You have set the heavens in motion and surrounded them with the fullness of beauty in a band of angels who, even as they surround You in a band of praise, cannot cease to be amazed that You created us humans in such a way. With the same band of praise You have girded us in place of the angels who rejected and renounced the teaching of heaven. You have so strengthened us with Your garment that we shall not in the future cease our song of praise. But the angels are astonished that You have taken Your garment from the mortal Adam even though You did this so that Adam, despite his offense, might receive again new life, and so that the divine splendor — to which no inquiry can even set a limit — might once again shine forth to the angels in heaven.

For this reason you said: "You are always before My countenance; hence You do not need to be called back like the one [Adam] who was found again through My garment. He did not completely deny Me even when he was led astray by another. Because he wished to be like Me, he fell victim to mortality. Therefore, he had to be called back through the suffering of My garment. The brotherly association with you should not be lost in him. For even though I created you without a body and him [Adam] with a body, I formed each of you as an individual being."

The hidden Godhead is totally just and is only seen to the extent it allows itself to be unveiled. Now in this way the Godhead reveals itself to the angels who remained in heaven without undergoing the fall from grace. In the all-embracing power of its justice, the Godhead possesses completeness to such an extent that no one who looks at the Godhead with the eyes of faith can go astray. But those who do not look at the Godhead with the eyes of faith vanish before the countenance of the Godhead, just as the fallen angel went astray and all who agree with him. For God, who has created everything, has also arranged everything well: Those who look to God receive the reward of their service. But those who wish to take no account of God will be judged. This is what this image means.

Vision Seven: 12

All of this has been revealed by the only begotten Son of God. Whoever believes in Him will be saved, and whoever turns away from Him will be damned. For He has not emerged from an earthly root but from the intact Virgin according to the will of God. Together with God He created everything before the Incarnation. After the Incarnation He saved the human species, which He had formed. Sinless He accepted a human form and as a human being — the very creature He had made — He achieved the redemption. No one could have done it but the One who created the human species.

When Adam was a simple-hearted and shining child, he experienced a stage of growth and another stage of sleep. Through the mind he was to be conscious of the world when in the waking stage; when he was asleep, his flesh was to be refreshed. In this way he was brought to an immutable Earth of bliss so that he could attain through his mind the perception of immortality and also become aware of the invisible aspect of life through his external eyesight. Immortal existence has no nebulous kind of light, as is the case with our earthly eye, which can only see for a certain limited time until the darkness again overtakes it. And we have to endure this because our eye is covered by a dark lid. The pupil indicates our inner eyesight, which is unknown to corporeal experience. But the eyelid indicates our corporeal sight, which faces outwardly.

Every deed we do is accomplished through these two forms of perception. The perception of our inner vision teaches us what is divine, the aspect which our flesh, in turn, seeks to block. But our deluded perception accomplishes the deeds of the night, resembling a snake that does not look at the light. Hence, our deluded perception seeks to turn away from the deeds of the light as much as possible. This is what happened to Adam when a deluded perception destroyed for him the light of living perception. Perception was in Adam like a prophecy that has lasted until the Incarnation of the Son of God. The Son was to bring to the light the gift of prophecy through His essence, just as the sun illuminates the whole Earth. Thus all promises were perceived as taking place both before and after the Law. And thus the Son was to complete the Law in a spiritual way in His own essence when He offered himself up totally to God, according to the following written statement:

Vision Seven: 13

"Using the clouds as Your chariot, You advance on the wings of the wind" (Psalm 104:3). This statement has the following meaning: Lord, You have arranged things in such a way that the just and proper desires of believers are the wings by which You can rule over their hearts. You direct Your ways by means of the words and writings of the sages, whom You raise up. For You change without blemish and perceive no sin within Yourself. Hence, the clouds are the offspring of the wings which You made for Yourself when You, O Son of God, climbed above them in Your garment. You adopted it from the unique, intact Virgin whose womb was never opened or touched. Just like the dew of the Earth, You entered her. You are not based on a man's root but on the Godhead, as a sun's ray warms the Earth so that its seed may sprout. From this seed You grew within her without harm or pain, so to speak, in a sleep, just as Eve was taken from the sleeping man. And just as the man, who was uninjured, joyfully beheld that [first] woman, this unique Virgin, who was also full of joy, enclosed her Son within the womb.

Eve, too, was not created from a man's seed but from the flesh of a man. For God created her by the same power through which God sent the Son to the Virgin. Neither Eve, the virgin and mother, nor Mary, the mother and Virgin, has found any woman like herself. In this way God put on a human form. God covered the divine Godhead with the Virgin in the sight of the angels in heaven, where God lives. Hence, humility, which God formed in its height and width and depth, is also God's abode.

Vision Seven: 14

The Son of God who became man has fulfilled in Himself all the historic wonders that preceded Him, as has been described above....

[The deception of the Magi by Herod indicates the Devil's deception. The period from Adam to Noah resembles Jesus' childhood. The youth symbolizes the period from Noah to Abraham. He (Jesus) surrendered to the waters and made them holy with His body. The time of His miracles resembles the Law of Moses; His Passion, the

Babylonian captivity; the Resurrection, the liberation of the people of Israel. The infusion of the Spirit and the sending forth of the disciples are an indication of the Old Covenant that is expiring and of the conversion to a spiritual way of life....]

Now God received the Son again into the divine heart whence the Son had gone forth, even though He had remained always present within God's heart, just as we humans receive our breath back into ourselves [when we breathe]. For all the choirs of angels and all the powers of heaven looked upon the Son as both God and man. Therefore, the Son inspired His disciples with the same fire He had received within His mother's womb. He poured out a mighty power through the tongues of fire. And this power was mightier than that of a lion, which has no fear of other wild animals but preys upon them. This was so that the disciples would have no fear of other people but would overcome them. The Holy Spirit changed the disciples' life into another kind of life that they had not previously known. Through the breath of the spirit the Holy Spirit awakened them so that they no longer were sure whether they were still human. The Spirit inflicted on them a bigger and greater lot in life than it had ever inflicted on anyone in the past or than it would ever inflict on anyone in the future. Although the prophets had made many predictions about the Holy Spirit, and although many individuals have worked great wonders since the disciples, no one has ever seen the tongues of fire. Because the disciples did so with their outer eyes, they were strengthened inwardly so that they no longer felt fright or anxiety in the face of danger. For the divine power had impressed on them so much power by the fiery tongues.

But God was pleased to preserve the Twelve associated with the Son. This was so that the disciples, in turn, might teach others what they had learned from the Son. Thus God has ordered the firmament. The divine celebrations are preserved by the blowing of the twelve winds and the twelve signs of the recurring months. Just as the firmament accomplishes all God's tasks by the power of fire, the Twelve were strengthened for all their wondrous deeds by the fire of the Holy Spirit. For their teaching was to stream forth over the Earth like the blowing of a wind. Just as the sun shines, their martyrdom burned, so to speak, with the south wind.

As the months accomplish their cycle by everything that holds the firmament together, God, too, accomplished all the divine signs of the Catholic faith by those steadfast men. Through the Son, God brought back to heaven the tenth part — the human species — indicated by the [lost] drachma and rediscovered by Wisdom. And thus the only begotten Son of God is also the son of the Virgin whose name is "star of the sea"* from which all rivers flow and into which they will all return. In the same way this only begotten Son of God abides with God and from the Son comes salvation for all souls. He brought to fulfillment in Himself everything announced in advance either under the Law or prior to it. He brought everything to a better situation. And thus He is wafted on the blowing of the winds. This means that by His wondrous deeds mentioned above He goes beyond the deeds of the patriarchs, the words of the prophets, and the testimony and writings of all the scholars. In His humanity He is raised above all creation — and this is a human being! From God He receives all creation as His heritage, just as He Himself told His disciples.

Vision Seven: 16

In this way God created a superterrestrial abode and a Paradise, just as we do when we build a house for our dependents. To this home the Son of God, at God's command, brought the souls of believers after snatching them out of hell. This is what we ourselves do; after we have founded a city with a few settlers, we then bring to it a great many inhabitants. Almighty God decided all these things before the Incarnation of the divine Son, giving to us humans the advantage of being able to cooperate in the task of creation. Only we humans approach this task with our heads held high and looking up to heaven while the other living creatures are bent toward the Earth and are subject to us.

And thus we are imperishable through the rational breath of the mind, but are given over to the maggots of decay through the flesh. Wisdom is like the words of children who as yet cannot understand the meaning of words. But when they grow up, they understand what they are saying. Thus Wisdom was incomprehensible before the Incarnation of God's Son, but it was revealed in Christ since

---

*"Stella Maris" is a traditional name for Mary.

His is the root of all good fruit. The root first gives rise to the stem of a plant, the stem to the shoot, the shoot to the branches, the branches to the blossoms, and the blossoms to the fruit. Thus the root indicates Adam, the stem the patriarchs, the seed the prophets, the branches the sages, and the blossoms the Law. But the fruit indicates the incarnate Son of God who gave to true believers the forgiveness of sins by means of water. Just as a fire is put out by water, original sin and other sins are washed away in the cleansing waters of baptism. And because the Holy Spirit entered the water, it purified us from sin by means of circumcision. The Holy Spirit also healed our soul, which has been poisoned by the cunning of the old snake. As a result, our soul will thereafter be a temple of the Holy Spirit in the community of true faith. Therefore, David makes the following statement, under My inspiration, about human beings whose sins are not washed away by baptism.

Vision Seven: 17

"You bring darkness on, night falls, all the forest animals come out" (Psalm 104:20). This verse is to be understood in the following way:

[Unbelievers persist in the night and are victims of forgetfulness. But believers convert to life by permitting themselves to be purified in the waters of baptism. Only through water in the Holy Spirit can they share in salvation....]

Believers should accept these words in the humility of their hearts because this statement was revealed for the benefit of believers by One who is the First and the Last.

Translated by Robert Cunningham

Mechthild of Magdeburg

As far as can be established with any likelihood, Mechthild of Magdeburg was born around 1207 into the north German nobility and grew up the product of courtly society. At the age of twelve, she had her first visionary experience, leaving home some eleven years later to take up an ascetic life as a Beguine in Magdeburg. It was there that she began to commit her recurring visions to writing at the urging of her confessor, Heinrich of Halle, but her work on the project was interrupted by sickness as well as various attacks made against her by her critics. She completed it only shortly before her death in about 1282, by which time she had changed her affiliation and entered the Cistercian cloister at Helfta. The resulting text, *The Flowing Light of the Godhead* (originally written in Middle Low German), claims for itself the status of "revelation." Although formally varied, it is thematically unified in its depiction of the *unio mystica* as heavenly marriage between the soul, or Bride, and Christ, the Bridegroom: a depiction drawing heavily on the language and imagery of the Song of Songs. With her passionate elaboration on this traditional allegorical subject, Mechthild secures her place as representative *par excellence* of German "love mysticism."

From The Flowing Light of the Godhead

This Is the First Part of the Book

This book is to be joyfully welcomed for God Himself speaks in it

This book I now send forth as a messenger to all spiritual people both good and bad — for if the pillars fall,* the building cannot stand. The book proclaims Me alone and shows forth My holiness with praise. All who would understand this book should read it nine times.

This Book is called The Flowing Light of the Godhead

Ah! Lord God! Who has written this book? I in my weakness have written it, because I dared not hide the gift that is in it. Ah! Lord! What shall this book be called to Thy Glory? It shall be called *The Flowing Light of My Godhead* into all hearts which dwell therein without falseness.

1. *How Love and the Soul, who sits enthroned as Queen, speak together*†

SOUL

God greet thee Lady, thy name
Is known to me, it is Love!

---

*The clergy and rulers of the Church. (Menzies)
†Mechthild's language here is that of the Minnesingers, of court life. Love appears as a lady of rank at the court of heaven, wooing a royal bride for her lord. (Menzies)

LOVE

God reward thee, O Queen!

SOUL

Love! I am happy to meet thee!

LOVE

And I by the greeting, much honored.

SOUL

Love, thou didst wrestle long years
With the Holy Trinity
Till the overflow fell once for all
In Mary's humble lap!

LOVE

But, O Queen, these things were done
For thy honor and thy delight.

SOUL

Ah Love! thou hast taken from me
All I had won on earth!

LOVE

A blessed exchange, O Queen!

SOUL

To deprive me of my childhood?

LOVE

In exchange for heavenly freedom!

SOUL

Thou hast taken away my youth!

LOVE

In exchange for many virtues.

SOUL

Thou hast taken my friends and relations!

LOVE

Queen! that is a false charge!

SOUL

And taken from me the world,
Honor and all my possessions!

LOVE

These all I shall, O Queen,
In one hour by as much as thou wilt
Of the Holy Spirit, make good to thee.

SOUL

Love, thou hast tried me so sore
Through suffering, that now my body
Can barely support its weight.

LOVE

Against that loss, O Queen,
Thou hast gained great understanding.

SOUL

Ah Love! thou hast consumed
My very flesh and blood!

LOVE

Thereby art thou enlightened
And raised up to God.

SOUL

But Love, thou art a robber,
Make thou that good to me!

LOVE

That will I do, O Queen,
I pray thee — take myself!

SOUL

Now even here on earth
Thou'st paid me back again
A hundredfold, O Love!

LOVE

My Queen, now God and all
His heavenly realm are thine.

5. *Of the torment and reward of Hell**

My body is in long torment, my soul in high delight, for she has seen
and embraced her Beloved. Through Him, alas for her! she suffers
torment. As He draws her to Himself, she gives herself to Him. She
cannot hold back and so He takes her to Himself. Gladly would she
speak but dares not. She is engulfed in the glorious Trinity in high
union. He gives her a brief respite that she may long for Him. She
would fain sing His praises but cannot. She would that He might
send her to Hell, if only He might be loved above all measure by all
creatures. She looks at Him and says, "Lord! Give me Thy blessing!"
He looks at her and draws her to Him with a greeting the body
may not know —

> Thus the body speaks to the soul
> "Where hast thou been? I can bear this no more!"
> And the soul replies "Silence! Thou art a fool!
> I will be with My Love
> Even shouldst thou never recover!
> I am His joy; He is my torment — "

> This is her torment,
> Never must she recover from it
> But must ever endure it
> And never escape from it.

13. *How God comes to the soul*

> I come to My love
> As dew on the flowers.

*Such dramatic shifts in tone and alternations among voices are typical, as
Mechthild now directly, now indirectly, identifies herself with the soul or Bride.

14. *How the soul receives and praises God*

Ah! joyful sight and happy greeting! Ah! loving embrace! Lord! Thy glory has wounded me; Thy mercy has overwhelmed me! Thou mighty Rock! so gloriously cleft, wherein none may nest but the dove and the nightingale!

15. *How God receives the soul*

Welcome sweet dove!
Thou hast flown so long over the earth
That thy wings have grown strong enough
To carry thee up to Heaven!

16. *How God compares the soul to four things*

Thou art sweet as the grape;
Fragrant as balsam;
Bright as the sun —
    Thou art a heightening of My highest love!

17. *The soul praises God in five things*

O God! so generous in the outpouring of Thy gifts!
So flowing in Thy love!
So burning in Thy desire!
So fervent in union!
O Thou who dost rest on my heart
    Without whom I could no longer live!

18. *God compares the soul to five things*

O lovely rose on the thorn!
O hovering bee in the honey!
O pure dove in thy being!

O glorious sun in thy shining!
O full moon in thy course!
From thee I will never turn away.

19. *God caresses the soul in six things*

Thou art My resting place, My love, My secret peace, My deepest longing, My highest honor. Thou art a delight of My Godhead, a comfort of My manhood, a cooling stream for My ardor.

20. *The soul replies praising God in six things*

Thou art a mirror of my vision, a delight of my eyes, an escape from myself, a tempest of my heart, a fall, a weakening of my power — and yet my highest security!

22. *Of the mission of the Virgin Mary;*
how the soul was made in honor of the Trinity

The sweet dew of the uncreated Trinity distilled from the spring of the eternal Godhead in the flower of the chosen Maid. And the fruit of the flower is an immortal God and a mortal man and a living comfort of everlasting love; our Redeemer is become our Bridegroom!

The Bride is intoxicated by the sight of His glorious countenance. In her greatest strength she is overcome, in her blindness, she sees most clearly; in her greatest clearness, she is both dead and alive. The richer she becomes, the poorer she is.... The more she storms, the more loving God is to her. The higher she soars, the more brightly she shines from the reflection of the Godhead the nearer she comes to Him. The more she labors, the more sweetly she rests. The more she understands, the less she speaks. The louder she calls, the greater wonders she works with His power and her might. The more God loves her, the more glorious the course of love, the nearer the resting place, the closer the embrace. The closer the embrace, the sweeter the kiss. The more lovingly they gaze at each other, the more difficult it is to part. The more He gives her, the more she spends, the more she has. The more humbly she takes leave, the sooner she returns. The more the fire burns, the more her light increases. The more love consumes her, the brighter she shines. The vaster God's praise, the vaster her desire for Him.

Ah! whither fares our Bridegroom and Redeemer in the Jubilation of the Holy Trinity? As God willed no longer to remain in Himself, alone, therefore created He the soul and gave Himself in great love to her alone. Whereof art thou made, O Soul, that thou soarest so high over all creatures and whilst mingling in the Holy Trinity, yet remainest complete in thyself?

SOUL. — Thou hast spoken of my beginning, I was created in love, therefore nothing can express or liberate my nobleness save Love alone. Blessed Mary! Thou art the mother of this Wonder. When did that happen to thee?

THE VIRGIN MARY. — When our Father's joy was darkened by Adam's fall, so that He was angered, the everlasting wisdom of Almighty God was provoked. Then the Father chose me as Bride that He might have something to love, because His noble Bride, the soul, was dead. Then the Son chose me as mother and the Holy Spirit received me as friend. Then was I alone the Bride of the Holy Trinity and the mother of orphans whom I bore before the sight of God (that they might not quite disappear as some did). As I thus became the mother of many noble children, I was so full of the milk of compassion that I nurtured the wise men and prophets before the birth of the Son of God. After that, in my youth, I nurtured Jesus; later, as the Bride of God, I nurtured holy Church at the foot of the Cross; but from that I became dry and wretched, for the sword of the human agony of Jesus spiritually pierced my soul....But it was reborn of His life-giving wounds and lived again, young and child-like. But were it fully to recover, God's mother must be its mother and its nurse. Ah! God! it was so and it was just! God is the soul's rightful Father and the soul His rightful Bride who resembles Him in all her sorrows.

Ah! blessed Mary! In thine old age thou didst nurture the holy Apostles with thy maternal wisdom and thy powerful prayer, so that God's honor and will should be fulfilled in them. Likewise didst thou then, as now, nurture the martyrs with strong faith in their hearts; the confessors by thy protection of their ears, the maidens by thy purity, the widows with constancy, the perfect with gentleness, sinners through thy intercession. Ah! Lady! thou must still nurture us...till the Last Day. Then shalt thou see how God's children and thy children are weaned and grown up into everlasting life. Then shall we see and know in unspeakable joy, the milk and e'en the self-same breast, which Jesus oft as infant kissed.

29. Of the comeliness of the Bridegroom and how the Bride should follow Him

Vide mea sponsa! See, my Bride! how beautiful are My eyes! How comely My mouth! How fiery My heart! How delicate My hands! How swift My feet!* And follow Me!

Thou shalt be martyred with Me; betrayed through envy; tempted in the desert; imprisoned through hate; denounced through slander; thine eyes shall be bound that thou mayest not recognize the truth; thou shalt be beaten by the fury of the world; brought to judgment in confession; thy head struck with rods; sent before Herod in derision; stripped in dereliction; scourged with poverty; crowned with temptation; spat on with contempt. Thou shalt bear thy cross in hatred of sin; be crucified in renunciation of all things by thine own will; nailed on the cross by the holy virtues; wounded through love; thou shalt die on the cross in holy constancy; be pierced to the heart by constant union; taken down from the cross in true victory over all thine enemies; buried in meekness; raised up from the dead to a blessed end; drawn up to Heaven by the breath of God.

31. Thou shall not heed contempt

I was greatly despised; then our Lord said: "Be not surprised! Seeing that the sublime vessel of the Chrism was cruelly cast down and spat upon, what could happen to a vessel containing only vinegar, in which there is nothing good of itself?"

*A variation on Song of Songs 4:1ff.?

32. *Thou shalt heed neither honor nor sorrow, but avoid sin*

Should honor be offered thee, be ashamed! Shouldst thou be tormented, rejoice! Should any do good to thee, be afraid. But if thou sin against Me, thou must grieve from thy heart. If thou dost not grieve, reflect how long and how deeply I was grieved through thee!

33. *Of the trust and love of a receiver of benefits*

My soul spake thus to her Love: "Lord! Thy tenderness is a wonderful trust to my body, Thy compassion an unspeakable comfort to my soul; Thy love to my whole being, rest eternal!"

35. *The desert has twelve things*

Thou shalt love the naughting,
And flee the self.
Thou shalt stand alone
Seeking help from none,
That thy being may be quiet,
Free from the bondage of all things.

Thou shalt loose those who are bound,
And exhort the free.
Thou shalt care for the sick
Yet dwell alone.
Thou shalt drink the waters of sorrow,
And kindle the fire of love
With the faggot of virtue —
    Thus shalt thou dwell in the desert.

From the Second Part

*Of the voices of the Godhead; the light of Truth; the four rays
of God in the nine Choirs; of the Holy Trinity and of St. Mary*

O soaring eagle! darling lamb!
O glowing spark! Set me on fire!
How long must I endure this thirst?
One hour is already too long,
A day is as a thousand years
When Thou art absent!

Should this continue for eight days
I would rather go down to Hell —
(Where indeed I already am!)
Than that God should hide Himself
From the loving soul;
For that were anguish greater than human death,
Pain beyond all pain.
The nightingale must ever sing
Because its nature is love;
Whoso would take that from it
Would bring it death.
    Ah! Mighty Lord! Look on my need!

Then the Holy Spirit spoke to the soul —
"Come, noble maid! Prepare thyself,
Thy Lover comes!"
    Startled but inwardly rejoicing
She said: "Welcome, faithful messenger,
Would that it were ever so!
I am so evil and so faithless
That I can find no peace of mind
Apart from my Love.
The moment it seems that I cool
But a little from love of Him,
Then am I in deep distress
And can do nothing but seek for Him lamenting."
    Then the messenger spoke:
"Thou must purify thyself,

Sprinkle the dust with water,
Scatter flowers in thy room."
   And the exiled soul replied:
"When I purify, I blush,
When I sprinkle, I weep,
When I pray, then must I hope,
When I gather flowers, I love.
When my Lord comes
I am beside myself
For there cometh with Him such sweet melody
That all carnal desire dieth within me:
And His sweet music puts far from me
All sorrow of heart.
   The mighty voice of the Godhead
Has spoken to me in powerful words
Which I have received
With the dull hearing of my misery —
A light of utmost splendor
Glows on the eyes of my soul
Therein have I seen the inexpressible ordering
Of all things, and recognized God's unspeakable glory —
That incomprehensible wonder —
The tender caress between God and the soul,
The sufficiency in the Highest,
Discipline in understanding,
Realization with withdrawal,
According to the power of the senses,
The unmingled joy of union,
The living love of Eternity
As it now is and evermore shall be."

   Then were seen four rays of light
Which shot forth all at once
From the noble crossbow of the Trinity
From the Divine Throne through the nine Choirs.
There none is so poor nor so rich
That he is not met by Love;
The rays of the Godhead illuminate him
With inconceivable light;

The humanity of the Son greets him
In brotherly love;
The Holy Spirit flows through him
With the miraculous creative power
Of everlasting joy!
The undivided Godhead welcomes him
With the glory of His Divine Countenance
And fills him with the blessedness
Of His life-giving breath.

Love flows from God to man without effort
As a bird glides through the air
Without moving its wings —
Thus they go whithersoever they will
United in body and soul
Yet in their form separate —
As the Godhead strikes the note
Humanity sings,
The Holy Spirit is the harpist
And all the strings must sound
Which are strung in love.

There was also seen
That sublime vessel
In which Christ dwelt nine months on earth
In soul and body,
As it ever shall remain
Only without the great glory
Which at the last day
The heavenly Father will give to all
The bodies of the redeemed.
This our Lady must also lack
So long as the earth floats above the sea.

Then it was seen how nobly our Lady stood by the Throne on the
left of the heavenly Father, in all her maidenly beauty, and how her
human body was formed and tempered in the noble likeness of her
soul; how her comely breasts were so full of sweet milk that drops
of it flowed down to the glory of the Father, for the love of man,
that man might be welcomed above all creatures. Though those

great princes the Archangels marveled that human beings should be raised above them, yet is it laudable that we should be fully represented there.

On the right hand of God stood Jesus our Redeemer with open wounds —

> Bleeding, unbound,
> To overcome the judgment of the Father,
> (Which touches many sinners so nearly!)
> For so long as sin endures on the earth
> So long will the wounds of Christ
> Remain open and bleeding —
> But after the Day of Judgment
> Christ shall put on so glorious a garment
> As never before was seen.
>   Then the sweet wounds will heal
> As if a rose-leaf
> In place of the wounds there lay.
>   Then shall we see rejoicings
> Which shall never die away,
> Then will the uncreated God
> Make all His creation new
> That it shall never grow old.

Here German fails me and Latin I know not. If anything good is in this writing, it is not owing to me! But no dog ever was so bad that if its master enticed it with a piece of bread, it would not come gladly.*

---

*Under the influence of the Dominican Order (popularly known as the "Dogs of the Lord"), Mechthild often compares herself to a dog. (Menzies) Her confessor Heinrich of Halle was a Dominican.

*25. The plaint of the loving soul when God appears to shun it
and withdraw His gifts; how the soul asks God who and what it
is; of a garden of flowers and of the singing of maidens*

O Thou countless treasure in Thy riches! Thou manifold and incomprehensible Wonder! Thou endless honor in the Majesty of Thy Glory! How bitter then to me, when Thou dost shun me!

> Even should all creatures lament for me
> None could fully tell Thee
> What inhuman need I suffer;
> Human death were far gentler to me.
> I seek Thee in my thoughts
> As a bride seeking her groom;
> When bound to Thee I suffer grievously,
> For the bond is stronger than I.
> Therefore can I never free myself from Love.

> I call Thee with profound desire
> And piteous voice.
> I wait for Thee with a heavy heart,
> I cannot rest, I burn without respite
> In Thy flaming love.
> I seek Thee with all my might,
> Had I the power of a giant
> Thou wert quickly lost
> If I came upon Thy footprints.

> Ah! Love! Run not so far ahead
> But rest a little lovingly
> That I may catch Thee up!

Ah! Lord! seeing Thou hast taken from me all that I had of Thee, give me of Thy grace, the gift every dog has by nature, that of being true to my Master in my need, when deprived of all consolation. This I desire more fervently than Thy heavenly Kingdom!

> "Sweet dove! now hark to me!
> My Divine Wisdom soars so far above thee
> That I must needs order My gifts to thee
> Else couldst thou not bear them in thy poor body.

Thy secret seeking must needs find Me,
Thy heart's distress must needs compel Me;
Thy loving pursuit has so wearied Me
That I long to cool Myself
In thy pure soul in which I am imprisoned.
The throbbing sighs of thy sore heart
Have driven My justice from thee.
That is well for us both,
For I cannot be sundered from thee;
However far we are parted
Never can we be separated.
However lightly I touch thee
I cause thee bitter pain,
But were I to give Myself to thee
As oft as thou wouldest
Then would I deprive Myself of the dear refuge
I find in thee in the world.
For even a thousand beings could not contain
The desire of a loving soul,
The higher the love, the more blessed the pain!"
   "Ah! Lord! Thou sparest too much my dark prison
Wherein I drink the sorrows of the world
And eat with lamentation
The ashy bread of my deficiency,
And am wounded to death
By the fiery rays of Thy Love.
— Now leave me here, O Lord,
Unanointed and in torment!"
      "Dear heart! My Queen!
How long wilt thou be thus impatient?
If I wound thee so sore
Do I not heal thee most lovingly
In the selfsame hour?
The greatness of My Kingdom is all thine
And thou shalt have power over Me Myself!
I am lovingly inclined to thee;
If thou hast the weights, I have the gold.
All thou hast done and lost and suffered for Me
Will I give thee again,

And will Myself grant thee everlasting forgiveness
For everything thou wilt."

"Lord! I would ask Thee two things,
Teach me them in Thy mercy —
Should my eyes weep miserably,
And my lips keep silence in simplicity,
And my tongue be full of lamentation,
And my senses ask me from hour to hour
What is wrong with me — All that, O Lord,
I have from Thee!
Should my flesh fall from me, my blood evaporate,
My limbs shrivel, cramp torture every vein,
My heart dissolve in Thy love,
My soul burn as the roar of a hungry lion —
How shall it be with me then?
Where wilt Thou be then? Beloved, tell me!"

"Then art thou like a new-wed bride
Whose lover has left her sleeping —
He to whom she has given herself in all trust;
She cannot suffer that he should part from her
Even one hour. When she awakes
And finds herself alone, she laments bitterly,
It is more than she can bear.*
But the while the youth is not by her side,
Yet is she ever with him, his Bride!
He says: 'I come to thee at My pleasure, when I will!
Thou must be modest and still;
If thou but hide thy grief,
The power of love will grow in thee!
Now I will tell thee where I will be:
I am in Myself, in all places, all things,
As I ever was, without beginning.
And I await thee in the garden of love
And pluck thee the flower of sweet union,
And make thee a resting place
In the pleasant meadow of Holy Understanding.

*Cf. Song of Songs 3:1.

And the bright sun of My Eternal Godhead
Shall shine on thee
With the hidden wonder of My love
Which thou hast secretly engendered in Me.
    Then I bend down to thee
The highest branch of My Holy Trinity
From which thou shalt pluck
The green and white and red apples
Of My gentle humanity.
And the power of My Holy Spirit shall over-
shadow thee
From all earthly sorrow,
That thou canst no more think of it.
Once thou embrace the tree
I will teach thee the song of the maidens,
The way, the words, the sweet melody
Which some of themselves, those still troubled by desire
May not yet understand;
But they shall yet have a rich exchange.
Come love! Sing on and let Me hear
How thou canst sing this song!' "

"Alas! beloved! My throat is parched
From my maidenly innocence....
Yet the sweetness of Thy gentleness
Brings back music to my voice
So that I now can sing this song —
    Lord! Thy blood and mine is one unstained;
    Thy love and mine is one and undivided;
    Thy robe and mine is one, unspotted,
    Thy lips and mine are one, unkissed...."

Such are the words of the song of love:
May the sweet music of the heart ever remain in it,
For no earthly pen could ever describe it!

From the Third Part

9. *Of the beginning of all things God has made*

Ah! Father of all Good! I, an unworthy creature, thank Thee for all the faithfulness with which Thou hast drawn me out of myself into Thy marvels; that in Thy undivided Trinity I heard and saw the sublime Council which ruled before our time, when Thou, O Lord, wert enclosed in Thyself alone and hadst no one to share in Thine unspeakable Joy.

> Then the Three Persons shone so brightly in One
> That each shone through the other
> And yet was complete in itself.

The Father was adorned in Omnipotence, the Son was like the Father in unspeakable Wisdom; the Holy Spirit was like both in perfect gentleness.

Then the Holy Spirit put a plan gently before the Father and struck the Holy Trinity asunder and said, "Lord and Father, I will give Thee of Thyself, a gentle counsel: We will no longer be unfruitful! We will have a creative Kingdom and make angels after My pattern that they be one spirit with me; the second spirit shall be man.

> For that alone is Joy
> Which in great love and inconceivable happiness
> We share with others in Thy Presence."

Then the Father spoke: "Thou art one Spirit with Me; what Thou dost counsel pleases Me. When the angel was created, Thou knowest what happened. Even had the fall of the angel been prevented, man had to be created. The Holy Spirit gave the angels His goodness that they might serve Us and delight in Our blessedness."

Then the everlasting Son spoke with conviction: "Dear Father! My nature, too, must bear fruit. As We are now to work wonders, let Us fashion man after My Pattern! Although I foresee great trouble yet I must love man eternally."

Then the Father spoke: "Son! I, too, have a great longing in My Divine heart and I hear the call of love. We will become fruitful so that man will love Us in return and recognize in some measure Our great glory. I will make Myself a Bride who shall greet Me with her mouth and wound Me with her glance. Then first will love begin."

Then the Holy Spirit spoke, "Dear Father, I will lead Thy Bride to Thee."

And the Son spoke, "Father! Thou knowest that I am yet to die for love. Yet let Us begin these things in great joy and holiness."

Then the Holy Trinity gave itself to the creation of all things and made us body and soul in infinite love. Adam and Eve were fashioned nobly after the pattern of the Everlasting Son, begotten of the Father without beginning. The Son shared His heavenly wisdom and His earthly form with Adam —

> That he might have in perfect love
> True knowledge and holy senses
> To offer to all earthly creatures —
> That is now very dear to us!

Then the Lord gave Adam in love, a modest, noble, little maid. That was Eve. He gave her the same humble love He Himself bore in honor of the Father. Their bodies should remain pure for God did not create anything that should shame them and they were clothed as angels. They should conceive their children in holy love as the sun plays upon the waters and leaves them untroubled. But from the time they ate the forbidden fruit, their bodies were altered so that they did feel shame, as we still do today. Had the Holy Trinity made us like the angels, owing to the noble nature of that creation, we would have had no need to be ashamed.

The heavenly Father shared His divine love with the soul and said, "I am the God of all gods; thou art the goddess of all creatures and I give thee My solemn vow that I will never forsake thee. That thou mayst not lose thyself, My angels shall ever serve thee. I will give thee My Holy Spirit as thy guardian that thou mayst not unwittingly fall into mortal sin and I also give thee . . . free will. Thou shalt love Love before all things and go forward with prudence.

> Thou shalt keep a simple law
> Which thou must always remember —
> That I am thy God!
> The soul which feeds on the pure food
> God left for it in Paradise,

Shall remain in great holiness
In its mortal body.
But as Adam and Eve ate the food
Not intended for them
They lost angelic purity
And forgot chastity."

Then for many years
The soul called for her love
With plaintive voice
And in great darkness, saying,
"Ah! Lord! whence came Thy sweet love?
How sorely hast Thou banished Thy rightful Queen!

(This is the meaning of the Prophets)
Ah! Lord! how canst Thou suffer this long distress
That Thou dost not slay our death?
Thou didst will to be born —
But, Lord, all Thy doing is accomplished,
Yea! Even Thy wrath!"

Then began a solemn council in the Holy Trinity.
The Father spoke: I repent Me of My work
For I had given the Holy Trinity
So noble a Bride
That the highest angels
Should have been her waiting-maids;
Had Lucifer remained in his place of honor
She should have been his goddess.
For her alone was the nuptial couch prepared
— But she wished no longer to be like Me...
Now is she horribly misshapen —
Who would accept such dirt?

Ah! then the everlasting Son knelt before His Father and said: "I
will take her! Give Me Thy blessing! I will gladly take blood-stained
humanity upon Myself and will heal its wounds with My innocent
blood and will bind them up to the end with the cloth of humility.
And I will requite human sin to Thee, by human death."

Then the Holy Spirit spoke: "O Almighty God! We will make a noble procession and will proceed in glory down from these heights. I have once already waited on the Virgin Mary."

Then the Father bowed in great love to both their wills and said to the Holy Spirit: "Carry My light before My dear Son into all those hearts He shall touch with My words. But Thou, Son, shalt take up Thy Cross. I will go with Thee in all Thy ways and will give Thee a pure maid as mother, that Thou mayst more nobly uphold ignoble humanity."

Then the procession moved with great joy into the Temple of Solomon. And there Almighty God took shelter for nine months....

10. *The Passion of the loving soul which it has from God; how it rises and goes to Heaven*

The longing soul is betrayed in true love, in sighing after God. She is sold in holy lamentation for her love. She is besought by many tears for her dear Lord whom she longs to find. She is caught in the first moment of recognition when God kisses her in sweet union. She is seized by many holy thoughts as she mortifies the flesh that she may not waver. She is bound by the power of the Holy Spirit and her delight is manifold. She is overwhelmed by great weakness so that she cannot bear the everlasting Light without intermission. She is dragged before the Judge in trembling shame because God is so often withdrawn from her on account of her sins. She answers all things modestly and would not willingly vex any. Her cheeks are buffeted in the Tribune when devils assail her spirit. She is taken before Herod when she recognizes herself as worthless and unworthy and despises herself in thinking of her great Lord. She is taken before Pilate for she must attend to earthly things. She is shouted at, beaten and sore wounded, when she must return to her body. She is clothed with the purple of great love. She is crowned with manifold fidelity so long as she does not ask God to reward her for her faithfulness but to accept it to His praise. She is scoffed at because she loses herself so utterly in God that she forgets earthly wisdom. She kneels at the feet of all creation to the mockery of others. Her eyes are bound with the unworthiness of her body wherein she lies imprisoned in darkness. She bears her cross along a pleasant way because in all her

suffering she gives herself utterly to God. Her head is struck with a
rod because in her great holiness she seems like a fool. She is nailed
so firmly to the cross by the hammer of Almighty Love that not all
creatures can release her. She thirsts greatly on the Cross of Love
and would fain drink the pure wine of all God's children.

> Then they all come
> And offer her gall.
> Her body is slain
> In living Love,
> And her spirit is raised up
> Above all human comprehension.
> After this death she goes to Hell
> And comforts sorrowing souls
> With her prayers of God's goodness,
> Though her body knows nothing of it.
> She is pierced in her side
> By one blind to innocent love
> And from her heart there pours forth
> Much holy teaching.

She hangs high on the Cross of Love in the pure air of the Holy
Spirit, turned toward the Son of the living Godhead, oblivious of
all earthly things. Thus, in a holy end, she is taken down from the
Cross and says: "Father, receive my spirit. It is finished." She is laid
in a sealed grave of deep humility for she has ever known herself
the most unworthy of all creatures.

She rises happily on Easter Day having joyfully conversed with her
Love in the night. In the early morning, with Mary Magdalene she
comforts her maidens when she is assured that God has blotted out
all her sins through the remorse of love.... Thus she goes out from
the Jerusalem of Holy Church with a brave troop of virtues. Her
body distresses her for with its ignoble art it would gladly command
her will. But she insists to the virtues, "I am your Mistress; Ye must
obey me in all things. If I did not go to my Father ye would ever
remain fools!"

Then she ascends into Heaven where God supernaturally takes all
earthly things from her. She is received into a white cloud of holy
protection whence she is lovingly borne aloft and returns free from

all care. Then the angels come and comfort the Man of Galilee, when we remember God's chosen friends and their holy example.

Such a passion must be suffered by every soul truly penetrated by the love of God.

15. *Thou shalt go to God's Table with eight virtues*

Ah, foolish Beguines! How can ye be so bold that ye do not tremble before our Almighty Judge when, as so often, ye receive the Body of the Lord as a matter of blind habit? Now I, who am the least of you all, am ever ashamed! I blush! I tremble! On one great Festival I was so afraid that I did not dare to receive because I was ashamed of even my greatest merit before the eyes of our Lord. Then I begged my Beloved that He would show me His will. He said: "Truly, when thou goest before Me in humble lamentation and holy fear, I must fain follow thee as the flood, the millstream. But if thou meet Me with the flowering desire of flowing love, then must I touch thee with My divine nature as My Queen." If I am truly to show forth the goodness of God, then I am obliged to speak of myself. But that hinders me now truly no more than it hinders a hot oven to fill it with cold dough.

I went to God's Table with a noble band. They took care of me and saved me from many dangers. Truth censured me; Fear rebuked me; Shame drove me on; Remorse judged me; Desire drew me; Love led me to the goal. Christian Faith protected me; the true meaning of all good things prepared me; and all my good works cried Alas! and Alas! over me. Almighty God received me; His pure humanity united itself with me and His Holy Spirit comforted me.

Then I said: "Lord! now Thou art mine for Thou art given to me this very day on which it was declared unto us *Puer natus est nobis*, Unto us a Child is born!* Now I desire, O Lord, Thy praise, not my gain; that this day Thy Blessed Body may comfort poor souls. Thou art truly mine, now this day Thou shalt be a ransom for prisoners."

Then the soul won such power that she led Him by His might till they came to the most dreadful place my eyes ever lit upon. A bath was there prepared of fire and pitch, dirt, smoke, and

*Isaiah 9:6.

stench. A thick black cloud hung over it like a black skin. And therein lay souls like toads in filth. Their form was human, yet they were apparitions and had the devil's likeness in them. They stewed and roasted together. They cried out and suffered unspeakable things because of their bodies through which they had fallen so low. Their flesh had blinded their spirits; therefore they seethed here.

Then the human spirit spoke: "O Lord! how many of these poor creatures are there? Thou art my true ransom! Thou must take pity!" Then our Lord spoke: "Their number is above all human counting, thou canst not even grasp it because thou too art of the earth. These were all broken vessels who on earth forgot their spiritual life. They are from all ages and all lands."

Then the human spirit asked: "But, dear Lord, where are the hermits of whom I see no trace?" Our Lord answered: "Their sins were secret, therefore they are bound in a separate place...." Then the spirit was deeply distressed and laid itself down at our Lord's feet and longed mightily to be of loving service and said, "Ah, Lord! Thou knowest well what I desire!" And our Lord said: "Thou didst well to bring Me here. I will not be unmindful of them."

A great troop of devils stood round about and tormented the souls in the accursed bath. They were more than I could count and they rubbed and tweaked and nagged the souls and struck them with fiery thongs. The human spirit spoke to them: "Listen ye sin-eaters! Look on this ransom! Is it not precious enough to satisfy you?" Then they were terrified, quaking in utter shame and said: "Now we must flee from here. For however accursed we are, we must give way to Truth."

Then out of His Divine heart our Lord fulfilled the desire of the poor souls and they rose up in love and joy. The soul said: "Ah, dear Lord! whither shall they go now?" And He replied, "I will lead them to a hillside covered with flowers; there they will find joy greater than I can say." Then He waited on them and was their servant and their beloved companion. He said to me there were seventy thousand of them. Whereupon I asked how long their sufferings had lasted and He said: "For thirty years they have been separated from their bodies; they should have stayed another ten years in torment had not so noble a ransom been given for them." Then the devils fled, afraid to take the ransom. "Beloved," said the soul, "how long must they still stay here?" And our Lord answered, "As long as seems good to Us."

24. *Two kinds of persons are offered two kinds of spirit by God*

Now I will write of a truly spiritual sister and a worldly Beguine who conversed together. The sister spoke from the true light of the Holy Spirit without sorrow, but the Beguine spoke materially in the spirit of Lucifer, in a complaining way. There are two kinds of spiritual persons on Earth; they are offered two kinds of spirit. God offers His Holy Spirit to those pure beings who live in faithful holiness. Thus two pure natures come together, the glowing Fire of the Godhead and the gradual growth of the loving soul. If there is thus a pure dwelling ready for humility, a bright light will be kindled which will be seen from far. Then, O loving soul, thou wilt be rich with riches which no one can take from thee, even wert thou the poorest of the poor. Through humility one becomes rich; through discipline and a well-ordered life one becomes noble and modest; through love one becomes lovely and praiseworthy; through undeserved contempt one is raised up on high before God. Think of this, sister, and let no one drive thee from thy good habits. So shalt thou remain holy.

> The devil also offers his spirit
> To those who in hatred and proud desire
> Are ready for the worst.
> Such know not that love leads to all good,
> They become poor from hatred
> And the fury of the devil,
> So that it becomes impossible
> They should ever again find or follow
> The love of God.
> True love praises God constantly;
> Longing love gives the pure heart sweet sorrow;
> Seeking love belongs to itself alone;
> Understanding love loves all in common;
> Enlightened love is mingled with sadness;

Selfless love bears fruit without effort;
It functions so quietly
That the body knows nothing of it.
Clear love is still, in God alone,
Seeing that both have one will
And there is no creature so noble
That it can hinder them.
    This is written by Knowledge
Out of the everlasting book.
Gold is often heavily flecked by copper,
Just as falseness and vain honor
Blot out virtue from the human soul.
The ignoble soul to whom passing things are
so dear
That it never trembled before Love
Never heard God speak lovingly in it —
Alas! to such this life is all darkness!

From the Fourth Part

12. *How the Bride who is united with God refuses all creaturely comfort and accepts it of God alone; how she sinks under suffering*

Thus speaks the Bride of God who has dwelt in the enclosed sanctuary of the Holy Trinity — "Away from me all ye creatures! Ye pain me and cannot comfort me!" And the creatures ask, "Why?" The Bride says, "My Love has left me while I rested beside him and slept." But the creatures ask, "Can this beautiful world and all your blessings not comfort you?" "Nay," says the Bride, "I see the serpent of falsehood and false wisdom creeping into all the joy of this world. I see also the hook of covetousness in the bait of ignoble sweetness by which it ensnares many."

"Can even the Kingdom of Heaven not comfort thee?" ask the creatures. "Nay! it were dead in itself were the living God not there!" "Now, O Bride, can the saints not comfort thee?" "Nay! for were they separated from the living Godhead which flows through them,

they would weep more bitterly than I for they have risen higher than
I and live more deeply in God."

"Can the Son of God not comfort thee?"
Yea! I ask Him when we shall go
Into the flowery meadows of heavenly knowledge
And pray Him fervently,
That He unlock for me
The swirling flood which plays about the Holy Trinity,
For the soul lives on that alone.
  If I am to be comforted
According to the merit to which God has raised me,
Then His breath must draw me effortlessly into Himself.
For the sun which plays upon the living Godhead
Irradiates the clear waters of a joyful humanity;
And the sweet desire of the Holy Spirit
Comes to us from both....
Nothing can satisfy me save God alone,
Without Him I am as dead.
Yet would I gladly sacrifice the joy of His presence
Could He be greatly honored thereby.
For if I, unworthy, cannot praise God with all my might,
Then I send all creatures to the Court of Heaven
And bid them praise God for me,
With all their wisdom, their love,
Their beauty; all their desires,
As they were created, sinless by God,
To sing with all the sweetness of their voices
As they now sing.
Could I but witness this praise
I would sorrow no more.

Neither can I bear that a single consolation be given me save by
Love alone. I love my earthly friends in a heavenly fellowship and
I love my enemies with a holy longing for their salvation. God has
enough of all good things save of intercourse with the soul; of that
He can never have enough.

When this wonder and this consolation had continued for eight
years God wished to comfort me more mightily, far above my
deserts. "Nay, dear Lord! do not raise me up too high!" cried this

unworthy soul. "It is even now too much for me here in the lowest place. Gladly will I stay here to Thy honor." Then the soul fell down below the ill-fated souls who had forfeited their reward, and it seemed good to her so. There our Lord followed her as some others also did, who, so far as they could bear it, had gone to the state of least joy. For God appeared to them all beautiful and glorious, according as they had here been sanctified in love and ennobled in virtue. St. John says, "We shall see God as He is" (1 John 3:2). That is true, but the sun shines after the storm and there are many kinds of storms in this world, just as there are many mansions in Heaven. According as I can bear it and see it, so is it with me.

Then our Lord said: "How long wouldst thou stay here?" The Bride answered: "Ah! leave me dear Lord and let me sink further down, to Thy Glory!" Then soul and body came into such gross darkness that I lost light and consciousness and knew no more of God's intimacy; ever-blessed Love also went its way. Then the soul spoke: "Constancy! where art thou? I entrust to thee the mission of love; thou shalt uphold the glory of God in me!" Then this servitor Constancy strengthened her mistress with such holy patience and joyful forbearance that she lived without care. But Unbelief came and surrounded me with such darkness and roared at me in such fury that his voice frightened me and I said to myself, "If thy former grace had been from God He would not so utterly have forsaken thee!"

Then my soul cried: "Where art thou now, O Constancy? Bid true Faith to come to me!" And the heavenly Father spoke to the soul: "Remember what thou didst see and experience when there was nothing between Me and thee!" Then spoke the Son: "Remember what thy body has suffered for My pain." And the Holy Spirit said: "Remember what thou hast written!" Then both soul and body answered with the true faith of Constancy: "As I have praised and loved, enjoyed and known, thus will I go unchanged from here!"

After this came the state of Forsaken-ness of God and so surrounded the soul that it cried: " Welcome blessed Forsaken-ness! Well for me that I was born and that thou, Constancy, shalt now be my waiting-maid, for thou bringest me unaccustomed joy and inconceivable wonders and sweetness beyond what I can bear. But, Lord, Thou must take this sweetness from me and leave me only Forsaken-ness. Well for me, O faithful Lord, that after the transformation of love I can yet bear it in the palate of my soul."

And here I asked all creatures to praise our Lord in the *Te Deum Laudamus*. But they would not and turned their backs on me. Then my soul was glad and said: "Well for me that ye despise me and turn your backs on me, for that praises our Lord immeasurably!"*

Now is God marvelous to me and his Forsaken-ness better even than Himself. That the soul knew full well. For as God was about to comfort her she said: "Remember, O Lord, how lowly I am and withhold Thyself from me!" Then our Lord spoke to me: "Grant me that I may cool the glow of My Godhead, the desire of My humanity and the delight of My Holy Spirit in thee." The soul answered: "Yea, Lord, but only if that is well for Thee alone — and not for me!"

After that the Bride came into such great darkness that sweat and cramp racked her body. She was asked by some if she would be a messenger from them to God. She said: "Pain! I command thee that thou now release me, seeing that thou hast reached thy highest power in me." Then Pain rose from soul and body like a dark cloud and went to God and cried with a loud voice: "Lord! Thou knowest well what I desire!" Our Lord met Pain before the gate of the Kingdom and said: "Welcome, Pain! Thou art the garment I wore on My body upon earth: the contempt of the whole world was My most glorious cloak. But however much I prized thee there, thou canst not enter here. But to the maid who will do two things I will give two things. She must be modest and wise and it would help her if thou wouldst be her messenger; then will I embrace her and take her to My heart in union." Pain spoke thus: "Lord! I make many holy, though I myself am not holy and I nourish many holy bodies though I myself am evil, and I bring many to heaven, though I may never enter in myself." To this our Lord answered: "Pain! thou wast not born in Heaven, therefore canst thou not enter therein. Moreover, thou wast born out of Lucifer's heart, there thou must return and live forevermore."

Ah! blessed Forsaken-ness of God! how lovingly I am bound to thee! Thou strengthenest my will in suffering and makest dear to me the long difficult waiting in this poor body. The nearer I come to thee, the greater and more wonderful God appears to me. Ah!

*The paradox of Mechthild's formulations becomes most apparent here.

Lord! even in the depths of unmixed humility, I cannot sink utterly
away from Thee —

> In pride I so easily lost Thee —
> But now the more deeply I sink
> The more sweetly I drink
> Of Thee!

14. *Of the Holy Trinity: of the birth and name of Jesus Christ and of the nobility of man*

I saw and see three Persons in the everlasting heights, before the Son
of God was conceived in the Virgin Mary. There they were recognized and differentiated by all the holy angels in their Unity and in
their names, that they three were One God. But however clear the
eyes of the angels, they did not see flesh nor bone nor color nor the
Lord's Name of Jesus. This was miraculously hidden from them in
the bosom of the Everlasting Father. They called the Father the Uncreated, Everlasting God and the Son, Wisdom-without-beginning.
Both together they called the real Art of Truth.

The angels of the highest rank were those who hovered over the
Love of the Godhead in a breath of the Trinity, angels who served
and looked on at the wonderful decree by which God became God-
and-man. Gabriel alone carried the message and the name of Jesus
down to earth and he was given neither flesh nor bone nor blood to
take with him. The second Person was from the beginning the everlasting Son, even before He had redeemed mankind. He was always
ours and yet was not given to us until Gabriel fulfilled his mission.
If this same second Person had come before the mission to redeem
us, He would have had a beginning. That was not so. This same second Person became one nature with Adam before he soiled himself
through sin. But what broke and changed Adam's nature was not of
God, therefore we could and can still return. God preserved Adam's
noble, loving nature, therefore He could not withhold Himself from
him: He threw Lucifer down to an everlasting dungeon, but He drew
Adam back and questioned him and brought him again to the right
way. Lucifer had only one nature in God; when he destroyed that,
he could never return.

Man has full being in the Holy Trinity and God condescended to form him with His own divine hands. When He lost that most holy work on us, He was constrained in Himself by a threefold desire; He wished to bring us back Himself, with His own feet and hands, that we might again be closely united to Him. If mankind had stayed in Paradise, God would have regarded him as His son and would have greeted his soul and rejoiced in his body. Thus I saw God coming from Heaven into Paradise like a glorious angel. The same nature still compels God to greet us here as friends, with holy fervor, in so far as we are prepared with holy virtues and true innocence.

When I reflect that the divine nature now has bone, flesh, body, and soul, then I am raised up with joy above what I deserve. The angel also is formed in some ways after the likeness of the Holy Trinity; yet he is pure spirit. The soul alone lives with its flesh in Heaven and sits by the everlasting Host whom it resembles. There eye meets eye, spirit flows into spirit, hand clasps hand, mouth speaks to mouth, heart greets heart. Thus the Host honors the humble housewife by His side. And the princes and servitors are the holy angels whom the Host has before His eyes. All the service as well as the praise of the angels are offered to the humble housewife as well as to the Host. The richer we are here in holy virtues, the greater the rank of those who serve us there.

15. *Pure love has four essentials. If thou givest thyself to God, He will give Himself to thee*

Pure love of God has four essentials which never change. The first is growing desire, the second incessant vexations, the third burning love in soul and body, the fourth constant union combined with strict watchfulness. None can reach this state save he who makes a complete exchange with God. If thou givest God all that thine is, within and without, God will truly give thee all that His is, within and without.

> When the blessed hour has passed
> In which God has granted the loving
> soul
> His sublime consolation;

Then is the soul so full of delight
That everything seems to it good
Which might hurt a loveless soul.
Art thou displeased? Then it is much to
be feared
The devil has anointed thee!

From the Fifth Part

22. *Of seven demands of the Law*

The noblest joy of the senses, the holiest peace of the heart, and the most loving luster of all good works come from the fact that the creature puts his heart into what he does. Here our Lord speaks and teaches me of seven things the blessed must have, those who would rather submit to the Last Judgment through Jesus Christ than any human judgment. Whosoever has not got these things must stand before the Judge as a hired servant before his master, for all who strive against God's Truth with ready lies, really sell these virtues.

The first demand is righteousness in the present; that is, if I see my friend act wrongly toward my enemy and God's enemy, then I blame my friend and lovingly help my enemy.

The second is compassion in need; if I see my friend and my enemy in equal need, I shall help both equally.

The third is faithfulness in friendship: I will never rebuke my friend except for his unfaithful soul.

The fourth is help in secret need; that we seek and find the stranger, the sick and the prisoner and comfort them with friendly words and prayers and beg them to tell Thee their secret needs that Thou mayest help them.

Alas! that any should ever leave the sick or outcast without tears and sighs and compassion —

This ill becomes spiritual people
And sets them aloof from God
So that they lose His sweet intimacy

And yet will not realize
That they incur His judgment.

The fifth demand is that one should be silent in irritation; that the harsh word which rises from a proud and angry heart should not be spoken; from this one finds endless grace in God.

The sixth is that one shall be filled with truth: that person is full of truth whose heart in his best moments gives way to no fault; who rejoices that God's eye sees right into his heart and has nothing of which to be ashamed even were all men to see into his heart.

The seventh is that one shall be the sworn enemy of lying; we should rebuke lying in everyone and not hide it in ourselves.

These seven virtues we shall practice and achieve
Against the will of our own rebellious flesh,
And against the pull and weakness of the senses,
Otherwise we shall not attain them.
But the nobility of the soul toward all good
Gives us with the gentleness of God's love,
The first counsel:
Our sinful nature neglects
In its ignoble way many a divine day.
When we think of the blessed hours
In which God out of the depths of His heart,
His wisdom and His joyful nature,
Ceaselessly pours forth all good,
And out of His sweet mouth
Spiritually tempers our souls,
— Wisely in the senses, usefully in our bodies —
Then must we be ashamed, outwardly of our evil habits
Inwardly of our faithless hearts.

We must also be ashamed of our senses
That we make such poor use
Of the noble and manifold gifts of God:
That they bring back so little fruit
To that place whence there flowed out on us
The very heart of God!
Alas! for my sinful sufferings!

Good will brings all virtue to its rightful end
A task for which the body alone
Has not the power.

From the Sixth Part

26. *Thoughts of death and a long life are good*

I ponder much and reflect in my human senses how wonderful my soul is. For when I think of death, my soul rejoices so greatly at the thought of going forth from this earthly life, that my body soars in a supernatural peace beyond words; and my senses recognize the marvels which attend the passing hence of the soul; so that I would most gladly die at the time foreseen by God. At the same time I would gladly live till the last great day and in my heart I long for the days of the martyrs that I might have shed my blood for Jesus whom I love. That I dare to say I love God is because a special gift forces me to do so. For when my burdens and sufferings are held before me, my soul begins to burn in the fire of true love of God in such blissful sweetness, that even my body soars in divine bliss. But my senses still continue to lament and pray for all who have injured or maligned me, that God would keep them from sin.

29. *Of ten characteristics of the Divine Fire and of the nobility of God*

An unworthy creature thought simply about the nobility of God. Then God showed him in his senses and the eyes of his soul, a Fire which burned ceaselessly in the heights above all things. It had burned without beginning and would burn without end. This Fire is the everlasting God who has retained in Himself Eternal Life from which all things proceed. The sparks which have blown away from the Fire are the holy angels. The beams of the Fire are the saints of God for their lives cast many lovely lights on Christianity. The coals of the Fire still glow; they are the just who here burn in heavenly love and enlighten by their good example: as they were chilled by sin they now warm themselves at the glowing coals. The crackling sparks which are reduced to ashes and come to nothing are the bodies of the blessed, who in the grave still await their heavenly reward. The Lord of the Fire is still to come, Jesus Christ to whom the Father entrusted the first Redemption and the last Judgment. On the Last Day He shall make a glorious chalice for the heavenly Father out of the sparks of the Fire; from this chalice the Father will on the day of His Eternal Marriage drink all the holiness which, with His Beloved Son, He has poured into our souls and our human senses.

> Yea! I shall drink from Thee
> And Thou shalt drink from me
> All the good God has preserved in us.
> Blessed is he who is so firmly established here
> That he may never spill out
> What God has poured into him.

The smoke of the Fire is made of all earthly things which man uses with wrongful delight. However beautiful to our eyes, however pleasant to our hearts, they yet carry in them much hidden bitterness. For they disappear as smoke and blind the eyes of the highest, till the tears run.

The comfort of the Fire is the joy our souls receive inwardly from God, with such holy warmth from the Divine Fire, that we too burn with it and are so sustained by virtues that we are not extinguished. The bitterness of the Fire is the word God shall speak on the Last Day, *Depart from Me ye cursed into everlasting fire!* (Matthew 25:41). The radiance of the Fire is the glowing aspect of the divine countenance of the Holy Trinity, which shall so illumine our souls and bodies that we may then see and recognize the marvelous blessedness we cannot even name here.

These things have come out of the Fire and flow into it again according to God's ordinance in everlasting praise.

> Wouldst thou know my meaning?
> Lie down in the Fire
> See and taste the Flowing
> Godhead through thy being;
> Feel the Holy Spirit
> Moving and compelling

Thee within the Flowing
Fire and Light of God.

From the Seventh Part

57. *A little of Paradise*

This was shown to me and I saw how Paradise was made. There is no limit to its length or breadth. First I came to a place which was between this world and the beginning of Paradise. There I saw trees and leaves, clover and grass, but no weeds. Some trees bore apples but most of them only fragrant leaves. Swiftly flowing streams ran through this Paradise and warm winds blew from south to north. In the waters earthly sweetness was mingled with heavenly bliss. The air was sweet beyond expression. But there were neither beasts nor birds for God had commanded it should be for human beings alone that they might live at peace therein.

Then I saw two men therein, Enoch and Elias.* Enoch sat and Elias lay on the ground in inward fervor. I asked Enoch how they lived according to their human nature. He said, "We eat a few apples and drink a little water that the body may be kept alive, but the greatest thing here is the power of God." I asked him how they came there. He answered, "I know not how I came till I found myself sitting here." I asked about his prayer. "Faith and Hope, we pray in them." I asked how he was, if he was ever troubled. And he said, "All is well with me, I have no sorrow." I asked, "Dost thou not fear for the strife that shall come upon the Earth?" He said, "God will arm me with His power that I can withstand the onslaught." I asked, "Dost thou pray for the Church?" He said, "I pray that God will loose it from sin and bring it into His Kingdom."

Then Elias rose up and his face shone with heavenly radiance; his hair was white as wool. Both were poorly clad as men who went about with pilgrims' staves begging their bread. I asked Elias how he prayed for the Church. "I pray with compassion, humbly, faithfully and obediently." I asked, "Dost thou also pray for souls?" And he

---

*The two are principals of the apocalyptic literature.

said, "Yes! the more I pray the more their suffering is lessened.... As I pray their suffering goes." I asked, "Will they be redeemed from their suffering?" And he said, "Yes, many of them." I asked, "Why did God bring you here?" And he said, "That we may help the Church and God before the Last Day."

I saw a twofold Paradise; I have spoken of the earthly part. The heavenly Paradise is above and protects the earthly Paradise from all adversity. The souls are in the highest part, those who did not need to go to Purgatory and yet were not ready for the Kingdom of God —

> They soar in bliss
> As the air in the sun.
> Lordship and honor, rewards and crowns
> They have not yet,
> Till they enter the Kingdom.
>   If all earth passed away
> And the earthly Paradise was no more,
> After God had fulfilled His law
> The heavenly Paradise too would pass away.
> All who would come to God
> Shall live in one mansion
> But there will be no sick-house any more
> For whoso comes to God's Kingdom
> Is free of all sickness.
>   Praised be Jesus Christ
> Who has given us His Kingdom!

Translated by Lucy Menzies

Meister Eckhart

Meister Eckhart (c. 1260–1327/28) is widely considered the most important figure in the history of German mysticism. His early life parallels that of other mystics who preceded him: he was born into a noble family in Hochheim (Thuringia) and entered the religious life at an early age, receiving his primary education from the Dominicans at Erfurt. After pursuing more advanced studies in Cologne and Paris, he returned to Erfurt to serve as Dominican Prior there and as Vicar of Thuringia (until 1302). His life thereafter remained peripatetic, as he alternated between interludes of teaching/study (notably again in Paris, where he received his master's degree and the title "Meister") and increasingly important administrative assignments in Germany. In 1326, while in Cologne, he became embroiled in Inquisition proceedings when various of his propositions came under suspicion of heresy. Despite answering the charges against him in a written "Defense," he was condemned posthumously, by papal bull, in 1329. Since the propositions under dispute were taken mainly from his German works (some Latin writings also survive), the selections included here may give a good indication of what some of his contemporaries found so jarring and heterodox about Eckhart's teaching. (The transmission of these rests largely on the transcripts of his students.) Whether in his treatises ("Talks of Instruction"; "About Disinterest") or his sermons, he articulates the mystical ideal in the classic terms of the speculative tradition, defining *unio mystica* as simple identification with God, beyond all striving and beyond all affect.

From "The Talks of Instruction"

2. *Of the strongest prayer and the most exalted work*

The strongest prayer, one well-nigh almighty in what it can effect, and the most exalted work a man can do proceed from a pure heart. The more pure it is, the more powerful, and the more exalted, useful, laudable and perfect is its prayer and work. A pure heart is capable of anything.

What is a pure heart?

A pure heart is one that is unencumbered, unworried, uncommitted, and which does not want its own way about anything but which, rather, is submerged in the loving will of God, having denied self. Let a job be ever so inconsiderable, it will be raised in effectiveness and dimension by a pure heart.

We ought so to pray that every member and faculty, eyes, ears, mouth, heart, and the senses shall be directed to this end and never to cease prayer until we attain unity with Him to whom our prayers and attention are directed, namely, God.

3. *Of undevoted people who are full of self-will*

People say: "Alas, sir, but I would prefer to stand well with God, to have the devotion and divine calm of some people," or "I wish I could be like this or as poor as that." Or they say: "It will never do if I cannot be here or there and do thus and so. I must get away — or go into a cloister or a cell."

The truth is that you yourself are at fault in all this and no one else. It is pure self-will. Whether you realize it or not, there can be no restlessness unless it come from self-will, although not every person understands this. This is what I mean: people fly from this to seek that — these places, these people, these manners, those purposes, that activity — but they should not blame ways or things;

for thwarting them. When you are thwarted, it is your own attitude that is out of order.

Begin, therefore, first with self and forget yourself! If you do not first get away from self, then whatever else you get away from you will still find obstacles and restlessness. People look in vain for peace, who seek it in the world outside, in places, people, ways, activities, or in world-flight, poverty and humiliation, whatever the avenue or degree; for there is no peace this way. They are looking in the wrong direction, and the longer they look the less they find what they are looking for. They go along like someone who has missed his road; the farther they go the more they are astray.

What, then, is to be done?

Let everyone begin by denying self and in so doing he will have denied all else. Indeed, if a man gave up a kingdom, or even the whole world and still was selfish, he would have given up nothing. If, however, he denies himself, then whatever he keeps, be it wealth, honor, or anything else, he is free from it all.

Commenting on St. Peter's words, "See, Lord, we have forsaken all," when he had forsaken nothing but his nets and smacks, a saint named Hieronymous* says: "To give up your little bit willingly is to give up not this alone but all that worldly people seek after, indeed all they could possibly desire." To give up one's will and deny self is to forsake all else as completely as if it had been his very own, and he possessed it with full authority. For what you do not desire you let go, and let go for the sake of God. Thus our Lord says: "Blessed are the poor in spirit" — that is, [those devoid] of will and there should be no doubt that if there were a better way, the Lord would have mentioned it. But He said: "If any man will come after me, let him first deny himself." It all comes down to that. Watch yourself, and where you find self [creeping in], reject it; for that is best.

4. Of the usefulness of denial, to be practiced inwardly and outwardly

Know that no man in this life ever gave up so much that he could not find something else to let go. Few people, knowing what this

*St. Jerome (340–420).

means, can stand it long, [and yet] it is an honest requital, a just exchange. To the extent that you eliminate self from your activities, God comes into them — but not more and no less. Begin with that, and let it cost you your uttermost. In this way, and no other, is true peace to be found.

People ought not to consider so much what they are to do as what they *are*; let them but *be* good and their ways and deeds will shine brightly. If you are just, your actions will be just too. Do not think that saintliness comes from occupation; it depends rather on what one is. The kind of work we do does not make us holy but we may make it holy. However "sacred" a calling may be, as it is a calling, it has no power to sanctify; but rather we *are* and have the divine being within, we bless each task we do, be it eating, or sleeping, or watching, or any other. Whatever they do, who have not much of [God's] nature, they work in vain.

Thus take care that your emphasis is laid on *being* good and not on the number or kind of thing to be done. Emphasize rather the fundamentals on which your work depends.

6. On solitude and the attainment of God

I was asked this question: "Some people withdraw from society and prefer to be alone; their peace of mind depends on it; wouldn't it be better for them to be in the church?" I replied, No! And you shall see why.

Those who do well, do well wherever they are, and in whatever company, and those who do badly, do badly wherever they are and in whatever company. But if a man does well, God is really in him, and with him everywhere, on the streets and among people, just as much as in church, or a desert place, or a cell. If he really has God and only God, then nothing disturbs him. Why?

Because he has *only* God and thinks only God and everything is nothing but God to him. He discloses God in every act, in every place. The whole business of his person adds up to God. His actions are due only to Him who is the author of them and not to himself, since he is merely the agent. If we mean God and only God, then it is He who does what we do and nothing can disturb Him — neither company nor place. Thus, neither can any person disturb him, for he thinks of nothing, is looking for nothing, and relishes nothing but God, who is one with him by perfect devotion. Furthermore, since God cannot be distracted by the numbers of things, neither can the person, for he is one in One, in which all divided things are gathered up to unity and there undifferentiated.

One ought to keep hold of God in everything and accustom his mind to retain God always among his feelings, thoughts, and loves. Take care how you think of God. As you think of Him in church or closet, think of Him everywhere. Take Him with you among the crowds and turmoil of the alien world. As I have said so often, speaking of uniformity, we do not mean that one should regard all deeds, places, and people as interchangeable. That would be a great mistake; for it is better to pray than to spin and the church ranks above the street. You should, however, maintain the same mind, the same trust, and the same earnestness toward God in all your doings. Believe me, if you keep this kind of evenness, nothing can separate you from God-consciousness.

On the other hand, the person who is not conscious of God's presence, but who must always be going out to get Him from this and that, who has to seek Him by special methods, as by means of some activity, person, or place — such people have not attained God. It can easily happen that they are disturbed, for they have not God and they do not seek, think, and love only Him, and therefore, not only will evil company be to them a stumbling block, but good company as well — not only the street, but the church; not only bad deeds and words, but good ones as well. The difficulty lies within the man for whom God has not yet become everything. If God were everything, the man would get along well wherever he went and among whatever people, for he would possess God and no one could rob him or disturb his work.

Of what does this true possession of God consist, when one really has Him? It depends on the heart and an inner, intellectual return to God and not on steady contemplation by a given method. It is impossible to keep such a method in mind, or at least difficult, and even then it is not best. We ought not to have or let ourselves be satisfied with the God we have thought of, for when the thought slips the mind, that god slips with it. What we want is rather the reality of God, exalted far above any human thought or creature.

Then God will not vanish unless one turns away from Him of his own accord.

When one takes God as He is divine, having the reality of God within him, God sheds light on everything. Everything will taste like God and reflect Him. God will shine in him all the time. He will have the disinterest, renunciation, and spiritual vision of his beloved, ever-present Lord. He will be like one athirst with a real thirst; he cannot help drinking even though he thinks of other things. Wherever he is, with whomsoever he may be, whatever his purpose or thoughts or occupation — the idea of the Drink will not depart as long as the thirst endures; and the greater the thirst the more lively, deep-seated, present, and steady the idea of the Drink will be. Or suppose one loves something with all that is in him, so that nothing else can move him or give pleasure, and he cares for that alone, looking for nothing more; then wherever he is or with whomsoever he may be, whatever he tries or does, that Something he loves will not be extinguished from his mind. He will see it everywhere, and the stronger his love grows for it the more vivid it will be. A person like this never thinks of resting because he is never tired.

The more he regards everything as divine — more divine than it is of itself — the more God will be pleased with him. To be sure, this requires effort and love, a careful cultivation of the spiritual life, and a watchful, honest, active oversight of all one's mental attitudes toward things and people. It is not to be learned by world-flight, running away from things, turning solitary and going apart from the world. Rather, one must learn an inner solitude, wherever or with whomsoever he may be. He must learn to penetrate things and find God there, to get a strong impression of God firmly fixed in his mind.

It is like learning to write. To acquire this art, one must practice much, however disagreeable or difficult it may be, however impossible it may seem. Practicing earnestly and often, one learns to write, acquires the art. To be sure, each letter must first be considered separately and accurately, reproduced over and over again; but once having acquired skill, one need not pay any attention to the reproduction [of the letters] or even think of them. He will write fluently and freely whether it be penmanship or some bold work, in which his art appears. It is sufficient for the writer to know that he is using his skill and since he does not always have to think of it, he does his work by means of it.

So a man should shine with the divine Presence without having to work at it. He should get the essence out of things and let the things themselves alone. That requires at first attentiveness and exact impressions, as with the student and his art. So one must be permeated with divine Presence, informed with the form of beloved God who is within him, so that he may radiate that Presence without working at it.

7. *How a person may work most intelligently*

There are many people who are not hindered by the things they handle, since those things leave no lasting impression on their minds. It is a stage easily reached if one desires to reach it, for no creature may find a place in a heart full of God. Still we should not be satisfied, for we shall profit by assuming that things are as we are, that they are what we see and hear, however strange and unfamiliar. Then and not until then shall we be on the right road — a road to which there is no end — on which one may grow without stopping, profiting more and more by making true progress.

In all his work, and on every occasion, a man should make clever use of his reason and have a conscious insight into himself and his spirituality and distinguish God to the highest possible degree in everything. One should be, as our Lord said, "Like people always on the watch, expecting their Lord." Expectant people are watchful, always looking for Him they expect, always ready to find Him in whatever comes along; however strange it may be, they always think He might be in it. This is what awareness of the Lord is to be like and it requires diligence that takes a man's senses and powers to the utmost, if he is to achieve it and to take God evenly in all things — if he is to find God as much in one thing as in another.

In this regard, one kind of work does indeed differ from another but if one takes the same attitude toward each of his various occupations, then they will be all alike to him. Thus being on the right track and God meaning this to him, he will shine, as clear in worldly things as heavenly. To be sure, one must not of himself behave intemperately or as being worldly, but whatever happens to him from without, whatever he sees or hears, let him refer it to God. The man to whom God is ever present, and who controls and uses his mind to the highest degree — that man alone knows what peace is and he has the Kingdom of Heaven within him.

To be right, a person must do one of two things: either he must learn to have God in his work and hold fast to him there, or he must give up his work altogether. Since, however, man cannot live without activities that are both human and various, we must learn to keep God in everything we do, and whatever the job or place, keep on with Him, letting nothing stand in our way. Therefore, when the beginner has to do with other people, let him first commit himself strongly to God and establish God firmly in his own heart, uniting his senses and thought, his will and powers with God, so that nothing else can enter his mind.

10. *How the will is capable of anything and virtue lies in the will, if it is just*

A man has little reason to be afraid of anything if he knows his will to be good and he should not be disturbed if he cannot realize it in deed. Nor should he despise his virtue, knowing that virtue and every other good depend on good will. If you have good will, you shall lack for nothing, neither love, humility, nor any other virtue, what you will with all your strength you shall have, and neither God nor any creature can deprive you — if, again, your will is sound, divine and wrapt in God. Therefore, do not say "I would" — for that refers to the future; but say "I will" — that it may now be so. For notice this: If I set my heart on something a thousand miles away, it is more really mine than something I hold in my bosom but which I do not want.

Good will is not less powerful for good than bad will is for evil. Be sure of it, that even if I never do evil and yet, if I hold bad will, I shall have sinned just as much as if I had done the deed. With a will that is purely bad, I commit as great sin as if I were to murder all the people in the world, even though I did not lift a finger toward the crime. Why should not the same power reside in good will? It does — and much, incomparably more!

In fact, I may do anything at all with my will. I may bear the burdens of mankind, feed the poor, do the world's work and anything else I please. If I lack the power but not the will to do

[so], then before God I have done it and no one may deny or dispute it for a moment. To will to do something as soon as I may, and to have done it, are the same in God's sight. Furthermore, if I choose that my will shall be a match for the total will of the world, and if my desire is perfect and great, then it shall be so, for what I will have I have. And so, if I really want to love as much as the world has ever loved, and thereby I mean to love God, or what you please, then it is so, when my will is perfect.

You may now be asking when the will is perfect.

It is perfect and right when it has no special reference, when it has cut loose from self, and when it is transformed and adapted to the will of God. Indeed, the more like this the will is, the more perfect and true it is. With a will like this, anything is possible, whether love or anything else.

The next question is: How may I have this love when as yet I have no intimation of it, as I see other people have — their impressive actions betraying it — people in whom I discover impassioned devotion and wonder which I certainly have not?

At this point we must observe two things about love. The first is the nature of it and the second is the action which expresses the nature of love. The seat of love is in the will alone. To have more will is to have more love; but no one can tell whether another person has more love — for that is hidden in the soul, just as God lies hidden in the soul's core. Thus love depends altogether on the will; to have more will is to have more love.

There is, moreover, the effect or expression of love. It often appears like a bright light, as spirituality, devotion, or jubilation and yet, as such, it is by no means best! These things are not always due to love. Sometimes they come of having tasted nature's sweets. They can also be due to heavenly inspiration or to the senses, and people at their best are not the ones who experience them most. For *if* such things are really due to God, He gives them to such people to bait and allure them on and also to keep them away from [worse] company. But when such people increase in love, such [ecstatic] experiences will come less facilely, and the love that is in them will be proved by the constancy of their fidelity to God, without such enticements.

Supposing, however, that all such [experiences] were really of love, even then it would not be best. We ought to get over amusing our-selves with such raptures for the sake of that better love, and to accomplish through loving service what men most need, spiritually, socially, or physically. As I have often said, if a person were in such a rapturous state as St. Paul once entered,* and he knew of a sick man who wanted a cup of soup, it would be far better to withdraw from the rapture for love's sake and serve him who is in need.

No one should think that thereby he will be robbed of grace, for what we forego willingly for love's sake returns in more precious habit, as Christ said: "He who forsakes anything for my sake shall receive again a hundredfold."† Yes, indeed, whatever one gives up or lets pass for God's sake, even though it be the consolation he so greatly desires, or the rapture, or the spirituality he has done all he can to get, he shall actually have it as much as if he had always been fully possessed of it and as if it were the only good — especially if, when it seems that God will not give it, he is still cheerful about it, and foregoes it for God's sake.

Having willingly given up and discounted his own convenience for God, he receives again a hundredfold. For what one would like to have, what he takes comfort in and yet forswears for God's sake, whether it is physical or spiritual, he will find again in God, as if he had always had it and given it up of his own accord; for one ought to be willing to be despoiled of *anything* for God's sake and out of love, to let all comfort go and disdain it.

That we should be willing to give up [rapturous] experiences, the loving Paul tells us when he says: "I could wish that myself were cut asunder from Christ for the love of my brethren."‡ And this is what he meant — not love in the first sense of the word — a love from which he could not wish to be cut off even for a moment, for anything that might ever happen in Heaven or on Earth. He referred, rather, to the consolations [of Christ].

But remember that the friends of God are never without their comfort; whatever God wills is to them most consoling, whether it is comfort or discomfort.

---

*Acts 9:3–9.
†Matthew 19:29.
‡Romans 9:3.

15. *Of two kinds of certainty of eternal life*

In this life there are two kinds of certainty about eternal life. The first is based on the belief that God Himself tells man about it, or that He sends word through an angel, or reveals it in some special illumination. These rarely happen, and to few people.

The second kind is incomparably better and more useful and common among people who love wholeheartedly. It is based on the love for God and the intimacy with Him which binds man to Him, by which He has full confidence in God and is so completely certain of Him that he loves God, without making any differences, in all creatures. And even though creatures denied God and forswore Him, and even though God denied Himself, still he would not mistrust, because love cannot mistrust. Love is confidence itself in the good and therefore there is no need to speak of the Lover and the beloved; for once a man discovers that God *is* his friend, he knows what is good for him and all that belongs to his happiness. Of this you may be sure, that however dear you are to God, He is immeasurably dearer to you and He trusts you that much more; for He Himself is the confidence by which one is sure of Him, as sure as all who love him are.

This certainty is far stronger than the first kind, and more perfect, and true. It does not deceive. Verbal telling might well be deceptive and throw a false light on the whole matter. What is more, this certainty is to be found in all the soul's agents. That is why it will not deceive true lovers of God. They will no more doubt it than they would doubt God Himself, for love drives out all fear, or, as St. Paul says, love knows no fear.*

It is further written that love hides a multitude of sins.† Perfect love and confidence cannot be where sins are, but love does hide sin completely. Love knows nothing of sin — not that man has not sinned — but sins are blotted out at once by love and they vanish as if they had not been. This is because whatever God does He does completely, like the cup running over. Whom He forgives, He forgives utterly and at once, much preferring great forgiveness to little; for complete confidence is like that.

*The speaker is in fact John; see 1 John 4:18.
†1 Peter 4:8; James 5:20.

I regard this view as much better — nay, incomparably better — than the first, and more rewarding, more certain. Neither sin nor anything else is an obstacle to it. Those whom God finds alike in love, He rates as equals, whether their misdeeds are great or small. Moreover, to be forgiven much is to love much, as our Lord Jesus Christ said: "He to whom much has been forgiven will love much."*

17. How to be at peace and to follow after God when you discover that you are not taking the pains and doing as Christ and many of His saints have done

Anxiety and discouragement may easily come to people when they see how strict and diligent the lives of our Lord Jesus Christ and His saints have been, and that humanly we are not up to their level, nor even much inclined to be. When people find that they are otherwise disposed, they think they are apart from God — so far apart that they cannot follow Him. Let no one think that! No one may say at any time that he is apart from God, either because of his faults, or infirmities, or anything else. If, however, by reason of a great fault, you are an outcast, so that you are not able to approach God at all, then, of all times, consider that God is near you, for great harm comes of feeling that God is distant. For let a man go away or come back: God never leaves. He is always at hand and if He cannot get into your life, still He is never farther away than the door.

So it is with the strenuous life of discipleship. See how this applies to your discipleship. Notice, as you must have already, just what God exhorts you to do, for all people are not called to God by the same road, as St. Paul says. If you find that your shortest road is not via visible works and great efforts and privations, which things, after all, are of no great importance, unless one is specially required by God to do them — and one is strong enough to take it without disturbing his spiritual life — if, then, you find that this way is not for you, take it calmly and make nothing of it.

Perhaps you will say: If these things make no difference, why did our forebears and many of the saints do them?

Now consider: Our Lord was to them a pattern and also the

*Luke 7:47.

strength to follow it as they understood it and therefore that was the way they could do their best, but God never tied man's salvation to any pattern. Whatever possibilities inhere in any pattern of life inhere in all, because God has given it so and denied it to none. One good way does not conflict with another and people should know that they are wrong when, seeing or hearing of some good man that his way is not like their own, they say that his is just so much labor lost. Because that person's life pattern does not please them, they decry it, together with his good intentions. That is not right! We ought rather to observe the ways of other good people and despise none of them. Let each keep his own way and absorb into it the good features of other ways and thus include in his own the merits of all. A change of life pattern makes for unstable mind and character. What you get out of one pattern may be worked out in another, provided it, too, is good, praiseworthy, and directed toward God only — for not all people may travel the same road.

So it is with following the strenuous way of certain saints. You may admire the pattern of their lives; they may please you immensely; and still you may not be able to go their way. You may, however, say of the Lord Jesus Christ, that His way was always the highest and that we ought to follow Him in it. That may be true, but our Lord should be followed reasonably and not by details. He fasted forty days: no one is called upon to copy Him literally in that. There are other things He did, in which He meant us to follow Him spiritually and not literally. We should take care to follow Him intelligently, for He is much more intent on our love than on our actions. We are always to follow Him in our own way.

But how?

The manner and the method must be settled in each situation individually. As I have often said, I regard intelligent action as far better than literal actions. What does that mean?

Christ fasted forty days. Follow Him by observing what [bad habit] you are most inclined to and refuse to do that. But look well to yourself: it will profit you more to abstain from that [habit] without regret than to abstain from food completely.

Even so, it is often harder to keep back one word than it is to abstain from speech altogether. Sometimes people find it more difficult to pass over one little spiteful word, unimportant in itself, than to bear a heavy blow for which they are prepared, harder to be alone in a crowd than to be alone in a desert; harder to give up a little thing than a great one; harder to do a little job than one that seems important. So, in his weakness, a man may follow our Lord and not assume that He is far away.

"About Disinterest"

I have read much of what has been written, both by heathen philosophers and sages and in the Old and New Testaments. I have sought earnestly and with great diligence that good and high virtue by which man may draw closest to God and through which one may best approximate the idea God had of him before he was created, when there was no separation between man and God; and having delved into all this writing, as far as my intelligence would permit, I find that [high virtue] to be pure disinterest, that is, detachment from creatures. Our Lord said to Martha: *Unum est necessarium,*"* which is to say: to be untroubled and pure, one thing is necessary and that is disinterest.

The teachers praise love, and highly too, as St. Paul did, when he said: "No matter what I do, if I have not love, I am nothing."† Nevertheless, I put disinterest higher than love. My first reason is as follows. The best thing about love is that it makes me love God. Now, it is much more advantageous for me to move God toward myself than for me to move toward Him, for my blessing in eternity depends on my being identified with God. He is more able to deal with me and join me than I am to join Him. Disinterest brings God to me and I can demonstrate it this way: Everything likes its own habitat best; God's habitat is purity and unity, which are due to disinterest. Therefore God necessarily gives Himself to the disinterested heart.

---

*Luke 10:42. "But one thing is needful."
†1 Corinthians 13:1.

In the second place, I put disinterest above love because love compels me to suffer for God's sake, whereas disinterest makes me sensitive only to God. This ranks far above suffering for God or in God; for, when he suffers, man pays some attention to the creature from which his suffering comes, but being disinterested, he is quite detached from the creature. I demonstrate that, being disinterested, a man is sensitive only to God, in this way: Experience must always be an experience of something, but disinterest comes so close to zero that nothing but God is rarefied enough to get into it, to enter the disinterested heart. That is why a disinterested person is sensitive to nothing but God. Each person experiences things in his own way and thus every distinguishable thing is seen and understood according to the approach of the beholder and not, as it might be, from its own point of view.

The authorities also praise humility above other virtues, but I put disinterest above humility for the following reasons. There can be humility without disinterest but disinterest cannot be perfect without humility; perfect humility depends on self-denial; disinterest comes so near to zero that nothing may intervene. Thus, there cannot be disinterest without humility and, anyway, two virtues are better than one!

The second reason I put disinterest above humility is that in humility man abases himself before creatures, and in doing so pays some attention to the creatures themselves. Disinterest, however, stays within itself. No transference of attention (such as humility) can ever rank so high that being self-contained will not go higher. As the prophet puts it: *"Omnis gloria filiae regis ab intus,"** which means, "the glory of the king's daughter comes from within her." Perfectly disinterested, a man has no regard for anything, no inclination to be above this or below that, no desire to be over or under; he remains what he is, neither loving nor hating, and desiring neither likeness to this nor unlikeness to that. He desires only to be one and the same; for to want to be this or that is to want something; and the disinterested person wants nothing. Thus everything remains unaffected as far as he is concerned.

Someone may say: Surely our Lady had all the virtues and therefore she must have been perfectly disinterested. If then, disinterest

*Psalm 45:13.

ranks above virtue, why did the Lady glory in her humility rather than in disinterest? She said: "*Quia respexit Dominus humilitatem ancillae suae.*" That means: "He hath regarded the low estate of his handmaiden."*

I reply by saying that in God there is both disinterest and humility as well, to the extent that virtues may be attributed to God. You should know that it is loving humility that made God stoop to human nature, the same humility by which He created heaven and earth, as I shall later explain. And if our Lord, willing to become man, still remained unaffected in His disinterest, our Lady must have known that He desired this of her, too, and that therefore He would have regard to her humility rather than to her disinterest. Thus she continued, unmoved in her disinterestedness, and yet she gloried in humility.

If, however, she had said: "He hath regarded my disinterest," her disinterest would have been qualified by the thought and not perfect, for she would have departed from it. Any departure from disinterest, however small, disturbs it; and there you have the reason why our Lady gloried in humility rather than in disinterest. The prophet says: "*Audiam, qui loquatur in me Dominus Deus,*"† which means "I will be silent and hear what God the Lord will utter within me" — as if to say, "If God the Lord wants to speak to me, let Him come in, for I shall not go out." As Boethius puts it: "Ye people, why do you seek without for the blessing that is within you?"‡

I also put disinterest above mercy, for mercy is nothing but a man's going out to the want of a fellow and the heart is disturbed by it. Disinterest, however, is exempt from this, being self-contained and allowing nothing to disturb. To speak briefly: When I survey the virtues, I find none as flawless, as conducive to God as disinterest.

A philosopher named Avicenna§ said: "The rank of a disinterested mind is so high that what it sees is true, what it desires comes to pass, what it commands must be done." You may take this for the truth, that when a free mind is really disinterested, God is compelled to come into it; and if it could get along without contingent forms, it would then have all the properties of God Himself. Of course,

*Luke 1:48.
†Psalm 85:8.
‡Boethius, *Consolations* II, 5, 70.
§Ibn-Sina, Muslim physician and philosopher (980–1037).

God cannot give His properties away and so He can do nothing for the disinterested mind except to give Himself to it and it is then caught up into eternity, where transitory things no longer affect it. Then the man has no experiences of the physical order and is said to be dead to the world, since he has no appetite for any earthly thing. That is what St. Paul meant by saying: "I live; yet not I, but Christ liveth in me."*

You may ask: "What is this disinterest, that it is so noble a matter?" Know, then, that a mind unmoved by any contingent affection or sorrow, or honor, or slander, or vice, is really disinterested — like a broad mountain that is not shaken by a gentle wind. Unmovable disinterest brings man into his closest resemblance to God. It gives God His status as God. His purity is derived from it, and then His simplicity and unchangeable character. If man is to be like God, to the extent that any creature may resemble Him, the likeness will come through disinterest, and man proceeds from purity to simplicity and from simplicity to unchangeableness, and thus the likeness of God and man comes about. It is an achievement of the grace that allures man away from temporal things and purges him of the transitory. Keep this in mind: to be full of things is to be empty of God, while to be empty of things is to be full of God.

Bear in mind also that God has been immovably disinterested from the beginning and still is and that his creation of the heavens and the earth affected Him as little as if He had not made a single creature. But I go further. All the prayers a man may offer and the good works he may do will affect the disinterested God as little as if there were neither prayers nor works, nor will God be any more compassionate or stoop down to man any more because of his prayers and works than if they were omitted.

Furthermore, I say that when the Son in the Godhead willed to be human and became so, suffering martyrdom, the immovable disinterest of God was affected as little as if the Son had never become human at all.

Perhaps, then, you will say: "I take it, therefore, that prayers and good works are so much lost motion; God pays no attention to them and will not be moved by them. And yet they say that God wants us to pray to Him about everything."

*Galatians 2:20.

Now pay close attention and understand what I mean, if you can. When God first looked out of eternity (if one may say that He ever *first* looked out), He saw everything as it would happen and at the same time He saw when and how he would create each thing. He foresaw the loving prayers and the good deeds each person might do and knew which prayers and which devotions He would heed. He foresaw that tomorrow morning you will cry out to Him in earnest prayer and that tomorrow morning He will not heed you because He had already heard your prayer in His eternity, before you became a person; and if your prayer is neither honest nor earnest, He will not deny it now, for it is already denied in eternity. In that first eternal vision, God looked on each thing-to-be and therefore He does what He now does without a reason. It was all worked out beforehand.

Still, even if God remains forever unmoved, disinterested, the prayers and good works of people are not lost on that account, for well-doing is never without its reward. Philippus* says: "God the Creator holds things to the course and order He ordained for them in the beginning." To God there is neither past nor future and He loves the saints, having foreseen them before ever the world began. Then, when events, foreseen by God in eternity, come to pass in time, people think that God has taken a new departure, either to anger or toward some agreeable end; but it is we who change, while He remains unchanged. Sunshine hurts ailing eyes but is agreeable to sound ones, and yet it is the same sunshine in both cases. God does not see through time, nor does anything new happen in His sight.

Isidore† makes the same point in his book on the highest good. He says: "Many people ask what God was doing before He created Heaven and Earth. Where did He get his new impulse to make creatures? This is the answer: There never was a departure in God, nor a change of intention, and if there ever was a time when creatures did not exist as they do now, still they existed forever in God, in the mind of God." God did not make Heaven and Earth as our time-bound speech describes creation; they came into being when He spoke the word out of eternity. Moses said to our Lord, "Lord if Pharaoh asks who you are, what shall I tell him?" The Lord replied:

---

*Marcus Julius Philippus, Emperor of Rome, 244–49? Said by Christian writers to be a convert to Christianity. (Blakney)

†Isidore of Seville, Spanish bishop (560–636). His *Sentences* were very popular in the Middle Ages. (Blakney)

"Tell him that *he-who-is* sent you." We might say: The unchanging One hath sent me!

Someone well may ask: had Christ this unmoved disinterest when He said: "My soul is sorrowful even unto death"?* Or Mary, when she stood underneath the cross? Much has been made of her lamentations. How are such things compatible with unmoved disinterest?

On this point the authorities say that a person is not one, but two people. One is called the outward man — the sensual person. He is served by the five senses, which function by means of the soul's agents. The other is the inner man — the spiritual person. But notice this, that a man who loves God prefers not to use the agents of the soul in the outward man any more than necessary and then the inner man has recourse to the five senses only to the degree to which he can guide and lead them. He guards them against animal diversions — such as people choose when they live like animals without intelligence. Such people are more properly called animals than persons.

Whatever strength the soul possesses, beyond what it devotes to the five senses, it gives to the inner man. If this inner man is devoted to some high and noble enterprise, the soul recalls its agents and the person is said to be senseless or rapt because his enterprise or object is an unintelligible idea or is unintelligible without being an idea. Remember that God requires of every spiritual person a love which includes all the agents of the soul. Thus He said: "Love your God with all your heart."

There are people who squander the strength of their souls in the outward man. These are the people, all of whose desires and thoughts turn on transient goods, since they are unaware of the inner person. Sometimes a good man robs his outward person of all the soul's agents, in order to dispatch them on some higher enterprise; so, conversely, animal people rob the inner person of the soul's agents and assign them to the outward man. A man may be ever so active outwardly and still leave the inner man unmoved and passive.

Now both in Christ and our Lady, there was an outward man and an inner person and, while they taught about external matters, they were outwardly active but inwardly unmoved and disinterested.

*Mark 14:34.

This is how it was when Christ said: "My soul is sorrowful even unto death." And whatever the lamentations and other speeches of our Lady, inwardly she was still unmoved and disinterested. Take an illustration. A door swings to and fro through an angle. I compare the breadth of the door to the outward man and the hinge to the inner person. When the door swings to and fro, the breadth of the door moves back and forth, but the hinge is still unmoved and unchanged. It is like this here.

Now I ask what the object of pure disinterest is. I reply that it is neither this nor that. Pure disinterest is empty nothingness, for it is on that high plane on which God gives effect to His will. It is not possible for God to do His will in every heart, for even though He is almighty, He cannot act except where He finds preparations made or He makes them himself. I say "or makes them" on account of St. Paul, for God did not find him ready; He prepared St. Paul by an infusion of grace.* Otherwise, I say that God acts where He finds that preparations have been made.

God's activity is not the same in a man as in a stone; and there is a simile for that, too, in nature. If a bake oven is heated and lumps of dough are put into it, some of oatmeal, some of barley, some of rye, and some of wheat, then, even though there is only one heat for all in the oven, it will not act the same way on the various doughs; for one turns into a pretty loaf, another to a rough loaf, and others still rougher. That is not due to the heat but to the material, which differs. Similarly God does not work in all hearts alike but according to the preparation and sensitivity He finds in each. In a given heart, containing this or that, there may be an item which prevents God's highest activity. Therefore if a heart is to be ready for Him, it must be emptied out to nothingness, the condition of its maximum capacity. So, too, a disinterested heart, reduced to nothingness, is the optimum, the condition of maximum sensitivity.

Take an illustration from nature. If I wish to write on a white tablet, then no matter how fine the matter already written on it, it will confuse me and prevent me from writing down [my thoughts]; so that, if I still wish to use the tablet, I must first erase all that is written on it, but it will never serve me as well for writing as when it is clean. Similarly, if God is to write His message about the highest

*Galatians 1:15.

matters on my heart, everything to be referred to as "this or that" must first come out and I must be disinterested. God is free to do His will on His own level when my heart, being disinterested, is bent on neither this nor that.

Then I ask: What is the prayer of the disinterested heart? I answer by saying that a disinterested man, pure in heart, has no prayer, for to pray is to want something from God, something added that one desires, or something that God is to take away. The disinterested person, however, wants nothing, and neither has he anything of which he would be rid. Therefore he has no prayer, or he prays only to be uniform with God. In this sense we may understand the comment of St. Dionysius* on a text of St. Paul — "they which run in a race run all, but one receiveth the prize" — that is, all the soul's agents race for the prize but only the soul's essence receives it. Thus, Dionysius says: "This race is precisely the flight from creatures to union with the uncreated." When the soul achieves this, it loses its identity, it absorbs God and is reduced to nothing, as the dawn at the rising of the sun. Nothing helps toward this end like disinterest.

To this point we may quote a saying of St. Augustine: "There is a heavenly door for the soul into the divine nature — where some-things are reduced to nothings." On earth, this door is precisely disinterest, and when disinterest reaches its apex it will be unaware of its knowledge, it will not love its own love, and will be in the dark about its own light. Here, too, we may quote the comment of an authority: "Blessed are the pure in heart who leave everything to God now as they did before ever they existed." No one can do this without a pure, disinterested heart.

That God prefers a disinterested heart for His habitation may be seen from the question: "What is God looking for in everything?" I reply with these words from the Book of Wisdom: "I seek peace in all things."† There is, however, no peace except in disinterest. Therefore God prefers it to any other condition or virtue. Remember, too, that the more his heart is trained to be sensitive to divine influences, the happier man is; the further he pushes his preparation, the higher he ascends in the scale of happiness.

---

*Pseudo-Dionysius (sixth century), Neoplatonist mystic and author of *The Celestial Hierarchy*. One of Eckhart's favorites. (Blakney)

†Possibly Ecclesiasticus 24:7. (Blakney)

But no man can be sensitive to divine influence except by conforming to God, and in proportion to his conformity he is sensitive to divine influence. Conformity comes of submission to God. The more subject to creatures a man is, the less he conforms to God, but the pure, disinterested heart, being void of creatures, is constantly worshiping God and conforming to Him, and is therefore sensitive to His influence. That is what St. Paul means by saying: "Put ye on Jesus Christ"* — that is, conform to Christ! Remember that when Christ became man, He was not one man but took human nature on Himself. If you get out, therefore, and clear of creatures, what Christ took on Himself will be left to you and you will have put on Christ.

If any man will see the excellence and use of perfect disinterest, let him take seriously what Christ said to His disciples about His humanity: "It is expedient for you that I go away: for if I go not away, the Comforter will not come unto you"† — as if He said: "You take too much pleasure in my visible form and therefore the perfect pleasure of the Holy Spirit cannot be yours." Therefore discard the form and be joined to the formless essence, for the spiritual comfort of God is very subtle and is not extended except to those who despise physical comforts.

Heed this, intelligent people: Life is good to the man who goes, on and on, disinterestedly. There is no physical or fleshly pleasure without some spiritual harm, for the desires of the flesh are contrary to those of the spirit, and the desires of the spirit are contrary to the flesh. That is why to sow the undisciplined love of the flesh is to be cut off by death, but to sow the disciplined love of the spirit is to reap of the spirit, life eternal. The less one pays attention to the creature things, the more the Creator pursues him.

Listen to this, man of intelligence: If the pleasure we take in the physical form of Christ diminishes our sensitivity to the Holy Spirit, how much more will the pleasure we take in the comfort of transitory things be a barrier against God? Disinterest is best of all, for by it the soul is unified, knowledge is made pure, the heart is kindled, the spirit wakened, the desires quickened, the virtues enhanced. Disinterest brings knowledge of God; cut off from the creature, the soul

*Romans 13:14.
†John 16:7.

unites with God, for love apart from God is like water to a fire, while love with God is the honeycomb in the honey.

Hear this, every intelligent spirit: The steed swiftest to carry you to perfection is suffering, for none shall attain eternal life except he pass through great bitterness with Christ. Nothing pierces man like suffering and nothing is more honey sweet than to have suffered. The surest basis on which perfection rests is humility, and he whose nature kneels in deepest lowliness — *his* spirit shall rise up to the heights of divinity; for as love brings sorrow, sorrow also brings love. Human ways are various: one person lives thus and another so.

For him who wishes to attain the utmost in life in his time, I set down here several aphorisms, much abbreviated, and taken from many writings.

Among men, be aloof; do not engage yourself to any idea you get; free yourself from everything chance brings to you, things that accumulate and cumber you; set your mind in virtue to contemplation, in which the God you bear in your heart shall be your steady object, the object from which your attention never wavers; and whatever else your duty may be, whether it be fasting, watching, or praying, dedicate it all to this one end, doing each only as much as is necessary to your single end. Thus you shall come to the goal of perfection.

Someone may ask: "Who could long endure this unwavering contemplation of the divine object?" I reply: No one living in such times as these. I tell you privately about these things only to have you know what the highest is, so that you may desire it and aspire to it. And if this vision is withdrawn from you, if you are a good man, the withdrawal shall be to you as if the eternity of bliss were taken away, but you must return at once to the pursuit of it, so that it may return to you. Even so, set a perpetual watch over yourself and your thoughts and let your refuge be in this [vision], in which you abide as constantly as possible. Lord God, be thou praised forever! Amen.

Selected Sermons

1. *This is Meister Eckhart from whom God hid nothing**

Dum medium silentium tenerent omnia et nox in suo cursu
medium iter haberet....

— Wisdom of Solomon 18:14

"For while all things were wrapped in peaceful silence and night was
in the midst of its swift course...."

Because the same One, who is begotten and born of God the
Father, without ceasing in eternity, is born today, within time, in
human nature, we make a holiday† to celebrate it. St. Augustine says
that this birth is always happening. And yet, if it does not occur in
me, how could it help me? Everything depends on that.

We intend to discuss, therefore, how it does occur in us, or how it
is made perfect in a good soul, for it is in a good soul that God the
Father is speaking His eternal word. What I shall say applies to that
perfect person who has turned to the way of God and continues in
it, and not to the natural undisciplined person who is far from this
birth and ignorant of it. This, then, is the saying of the wise man:
"While all things were wrapped in peaceful silence...a secret word
leaped down from heaven, out of the royal throne, to me."‡ This
sermon is to be on that word.

Three points are, then, noteworthy. The first is: where does God
the Father speak His word in the soul, or where does this birth
take place — or what part of the soul is susceptible to this act? It
must be in the purest, noblest, and subtlest element the soul can
provide. Truly, if God could give the soul anything rarer out of His
omnipotence, and if the soul could have received into its nature

---

*Title supplied by Eckhart disciple. Evidently Eckhart wrote this and the following
two sermons in full. (Blakney)

†Christmas.

‡Eckhart seems never to quote by copying and hence his quotations are difficult
to identify precisely. (Blakney)

93

anything nobler from Him, He must have awaited its coming to be born. Therefore the soul in which this birth is to happen must have purity and nobility of life, and be unitary and self-contained; it must not be dissipated in the multiplicity of things, through the five senses. What is more, it must continue to be self-contained and unitary and of the utmost purity, for that is its station and it disdains anything less.

The second part of this sermon will discuss what one should do about this act of God, this inward utterance, this birth: whether it is necessary to co-operate in some way to merit and obtain the birth. Should one construct an idea in his mind and thinking-process and discipline himself by meditating upon it, to the effect that God is wise, almighty, and eternal? Or should one withdraw from all thought and free his mind of words, acts, and ideas, doing nothing but being always receptive to God and allowing Him to act? How shall one best serve the eternal birth?

The third part [of this sermon will discuss] the profitableness of this birth and how great it is.

In the first place, please note that I shall support what I have to say by citations from nature, which you may check for yourselves. Even though I believe more in the Scriptures than I do in myself, I shall follow [this policy] because you will get more out of arguments based on evidence.

Let us take first the test: "Out of the silence, a secret word was spoken to me." Ah, Sir! — what is this silence and where is that word to be spoken? We shall say, as I have heretofore, [it is spoken] in the purest element of the soul, in the soul's most exalted place, in the core, yes, in the essence of the soul. The central silence is there, where no creature may enter, nor any idea, and there the soul neither thinks nor acts, nor entertains any idea, either of itself or of anything else.

Whatever the soul does, it does through agents. It understands by means of intelligence. If it remembers, it does so by means of memory. If it is to love, the will must be used and thus it acts always through agents and not within its own essence. Its results are achieved through an intermediary. The power of sight can be effectuated only through the eyes, for otherwise the soul has no means of vision. It is the same with the other senses. They are effectuated through intermediaries.

In Being, however, there is no action and, therefore, there is none in the soul's essence. The soul's agents, by which it acts, are derived from the core of the soul. In that core is the central silence, the pure peace, and abode of the heavenly birth, the place for this event: this utterance of God's word. By nature the core of the soul is sensitive to nothing but the divine Being, unmediated. Here God enters the soul with all He has and not in part. He enters the soul through its core and nothing may touch that core except God Himself. No creature enters it, for creatures must stay outside in the soul's agents, from whence the soul receives ideas, behind which it has withdrawn as if to take shelter.

When the agents of the soul contact creatures, they take and make ideas and likenesses of them and bear them back again into the self. It is by means of these ideas that the soul knows about eternal creatures. Creatures cannot approach the soul except in this way and the soul cannot get at creatures, except, on its own initiative, it first conceives ideas of them. Thus the soul gets at things by means of ideas and the idea is an entity created by the soul's agents. Be it a stone, or a rose, or a person, or whatever it is that is to be known, first an idea is taken and then absorbed, and in this way the soul connects with the phenomenal world.

But an idea, so received, necessarily comes in from outside, through the senses. Thus the soul knows about everything but itself. There is an authority who says that the soul can neither conceive nor admit any idea of itself. Thus it knows about everything else but has no self-knowledge, for ideas always enter through the senses and therefore the soul cannot get an idea of itself. Of nothing does the soul know so little as it knows of itself, for lack of means. And that indicates that within itself the soul is free, innocent of all instrumentalities and ideas, and that is why God can unite with it, He, too, being pure and without idea, or likeness.

Whatever skill a master teacher may have, concede that skill to God, multiplied beyond measure. The wiser and more skillful a teacher is, the more simply, and with less artifice, he achieves his ends. Man requires many tools to do his visible work and, before he can finish it as he has conceived it, much preparation is required. It is the function and craft of the moon and sun to give light and they do it swiftly. When they emit their rays, all the ends of the world are filled with light in a moment. Higher than these are the angels who work with fewer instruments and also with fewer ideas. The highest seraph has only one. He comprehends as unity all that his inferiors see as manifold. But God needs no idea at all, nor has He any. He acts in the soul without instrument, idea, or likeness. He acts in the core of the soul, which no idea ever penetrated — but He alone — His own essence. No creature can do this.

How does God beget His Son in the soul? As a creature might, with ideas and likenesses? Not at all! He begets Him in the soul just as He does in eternity — and not otherwise. Well, then, how? Let us see.

God has perfect insight into Himself and knows Himself up and down, through and through, not by ideas, but of Himself. God begets His Son through the true unity of the divine nature. See! This is the way: He begets His Son in the core of the soul and is made One with it. There is no other way. If an idea were interposed, there could be no true unity. Man's whole blessedness lies in that unity.

Now you might say: "Naturally! But there is nothing to the soul but ideas." No! Not at all! If that was so, the soul could never be blessed, for even God cannot make a creature in which a perfect blessing is found. Otherwise, God Himself would not be the highest blessing, or the best of ends, as it is His nature and will to be — the beginning and the end of everything. A blessing is not a creature nor is it perfection, for perfection [that is, in all virtues] is the consequence of the perfecting of life, and for that you must get into the essence, the core of the soul, so that God's undifferentiated essence may reach you there, without the interposition of any idea. No idea represents or signifies itself. It always points to something else, of which it is the symbol. And since man has no ideas, except those abstracted from external things through the senses, he cannot be blessed by an idea.

The second point [of this sermon] is this: What should a man do to secure and deserve the occurrence and perfection of this birth in his soul? Should he co-operate by imagining and thinking about God, or should he keep quiet, be silent and at peace, so that God may speak and act through him? Should he do nothing but wait until God does act? I repeat, as I have said before, that this exposition and this activity are for those good and perfect persons only, who have so absorbed the essence of virtue that virtue emanates from them without their trying to make it do so, and in whom the useful life and noble teachings of our Lord Jesus Christ are alive. Such persons know that the best life and the loftiest is to be silent and to let God speak and act through one.

When all the agents [of the soul] are withdrawn from action and ideation, then this word is spoken. Thus he said: "Out of the silence, a secret word was spoken to me." The more you can withdraw the agents of your soul and forget things and the ideas you have received hitherto, the nearer you are to [hearing the word] and the more sensitive to it you will be. If you could only become unconscious of everything all at once and ignore your own life, as St. Paul did when he could say: "Whether in the body, or out of it, I cannot tell. God knoweth!"* His spirit had so far withdrawn all its agents that the body was forgotten. Neither memory nor intellect functioned, nor the senses, nor any [of the soul's] agents which are supposed to direct or grace the body. The warmth and energy of the body were suspended and yet it did not fail during the three days in which he neither ate nor drank. It was also this way with Moses, when he fasted forty days on the mountain and was none the worse for it. He was as strong on the last day as on the first. This is the way a man should diminish his senses and introvert his faculties until he achieves forgetfulness of things and self. So one authority said to his soul: "Draw back from the unrest of external actions," and also: "Fly from the storm of visible works and inward thoughts and hide yourself, for they only make turmoil."

There, if God is to speak His word to the soul, it must be still and at peace, and then He *will* speak His word and give Himself to the soul and not a mere idea, apart from Himself. Dionysius says: "God has no idea of Himself and no likeness, for He is intrinsic good, truth, and being." God does all that He does within Himself and of Himself in an instant. Do not imagine that when God made Heaven and Earth and all the creatures, that he made one today and another tomorrow. To be sure, Moses describes it thus, but he knew much better! He put it this way on account of the people who could neither understand nor conceive it otherwise. God did nothing more about it than just this: He willed and they were! God acts without instrumentality and without ideas. And the freer you are from ideas

*2 Corinthians 12:3.

the more sensitive you are to His inward action. You are nearer to it in proportion as you are introverted and unself-conscious.

It was to this point that Dionysius instructed his disciple Timothy, saying: "My dear son Timothy, you should soar above self with untroubled mind, above all your faculties, characteristics, and states, up into the still, secret darkness, so that you may come to know the unknown God above all gods. Forsake everything. God despises ideas."

But now, perhaps you say: "What can God do in the core and essence [of the soul] without ideas?" I couldn't possibly know, for the agents of the soul deal only in ideas, taking things and naming them, each according to its own idea. A bird is not known [as such] on the human idea [pattern], and thus, since all ideas come from the outside, [what God is doing in the core of my soul] is hidden from me and that is a great benefit. Since the soul itself does not know, it wonders and, wondering, it seeks, for the soul knows very well that something is afoot, even though it does not know how or what. When a person learns the cause of anything, he soon grows tired of it and looks for something else to work out, and is constantly uneasy until he knows all about that, and thus he lacks steadfastness. Only this unknown knowledge keeps the soul steadfast and yet ever on the search.

The wise man said: "In the middle of the night, while all things were wrapped in silence, a secret word was spoken to me." It came stealthily, like a thief. What does he mean by a word that is secret or hidden? It is the nature of a word to reveal what is hidden. "It opened and shone before me as if it were revealing something and made me conscious of God, and thus it was called 'a word.' Furthermore it was not clear to me what it was, because it came with stealth like a whisper trying to explain itself through the stillness." See! As long as it is concealed, man will always be after it. It appears and disappears, which means that we shall plead and sigh for it.

St. Paul says that we are to hunt it and track it down and never give up till we get it. Once he was caught up into the third Heaven* of the knowledge of God and saw everything. When he came back he had forgotten nothing but it had so regressed into the core of his soul that he could not call it up to mind. It was covered up.

---

*2 Corinthians 12:2–4.

Thus he felt constrained to pursue it within [his soul] and not with-out. It is always within and never outside — but always inward. When he was convinced of that, he said: "I am persuaded that nei-ther death...nor any affliction can separate me from what I find within me."*

One heathen authority once said something fine about this to another: "I am aware of something in myself *whose shine is my reason.* I see clearly that something is there, but what it is I cannot understand. But it seems to me that, if I could grasp it, I should know all truth." To which the other authority replied: "By all means keep after it! For if you do grasp it, you will possess the totality of all goods and life eternal!" St. Augustine also has something to say about this: "I am aware of something in myself, like a light dancing before my soul, and if it could be brought out with perfect steadiness, it would surely be life eternal. It hides, and then again, it shows. It comes like a thief, as if it would steal everything from the soul. But since it shows itself and draws attention, it must want to allure the soul and make the soul follow it, to rob the soul of self." One of the prophets also has something to say about this: "Lord, take from them their spirit and give them instead thy spirit!" This is what that loving soul† meant when she said: "When Love said that word, my soul melted and flowed away. Where he comes in, I must go out!" That is also what Christ meant, when He said: "Whosoever shall forsake anything for my sake, shall receive again a hundredfold and whosoever will have me, must deny himself of everything and whosoever will serve me must follow me and not seek his own."‡

Now perhaps you are saying: "My dear sir! You are trying to re-verse the natural course of the soul. It is the soul's nature to take things in through the senses and convert them into ideas. Do you want to reverse that sequence?"

No! But how do you know what precious things God has stored up in nature which have not yet been described — things still hid-den? Those who write about the aristocracy of the soul can get no further than their natural intelligence will take them. They can-not get into the core and therefore much must remain hidden from

---

*Romans 8:38–39.
†Perhaps a reference to Song of Songs 5:2–7. (Blakney)
‡Matthew 16:24, 19:29.

them and unknown. The prophet said: "I will sit and be silent and listen to what God shall say in me." That this word comes "at night and in the darkness" is expressive of its hiddenness. St. John says: "The light shone in the darkness. It came unto its own. And to as many as received it, to them power was given to become the Sons of God."*

See now the profit and fruit of this secret word and this darkness. Not only the Son of the heavenly Father is born in the darkness which is His own, but you, too, are born there, a son of the same heavenly Father, and to you also He gives power. Now see how great the profit is! For all the truth the authorities ever learned by their own intelligence and understanding, or ever shall learn up to the last of days, they never got the least part of the knowledge that is in the core [of the soul]. Let it be called ignorance or want of knowledge, still it has more in it than all wisdom and all knowledge without it, for this outward ignorance lures and draws you away from things you know about and even from yourself. That is what Christ meant when He said: "Whosoever forsaketh not himself and mother and father and all that is external is not worthy of me." It was as if He would say: "Whosoever will not depart from the externality of creatures cannot be born or received in this divine birth." By robbing yourself of self and all externalities you are admitted to the truth.

And I really believe it, and am sure that the person who is right in this matter will never be separated from God by any mode [of action] or anything else. I say that there is no way he can fall into deadly sin. He would rather suffer the most shameful death than commit the least of mortal sins, as did the saints. I say that he could not commit even a venial sin nor consent to one in himself or other people, if it could be prevented. He is so strongly attracted and drawn and accustomed to this way of life that he would not turn to another. All his mind and power are directed to this one end.

May God, newly born in human form, eternally help us, that we frail people, being born in Him, may be divine. Amen.

*John 1:12.

3. *This, too, is Meister Eckhart who always taught the truth**

In his, quae Patris mei sunt, oportet me esse.
— Luke 2:49

"I must be about my Father's businesss!" This text is quite convenient to the discussion in which I shall now engage, dealing with the eternal birth, which occurred at one point of time, and which occurs every day in the innermost recess of the soul — a recess to which there is no avenue of approach. To know this birth at the core of the soul it is necessary above all that one should be about his Father's business.

What are the attributes of the Father? More power is attributed to Him than to the other persons [of the Trinity]. Accordingly, no one can be sure of the experience of this birth, or even approach it, except by the expenditure of a great deal of energy. It is impossible without a complete withdrawal of the senses from the [world of] things and great force is required to repress all the agents of the soul and cause them to cease functioning. It takes much strength to gather them all in, and without that strength it cannot be done. So Christ said: "The kingdom of heaven suffereth violence and the violent take it by force."†

Now it may be asked about this birth: does it occur constantly or intermittently — only when one applies himself with all his might to forgetting the [world of] things while yet knowing that he does so?

There are certain distinctions to be made. Man has an active intellect, a passive intellect, and a potential intellect. The presence of the active intellect is indicated by [the mind] at work, either on God or creature, to the divine honor and glory. It is characterized chiefly by its drive and energy and therefore is called "active." But when the action at hand is undertaken by God, the mind must remain passive. On the other hand, potential intellect is related to both. It signifies the mind's potentialities, what it has the capacity to do, what God can do. In one case, the mind is at work on its own initiative; in the other, the mind is passive, so that God may undertake the work at hand, and then the mind must hold still and let God do it, but before the mind can begin and God can finish, the mind must have a previ-

---

*Title, again, by the editing disciple of Meister Eckhart. (Blakney)
†Matthew 11:12.

sion of what is to be done, a potential knowledge of what may be. This is the meaning of "potential intellect," but it is much neglected and therefore nothing comes of it. But when the mind goes to work in real earnest, then God is enlisted and He is both seen and felt. Still, the vision and experience of God are too much of a burden to the soul while it is in the body and so God withdraws intermittently, which is what [Christ] meant by saying: "A little while, and ye shall not see me: and again, a little while, and ye shall see me."*

When our Lord took three disciples up the mountain and showed them the transfiguration of His body, made possible by His union with the Godhead — which shall come to us also in the resurrection of the body — St. Peter at once, when he saw it, wanted to stay there with it forever.† In fact, to the extent that one finds anything good, he never wants to part with it. What one grows to know and comes to love and remember, his soul follows after. Knowing this, our Lord hides Himself from time to time, for the soul is an elemental form of the body, so that what once gains its attention holds it. If the soul were to know the goodness of God, as it is and without interruption, it would never turn away and therefore would never direct the body.

Thus it was with Paul. If he had remained a hundred years at that point where he first knew God's goodness, even then he would not have wanted to return to his body and would have forgotten it altogether. Since, then, the divine goodness is alien to this life and incompatible with it, faithful God veils it or reveals it when He will, or when He knows it will be most useful and best for you that He do so. He is like a trustworthy physician. The withdrawal does not depend on you but upon Him whose act it is. He reveals Himself or not as He thinks best for you. It is up to Him to show Himself to you or not, according as He knows you are ready for Him, for God is not a destroyer of nature but rather one who fulfills it, and He does this more and more as you are prepared.

You may, however, say: Alas, good man, if, to be prepared for God, one needs a heart freed from ideas and activities which are natural to the agents of the soul, how about those deeds of love which are wholly external, such as teaching and comforting those

*John 16:16.
†Matthew 17:4.

who are in need? Are these to be denied? Are we to forgo the deeds
that occupied the disciples of our Lord so incessantly, the work that
occupied St. Paul on behalf of the people, so much that he was like
a father to them? Shall we be denied the [divine] goodness because
we do virtuous deeds?

Let us see how this question is to be answered. The one [contem-
plation] is good. The other [deeds of virtue] is necessary. Mary was
praised for having chosen the better part but Martha's life was useful, for she waited on Christ and His disciples.* St. Thomas [Aquinas]
says that the active life is better than the contemplative, for in it one
pours out the love he has received in contemplation. Yet it is all one;
for what we plant in the soil of contemplation we shall reap in the
harvest of action and thus the purpose of contemplation is achieved.
There is a transition from one to the other but it is still a single process with one end in view — that God is, after which it returns to
what it was before. If I go from one end of this house to the other,
it is true, I shall be moving and yet it will be all one motion. In
all he does, man has only his one vision of God. One is based on
the other and fulfills it. In the unity [one beholds] in contemplation,
God foreshadows the harvest of action. In contemplation, you serve
only yourself. In good works, you serve many people.

The whole life of Christ instructs us in this matter, and the lives
of His saints as well, all of whom He sent out into the world to
teach the Many the one truth. St. Paul said to Timothy: "Beloved,
preach the word!"† Did he mean the audible word that beats the air?
Certainly not! He referred to the inborn, secret word that lies hidden
in the soul. It was this that he preached, so that it might instruct
the faculties of people and nourish them, and so that the behavior
of men might proclaim it and so that one might be fully prepared
to serve the need of his neighbor. It should be in the thoughts, the
mind, and the will. It should shine through your deeds. As Christ
said: "Let your light so shine before men!"‡ He was thinking of
people who care only for the contemplative life and not for the
practice of virtue, who say that they have no need for this, for
they have got beyond it. Christ did not include such people when
He said: "Some seed fell in good ground and brought forth fruit a

*Luke 10:38–42.
†2 Timothy 4:2.
‡Matthew 5:15.

hundredfold."* But He did refer to them when He spoke of "the tree that does not bear fruit and which shall be hewn down."†

Now some of you may say: "But, sir, what about the silence of which you have said so much?" Plenty of ideas intrude into that. Each deed follows the pattern of its own idea, whether spiritual or external, whether it be teaching, or giving comfort, or what not. Where, then, is the stillness? If the mind goes on thinking and imagining, and the will keeps on functioning, and the memory: does not this all involve ideation? Let us see.

We have already mentioned the passive and active intellects. The active intellect abstracts ideas from external things and strips them of all that is material or accidental and passes them on to the passive intellect, thus begetting their spiritual counterparts there. So the passive intellect is made pregnant by the active and it knows and cherishes these things. Nevertheless, it cannot continue to know them without the active intellect's continuing, renewing enlightenment. But notice this: all the active intellect does for the natural man, God does and much more too for the solitary person. He removes the active intellect and puts Himself in its place and takes over its complete function.

Now, if a person is quite unoccupied, and his mind is stilled, God undertakes its work, and becomes controller of [the mind's] agents and is Himself begotten in the passive intellect. Let us see how this is. The active intellect cannot pass on what it has not received, nor can it entertain two ideas at once. It must take first one and then the other. Even if many forms and colors are shown up by light and air at the same time, you can perceive them only one after the other. It is the same with the active intellect when it acts — but when God acts in lieu of it, He begets many ideas or images at one point. When, therefore, God moves you to a good deed, your [soul's] agents organize at once for good and your heart is set on goodness. All your resources for good take shape and gather at the same instant to the same point. This shows clearly and beyond doubt that it is not your own mind that is working, because it has neither the authority nor the resources required for that. Rather, it is the work which is begotten of Him who comprehends all ideas within

---

*Matthew 13:8.
†Matthew 7:19.

Himself simultaneously. St. Paul says: "I can do all things through Him that strengtheneth me and in Him; I am not divided."* Thus you may know that the ideas back of good deeds are not your own but are from the Superintendent of nature, from whom both the deed and the idea proceed. Do not claim as your own what is His and not yours. It is given you for a little while, but it was born of God, beyond time, in the eternity that is above all ideas or images.

You may, however, ask: "What is to become of my mind, once it has been robbed of its natural function and has neither ideas nor anything else to work on? It must always consist of something and the soul's agents are bound to connect with something on which they will go to work, whether the memory, the reason, or the will."

Here is the answer. The object and existence of the mind are essential and not contingent. The mind has a pure, unadulterated being of its own. When it comes across truth or essence, at once it is attracted and settles down to utter its oracle — for it now has a point of reference. If, however, the intellect does not discover any essential truth or touch some bedrock, so that it can say "this is this and therefore not something else," if it has to continue searching and expecting, arrested or attracted by nothing, it can only work on until the end, when it passes out, still searching and still expecting.

Sometimes a year or more is spent in working over a point about nature to discover what it is, and then an equal period has to be spent whittling off what it is not. Having no reference point, the mind can make no statement at this time, for it has no real knowledge of the core of truth. That is why the mind can never rest during this lifetime. For let God reveal Himself here ever so much, it is nothing to what He really is. There is Truth at the core of the soul but it is covered up and hidden from the mind, and as long as that is so there is nothing the mind can do to come to rest, as it might if it had an unchanging point of reference.

The mind never rests but must go on expecting and preparing for what is yet to be known and what is still concealed. Meanwhile, man cannot know what God is, even though he be ever so well aware of what God is not; and an intelligent person will reject that. As long as it has no reference point, the mind can only wait as matter waits

*Philippians 4:13.

for form. And matter can never find rest except in form; so, too, the mind can never rest except in the essential truth which is locked up in it — the truth about everything. Essence alone satisfies and God keeps on withdrawing, farther and farther away, to arouse the mind's zeal and lure it on to follow and finally grasp the true good that has no cause. Thus, contented with nothing, the mind clamors for the highest good of all.

Now you may say: "But, sir, you have often told us that the agents should all be still and yet here you have everything setting up a clamor and covetousness in the mind where quiet should be: there is a great hubbub and outcry for what the mind has not. Whether it be desire, or purpose, or praise, or thanks, or whatever is imagined or engendered in the soul, it cannot be the pure peace or complete quiet, of which you have spoken. Rather, the mind is despoiled of its peace."

This requires an answer. When you get rid of selfishness, together with things and what pertains to them, and have transferred all to God, and united with Him, and abandoned all for Him in complete trust and love, then whatever your lot, whatever touches you, for better or worse, sour or sweet, none of it is yours but it is all God's to whom you have left it.

Tell me: whose is the Word that is spoken? Is it his who speaks, or his who hears it? Even though it come to him who hears it, it still is his who speaks or conceives it. Take an illustration. The sun radiates its light into the air and the air receives it and transmits it to the earth, and receiving it, we can distinguish one color from another. Now, although light seems to be everywhere in the air, it is really in the sun. The rays are really emitted by the sun and come from it — not from the air. They are only received by the air and passed on to anything that can be lighted up.

It is like this with the soul. God begets His Son or the Word in the soul and, receiving it, the soul passes it on in many forms, through its agents, now as desire, now in good intentions, now in loving deeds, now in gratitude or whatever concerns it. These are all His and not yours at all. Credit God with all He does and take none for yourself, as it is written: "The Holy Spirit maketh intercession for us with groanings which cannot be uttered."* It is He that prays

*Romans 8:26.

in us and not we ourselves. St. Paul says that "no man can say that Jesus is the Lord but by the Holy Ghost."*

Above all, claim nothing for yourself. Relax and let God operate you and do what He will with you. The deed is His; the word is His; this birth is His; and all you are is His, for you have surrendered self to Him, with all your soul's agents and their functions and even your personal nature. Then at once, God comes into your being and faculties, for you are like a desert, despoiled of all that was peculiarly your own. The Scripture speaks of "the voice of one crying in the wilderness." Let this voice cry in you at will. Be like a desert as far as self and the things of this world are concerned.

Perhaps, however, you object: "What should one do to be as empty as a desert, as far as self and things go? Should one just wait and do nothing? Or should he sometimes pray, read, or do such virtuous things as listening to a sermon or studying the Bible — of course, not taking these things as if from outside himself, but inwardly, as from God? And if one does not do these things, isn't he missing something?"

This is the answer. External acts of virtue were instituted and ordained so that the outer man might be directed to God and set apart for spiritual life and all good things, and not diverted from them by incompatible pursuits. They were instituted to restrain man from things impertinent to his high calling, so that when God wants to use him, he will be found ready, not needing to be brought back from things coarse and irrelevant. The more pleasure one takes in externalities the harder it is to turn away from them. The stronger the love the greater the pain of parting.

See! Praying, reading, singing, watching, fasting, and doing penance — all these virtuous practices were contrived to catch us and keep us away from strange, ungodly things. Thus, if one feels that the spirit of God is not at work in him, that he has departed inwardly from God, he will all the more feel the need to do virtuous deeds — especially those he finds most pertinent or useful — not for his own personal ends but rather to honor the truth — he will not wish to be drawn or led away by obvious things. Rather, he will want to cleave to God, so that God will find him quickly and not have to look far afield for him when, once more, He wants to act through him.

*1 Corinthians 12:3.

But when a person has a true spiritual experience, he may boldly drop external disciplines, even those to which he is bound by vows, from which even a bishop may not release him. No man may release another from vows he has made to God — for such vows are contracts between man and God. And also, if a person who has vowed many things, such as prayer, fasting, or pilgrimages, should enter an order, he is then free from the vow, for once in the order, his bond is to all virtue and to God Himself.

I want to emphasize that. However much a person may have vowed himself to many things, when he enters upon a true spiritual experience he is released from them all. As long as that experience lasts, whether a week, or a month, or a year, none of this time will be lost to the monk or nun, for God, whose prisoners they are, will account for it all. When he returns to his usual nature, however, let him fulfill the vows appropriate to each passing moment as it comes, but let him not think for a moment of making up for the times he seemed to neglect, for God will make up for whatever time He caused you to be idle. Nor should you think it could be made up by any number of creature-deeds, for the least deed of God is more than all human deeds together. This is said for learned and enlightened people who have been illumined by God and the Scripture.

But what shall be said of the simple fellow who neither knows nor understands [the meaning of] bodily disciplines, when he has vowed or promised something such as a prayer or anything else? This I say for him: If he finds that his vow hinders him and that if he were loosed from it he could draw nearer to God, let him boldly quit the vow; for any act that brings one nearer to God is best. That is what Paul meant when he said: "When that which is perfect is come, then that which is in part shall be done away."*

Vows taken at the hands of a priest are very different. They are as binding as those vowed directly to God. To take a vow with the good intention of binding oneself to God is the best one can do at any time. If, however, a man knows a better way, one that experience has taught him is better, then the first way is at once superseded.

This is easy to prove, for we must look to the fruits, the inward truth, rather than to outward works. As St. Paul says: "The letter

---

*1 Corinthians 13:10.

killeth (that is, all formal practices) but the spirit maketh alive (that is, inner experience of the truth)."* Realize this clearly, that whatever leads you closest to this inner truth, you are to follow in all you do. Let your spirit be uplifted and not downcast, burning and yet pure, silent and quiet. You need not say to God what you need or desire, for He knows it all beforehand. Christ said to His disciples: "When ye pray, use not vain repetitions as the heathen do: for they think that they shall be heard for their much speaking."†

That we may follow this peace and inward silence, that the eternal Word may be spoken in us and understood, and that we may be one with Him, may the Father help us, and the Word, and the spirit of both. Amen.

4. *Eternal birth*

Et cum factus esset Iesus annorum duodecim, etc.
— Luke 2:42

We read in the Gospel that when our Lord was twelve years old He went to the temple at Jerusalem with Mary and Joseph and that, when they left, Jesus stayed behind in the temple without their knowledge. When they got home and missed Him, they looked for Him among acquaintances and strangers and relatives. They looked for Him in the crowds and still they could not find Him. Furthermore, they had lost Him among the [temple] crowds and had to go back to where they came from. When they got back to their starting point, they found Him.

Thus it is true that, if you are to experience this noble birth, you must depart from all crowds and go back to the starting point, the core [of the soul] out of which you came. The crowds are the agents of the soul and their activities: memory, understanding, and will, in all their diversifications. You must leave them all: sense perception, imagination, and all that you discover in self or intend to do. After that, you may experience this birth — but otherwise not — believe me! He was not found among friends, nor relatives, nor among acquaintances. No. He is lost among these altogether.

*2 Corinthians 3:6.
†Matthew 6:7.

Thence we have a question to ask: Is it possible for man to experience this birth through certain things which, although they are divine, yet they come into the man through the senses from without? I refer to certain ideas of God, such as, for example, that God is good, wise, merciful, or whatever — ideas that are creatures of the reason, and yet divine. Can a man have the experience [of the divine birth] by means of these? No! Truly no. Even though [these ideas] are all good and divine, still he gets them all through his sense from without. If the divine birth is to shine with reality and purity, it must come flooding up and out of man from God within him, while all man's own efforts are suspended and all the soul's agents are at God's disposal.

This work [birth], when it is perfect, will be due solely to God's action while you have been passive. If you really forsake your own knowledge and will, then surely and gladly God will enter with His knowledge shining clearly. Where God achieves self-consciousness, your own knowledge is of no use, nor has it standing. Do not imagine that your own intelligence may rise to it, so that you may know God. Indeed, when God divinely enlightens you, no natural light is required to bring that about. This [natural light] must in fact be completely extinguished before God will shine in with His light, bringing back with Him all that you have forsaken and a thousand times more, together with a new form to contain it all.

We have a parable for this in the Gospel. When our Lord had held friendly conversation with the heathen woman at the well, she left her jug and ran to the city to tell the people that the true Messiah had come. The people, not believing her report, went out to see for themselves. Then they said to her: "Now we believe, not because of thy saying: for we have seen Him ourselves."* Thus it is true that you cannot know God by means of any creature science nor by means of your own wisdom. If you are to know God divinely, your own knowledge must become as pure ignorance, in which you forget yourself and every other creature.

But perhaps you will say: "Alas, sir, what is the point of my mind existing if it is to be quite empty and without function? Is it best for me to screw up my courage to this unknown knowledge which cannot really be anything at all? For if I know anything in any way,

---

*John 4:42.

I shall not be ignorant, nor would I be either empty or innocent. Is it my place to be in darkness?"

Yes, truly. You could do no better than to go where it is dark, that is, unconsciousness.

"But, sir, must everything go and is there no turning back?" Certainly not. By rights, there is no return.

"Then what is the darkness? What do you mean by it? What is its name?"

It has no name other than "potential sensitivity" and it neither lacks being nor does it want to be. It is that possible [degree of] sensitivity through which you may be made perfect. That is why there is no way back out of it. And yet, if you do return, it will not be for the sake of truth but rather on account of the world, the flesh, and the devil. If you persist in abandoning it, you necessarily fall [a victim to spiritual] malady and you may even persist so long that for you the fall will be eternal. Thus there can be no turning back but only pressing on to the attainment and achievement of this potentiality. There is no rest [in the process] short of complete fulfillment of Being. Just as matter can never rest until it is made complete by form, which represents its potential Being, so there is no rest for the mind until it has attained all that is possible to it.

On this point, a heathen master says: "Nature has nothing swifter than the heavens, which outrun everything else in their course." But surely the mind of man, in its course, outstrips them all. Provided it retains its active powers and keeps itself free from defilement and the disintegration of lesser and cruder things, it can outstrip high heaven and never slow down until it has reached the highest peak and is fed and lodged by the highest good, which is God.

Therefore, how profitable it is to pursue this potentiality until, empty and innocent, a man is alone in that darkness of unself-consciousness, tracking and tracing [every clue] and never retracing his steps! Thus you may win that [something] which is everything, and the more you make yourself like a desert, unconscious of everything, the nearer you come to that estate. Of this desert, Hosea writes: "I will allure her, and bring her into the wilderness, and speak to her heart."* The genuine Word of eternity is spoken only in that eternity of the man who is himself a wilderness, alienated

*Hosea 2:14.

from self and all multiplicity. The prophet longed for this desolated alienation from self, for he said: "O that I had wings like a dove! for then would I fly away, and be at rest."* Where may one find peace and rest? Really only where he rejects all creatures, being alienated from them and desolate. So David said: "I would choose rather to sit at the threshold of the house of my God than to dwell with great honor and wealth in the tents of wickedness."†

But you may say: "Alas, sir, does a man have to be alienated from creatures and always desolate, inwardly as well as outwardly, the soul's agents together with their functions — must all be done away? That would put one in a hard position — if then God should leave him without his support, and add to his misery, taking away his light and neither speaking to him nor acting in him, as you now seem to mean. If a person is to be in such a state of pure nothingness, would it not be better for him to be doing something to make the darkness and alienation supportable? Should he not pray, or read, or hear a sermon or do something else that is good to help himself through it?"

No! You may be sure that perfect quiet and idleness are the best you can do. For, see, you cannot turn from this condition to do anything, without harming it. This is certain: you would like in part to prepare yourself and in part to be prepared by God, but it cannot be so, for however quickly you desire or think of preparing, God gets there first. But suppose that the preparation could be shared between you and God for the [divine] work of ingress — which is impossible — then you should know that God must act and pour in as soon as He finds that you are ready. Do not imagine that God is like a carpenter who works or not, just as he pleases, suiting his own convenience. It is not so with God, for when He finds you ready He must act, and pour into you, just as when the air is clear and pure the sun must pour into it and may not hold back. Surely, it would be a very great defect in God if He did not do a great work, and anoint you with great good, once He found you empty and innocent.

The authorities, writing to the same point, assert that when the matter of which a child is made is ready in the mother's body, God at once pours in the living spirit which is the soul — the body's form.

Readiness and the giving of form occur simultaneously. When nature reaches its highest point, God gives grace. When the [human] spirit is ready, God enters it without hesitation or waiting. It is written in the Revelation that our Lord told people: "I stand at the door and knock and wait. If any man let me in, I will sup with him."* You need not look either here or there. He is no farther away than the door of the heart. He stands there, lingering, waiting for us to be ready and open the door and let Him in. You need not call to Him as if He were far away, for He waits more urgently than you for the door to be opened. You are a thousand times more necessary to Him than He is to you. The opening [of the door] and His entry are simultaneous.

Still you may ask: "How can that be? I do not sense His presence. But look! To sense His presence is not within your power, but His. When it suits Him, He shows Himself, and He conceals Himself when He wants to. This is what Christ meant when He said to Nicodemus: "The wind [Spirit] bloweth where it listeth, and thou hearest the sound thereof but canst not tell whence it cometh and whither it goeth."† There is an [apparent] contradiction in what He says: "You hear and yet do not know." When one hears, he knows. Christ meant: by hearing a man takes in or absorbs [the Spirit of God]. It was as if He wanted to say: you receive it without knowing it. But you should remember that God may not leave anything empty or void. That is not God's nature. He could not bear it. Therefore, however much it may seem that you do not sense His presence or that you are quite innocent of it, this is not the case. For if there were any void under Heaven whatever, great or small, either the sky would have to draw it up to itself or bend down to fill it. God, the master of nature, will not tolerate any empty place. Therefore be quiet and do not waver lest, turning away from God for an hour, you never return to Him.

Still you may say: "Alas, sir, you assume that this birth is going to happen and that the Son [of God] will be born in me. But by what sign shall I know that it has happened?"

Yes! Certainly! There may well be three trustworthy signs, but let me tell about one of them. I am often asked if it is possible, within

*Revelation 3:20.
†John 3:8.

time, that a person should not be hindered either by multiplicity or by matter. Indeed, it is. When this birth really happens, no creature in all the world will stand in your way and, what is more, they will all point you to God and to this birth. Take the analogy of the thunderbolt. When it strikes to kill, whether it is a tree or an animal or a person, at the coming of the blow, they all turn toward it and if a person's back were turned, he would instantly turn to face it. All the thousands of leaves of a tree at once turn the required sides to the stroke. And so it is with all who experience this birth. They, together with all around them, earthy as you please, are quickly turned toward it. Indeed, what was formerly a hindrance becomes now a help. Your face is turned so squarely toward it that, whatever you see or hear, you only get this birth out of it. Everything stands for God and you see only God in all the world. It is just as when one looks straight at the sun for a while: afterwards, everything he looks at has the image of the sun in it. If this is lacking, if you are not looking for God and expecting Him everywhere, and in everything, you lack the birth.

Still you might ask: "While in this state, should one do penances? Isn't he missing something if he doesn't?"

The whole of a life of penitence is only one among a number of things such as fasting, watching, praying, kneeling, being disciplined, wearing hair shirts, lying on hard surfaces, and so on. These were all devised because of the constant opposition of the body and flesh to the spirit. The body is too strong for the spirit and so there is always a struggle between them — an eternal conflict. The body is bold and brave here, for it is at home and the world helps it. This earth is its fatherland and all its kindred are on its side: food, drink, and comforts are all against the spirit. Here the spirit is alien. Its race and kin are all in heaven. It has many friends there. To assist the spirit in its distress, to weaken the flesh for its part in this struggle so that it cannot conquer the spirit, penances are put upon the flesh, like a bridle, to curb it, so that the spirit may control it. This is done to bring it to subjection, but if you wish to make it a thousand times more subject, put the bridle of love on it. With love you may overcome it most quickly and load it most heavily.

That is why God lies in wait for us with nothing so much as love. Love is like a fisherman's hook. Without the hook he could never catch a fish, but once the hook is taken the fisherman is sure of the fish. Even though the fish twists hither and yon, still the fisherman is sure of him. And so, too, I speak of love: he who is caught by it is held by the strongest of bonds and yet the stress is pleasant. He who takes this sweet burden on himself gets further, and comes nearer to which he aims at than he would by means of any harsh ordinance ever devised by man. Moreover, he can sweetly bear all that happens to him, all that God inflicts he can take cheerfully.

Nothing makes you God's own, or God yours, as much as this sweet bond. When one has found this way, he looks for no other. To hang on this hook is to be so [completely] captured that feet and hands, and mouth and eyes, the heart, and all a man is and has, become God's own.

Therefore there is no better way to overcome the enemy, so that he may never hurt you, than by means of love. Thus it is written: "Love is as strong as death and harder than hell."* Death separates the soul from the body but love separates everything from the soul. It cannot endure anything anywhere that is not God or God's. Whatever he does, who is caught in this net, or turned in this direction, love does it, and love alone, and whether the man does or not, makes no difference.

The most trivial deed or function in such a person is more profitable and fruitful to himself and all men, and pleases God better, than all other human practices put together, which, though done without deadly sin, are characterized by a minimum of love. His rest is more profitable than another's work.

Therefore wait only for this hook and you will be caught up into blessing, and the more you are caught the more you will be set free. That we all may be so caught and set free, may He help us, who is love itself. Amen.

8. *The fruits of good deeds live on!*

Meister Eckhart once said, when he stood up to preach: I once declared in a sermon that I want to teach people who do good deeds while under mortal sin, how their good deeds, performed

*Song of Songs 8:6.

while under deadly sin, may be brought to life* again, together with the interval of time in which they were done. And now I shall set forth the facts of the matter, for I have been asked to explain the meaning of my assertion.

The authorities all say that when a person is under grace, the deeds he does are worthy of eternal life. And that is true, for God works through grace; and I agree with them. Generally speaking, the authorities also assert that, if one falls into mortal sin, his deeds are then dead, as he himself is dead, and none of them merits eternal life, because he is no longer under grace. In some sense this, too, is true, and I agree. They say further, that when God returns His grace to persons who have suffered for their sins, those deeds they did before they sinned mortally live again in the new grace as they did before — and here, too, I agree.

But when they say that good deeds done by one in mortal sin are lost eternally, time and deeds together, then I disagree. I, Meister Eckhart, assert as follows: Of all the good deeds a man does while in mortal sin not one is lost, once he has been restored to grace, no, nor even the interval of time in which they were done. See! This is contrary to all living authorities.

Now pay close attention to what I am going to say and you will understand what I mean.

I say, categorically, that all the good deeds anyone ever did or might do, together with the time used in doing them, are both lost, time and deeds, all together. I say also that no deed was ever either sacred or blessed and that no interval of time was ever sacred or blessed, nor did it hold more good than any other. And if they are neither sacred nor blessed, nor intrinsically good, how could either be preserved? Since good deeds pass away, along with the time consumed in doing them, how could the deeds done under mortal sin, or the time consumed in doing them, be restored? I say that both are lost, one with the other; deeds and time together, the bad with the good, deed for deed, and time for time, are lost forever.

Then we should raise the question: Why should deeds be qualified, so that one is "good," another "sacred," and another "blessed," and so on; and why speak in similar terms of the times at which they

---

*Living "under mortal sin" means to have committed a mortal sin and not yet to have been restored to the grace of God through the sacrament of confession and absolution. (Blakney)

were done? See! As I have said, neither the deed nor the time may so be qualified. "Holy," "blessed," and "good" are terms applied gratuitously either to deeds or time and do not necessarily belong to the nature of either.

Why? A deed, as a deed, is nothing in itself. It did not happen by any will of its own, nor did it happen just by itself. Itself, it knows nothing. Therefore, it is neither good, nor sacred, nor blessed nor unblessed, for these terms apply only to the spirit in which a deed is done, and the spirit is exempt from form, and does not appear after the deed itself. As soon as a deed is done it becomes nothing at all, together with the time consumed in doing it. It is neither here nor there, for the spirit has nothing more to do with the deed. Henceforth, whatever the spirit may do, it must appear in another deed at another time.

For this reason, deeds and time pass away. Bad and good, they are all lost together, for they have no duration in the spirit, nor in their own right, nor have they a place of their own. They are lost because God needs them not at all. If one does a good deed, he is purified, and by this purification he is made more as he was when he was born. To that extent, he is more blessed and better than he was before. This is why we say that a deed is sacred or blessed, or speak so of the time at which it happened. Still, this is not accurate, for the deed knows nothing, nor does the time of its occurrence, and it all passes away. Therefore, the deed itself is neither good, nor sacred, nor blessed, but rather, he is blessed in whom the fruit of good deeds remain — not as times or deeds, but rather as the capacity to do good, which belongs always to the spirit. For the spirit is in the doing of good and is the good itself.

See! In this way, a good deed is never lost, no, nor the time consumed in doing it — not that it is stored up as time or deed but it is stored up apart from time and deed, in the spirit, which is eternal. Then let us see how this applies to deeds done while under mortal sin. As deeds and time, these good deeds are lost, deeds and time together, but then, I have also said that deeds and time are nothing of themselves. And if they are nothing in themselves, then the person who loses them loses nothing! It is true. Still, I have gone further; neither time nor deed has any being or place of itself. In fact, they only issue from the spirit out into time. Whatever the spirit does afterwards, it must be in another deed at another time, and neither of these can ever get into the spirit in so far as it is either deed or time. Neither can it penetrate God, for no temporal deed ever got into Him, and for this reason alone it becomes nothing and is lost.

But now I have said that of all the good deeds a person does while under mortal sin not a single one remains, neither deeds nor time, and that is true in the meaning which I have just explained. I want to make it perfectly clear to you, even though it is contrary to every authority alive.

Now for a brief word about my meaning and why it is true. When a person does a good deed while under mortal sin, he does not do it because of the sin, for his deed is as good as the sin is bad. Rather, he does it because of his basic nature [the core of the soul] which is naturally good, even though he is not under grace and his deeds do not serve to bring in the Kingdom of Heaven at the time he does them. That, however, does not harm the spirit at all, for the fruit of the deed, quite apart from the fact or the time of it, remains in the spirit and is spirit with spirit and can be destroyed as little as the spirit can put itself out of existence. What is more, the spirit purifies itself when it gets rid of the act, which is the image of its own goodness under grace, and in this way is prepared for unity and equality [with God] in which neither deeds nor time are of further use. The more a person purifies himself and gets rid of his images, the nearer he is to God, who Himself is altogether free of them. The more a man forgets his deeds, as well as the occasion of their performance, the purer he is.

If and when grace comes again [to the mortal sinner], all that by nature is his partakes of grace. To the extent he has purified himself by doing good, even while under mortal sin, he has struck a blow for his ultimate union with God, which might not have been possible if he had not purified himself by doing good under mortal sin. He will need time to get rid of his images [the remembered good deeds], but if he has so purified himself while under mortal sin, he has saved some time in which he may do more good, now that he is pure — good that will further unite him with God. The fruits of deeds remain in the spirit. Only the deeds themselves and the time of them are not eternal. So the spirit lives on, out of which deeds are born and the fruit of the deeds, apart from either deeds or time, is full of grace as the spirit is also.

Now, then, we have set forth the meaning of my assertion clearly and it really is true. All who contradict it are hereby contradicted in return, for Truth itself bespeaks the truth of what I have said. If people really understood what spirit is, what deeds and time are, and how deeds are related to the spirit, they would never say that any good deed could ever be lost or go astray. Only the deed passes away with the time and is made nothing, but its result is that the spirit is ennobled by the deed it has projected. That is the power of deeds and why they are done. Their fruits remain in the spirit and can never be taken away. They will never be lost to the spirit itself. If you understand that, how could it ever be possible to assert again that a good work goes amiss, as long as the spirit has being and lives anew under grace?

That we may come to be one spirit with God and be found under grace, may God help us all! Amen.

13. *Truth is not merchandise*

Intravit Iesus in templum Dei et ejiciebat omnes vendentes et ementes, etc.

— Matthew 21:12

We read in the holy Gospel that our Lord went into the temple and drove out all those that bought and sold, and said to the vendors of doves: "Get these things out of here!" He gave them clearly to understand that He wanted the temple pure, just as if He had said: "I have a right to this temple and I alone will be in it, to have control of it."

What does that tell us? The temple in which God wants to be master, strong to work His will, is the human soul, which He created and fashioned exactly like Himself. We read that the Lord said: "Let us make man in our own image."* And He did it. He made the human soul so much like Himself that nothing else in heaven or on earth resembles Him so much. That is why God wants the temple to be pure, so pure that nothing shall be in it except He Himself. And that is the reason He is well pleased with it when it is really prepared for Him, and why He takes such comfort there — when He is there alone.

*Genesis 1:26.

Now let us see who the people were that bought and sold — and who they still are, but understand me correctly, I shall now speak only of the good people. Nevertheless, at this time I shall indicate who the merchants were that bought and sold, whom our Lord struck and drove out of the temple. He is still doing just that to those who buy and sell in it. He will not allow a single one of them to be there. See! The merchants are those who guard against mortal sins, who would like to be good people and do their good deeds to the glory of God, such as fasting, watching, praying, and the like — all of which are good — and yet they do these things so that the Lord will give them something they want in exchange, or do something they ardently want to have done.

They are all merchants. That is plain to see. They want to give one thing for another and to trade with our Lord but they will be cheated out of their bargain — for all they ever have or attain is *given* them by God and they do what they do only by means of God, and thus He is obligated to them for nothing. He will give them nothing and do nothing for them that He would not do or give of His own free will anyway. What they are they are because of God, and whatever they have they have from God and not by their own contriving. Therefore God is not in the least obligated to them for their deeds or their gifts. By reason of His grace, He will like to do for them, of His own free will — but certainly not for the sake of any act they perform or offering they bring. For [in these things] they are not giving what is their own and their acts do not come out of themselves. For God Himself says: "Without me, ye can do nothing."*

They are very foolish people who want to trade with our Lord and they know little or nothing of the truth. Therefore, God strikes them and drives them out of the temple. Light and darkness cannot exist side by side. God is the truth and a light in Himself. When He enters the temple, He drives out ignorance and darkness and reveals Himself in light and truth. Then, when the truth is known, the merchants must begone — for truth wants no merchandising!

God does not seek His own. In all His acts, He is innocent and free and acts only out of true love. That is why the person who is united with God acts that way — he, too, will be innocent and free,

*John 15:5.

whatever he does, and will act out of love and without asking why, solely for the glory of God, seeking his own advantage in nothing — for God is at work in him.

And what is more, as long as a man is looking for pay for what he does, or wants to get from God anything that God could or would give, he is like a merchant. If you want to be rid of the commercial spirit, do all you can in the way of good works, solely for the praise of God, and efface yourself as completely as if you did not exist. Whatever you do, you shall not ask anything in return for it and then your efforts will be both spiritual and divine. Then only are the merchants driven out of the temple and God is alone in it — when a person thinks only of God. See! This is how the temple is cleared of merchants: the man who thinks only of God, to revere Him, is free and innocent of any mercantilism in his various acts, for he "seeketh not his own."

Furthermore, as I said, our Lord spoke to the people who trafficked in doves, saying: "Get these all out of here!" Take them away! But in scolding and driving them out, He was really not too severe. Rather, He spoke quite kindly: "Take it all out!" — meaning, perhaps, "this is not so bad in itself, but it does constitute a hindrance to the simple truth." They were all good people, working impersonally for God and not for themselves, but they were working under their own limitations of time and number, antecedent and consequence. In their varied efforts, they are kept from the highest truth, from innocence and freedom such as our Lord Jesus Christ had. He was incessantly refreshed in spirit by His heavenly Father apart from time, and reborn into the perfection of His Father with each eternal moment — each passing Now. His praise to the fatherlike Highest was gratitude for like dignity.

Everybody who wants to be sensitive to the highest truth must be like this, conscious of neither "before" nor "after," unhindered by their past records, uninfluenced by any idea they ever understood, innocent and free to receive anew with each Now-moment a heavenly gift, and to consecrate them to God in the same light, with thankful praise to our Lord Jesus Christ. Thus the doves are cleared out, that is, the hindrances, the good deeds that smack of selfishness, which are good enough in their way to enable one to get what he wants for himself. But of these our Lord spoke gently, saying: "Take them all out — get rid of them!" He may have meant merely: "No harm done — but they are just some more obstacles."

When the temple is cleared of every hindrance, that is, of strangers and their properties, its appearance is beautiful and it shines so clear and pure above all, and in all God has created, that no one but the uncreated God can be reflected in it. To be sure, nothing is like this temple but the uncreated God Himself. Nothing lower than the angels can be compared to it. In some ways, but not in all, the highest angels are comparable to this temple — the aristocratic soul. That they are like the soul at all is due to knowledge and love, but a limit is set for them, beyond which they cannot go. Only the soul may surpass that limit; for let the soul be equated with the highest element in human nature existing within time: a person with his possibility of freedom may rise unspeakably higher than the highest angel, in every Now-moment — moments without number and without specified nature — rising above the angels and all creature minds. Since God alone is free and uncreated, He is like the soul in being free — but not in uncreatedness, for the soul is created.

Comes then the soul into the unclouded light of God. It is transported so far from creaturehood into nothingness that, of its own powers, it can never return to its agents or its former creaturehood. Once there, God shelters the soul's nothingness with His uncreated essence, safeguarding its creaturely existence. The soul has dared to become nothing, and cannot pass from its own being into nothingness and then back again, losing its own identity in the process, except God safeguarded it. This must needs be so.

As I said before, Jesus went into the temple and drove out those that bought and sold and began to say to the others: "Take this all away!" See! I have it in these words: "Jesus went in and began to say: 'Take all this away!' — and they took it away." Observe, too, that then there was nobody left but Jesus, and being alone, He began to speak in the temple of the soul. Observe this also, for it is certain: if anyone else is speaking in the temple of the soul, Jesus keeps still, as if He were not at home. And He is not at home in the soul where there are strange guests — guests with whom the soul holds conversation. If Jesus is to speak in the soul and be heard, then the soul must be alone and quiet. So He got in, and began to talk. What does Jesus say then?

He says that He is! Then what is He? He is the Father's Word.

In this Word, God expresses Himself, together with all the divine Being, all that God is, as only He can know it. And He knows it as it is, because He is perfect in knowledge and power. Therefore, He is also perfect in self-expression. When He utters His Word, He expresses Himself and everything else in a second Person, to whom He gives His own nature. He speaks, and all intelligent spirits, re-echoing the Word, repeat His idea, just as rays shining from the sun bear the sun in themselves. So each intelligent spirit is a Word in itself; even though it is not like God's Word in all respects, it has received the power to become a likeness of the Word of God, full of grace.* And thus the Father has completely expressed His Word, as it really is, with all that is in Him.

Since, then, the Father has expressed Himself, what does Jesus say in the soul? As I have said, the Father utters the Word and speaks in the Word and not otherwise. But Jesus speaks in the soul. What He says is a revelation of Himself and all the Father has said to Him, in proportion as one's soul is sensitive to it. He reveals the Father's majesty with unmeasured power. If, in his spirit, one discovers this power in the Son, he will have like power in whatever he does, power for all virtue and purity. Neither joy nor sorrow, no, nor anything God ever created in time, shall be able to disturb this person, for he remains, strengthened by divine power, opposed to which creature things are insignificant and futile.

Once again, Jesus reveals Himself in the soul in unmeasured wisdom, which He is. He reveals Himself in the wisdom which is God's self-knowledge or His knowledge of His own fatherly power. And that Word, of which we spoke, is also wisdom and welds all those things it touches into unique oneness. When wisdom is joined to the soul, all doubt, error, and darkness fly away and the soul is set in a pure clear light, which is God Himself. That is what the prophet says: "Lord, in thy light, we shall see light."† Thus God is known through God in the soul, and the soul, through this wisdom, comes to know itself; and thence, too, the soul knows the paternal glory in its fruitful procreation, and the real is-ness‡ in its simple unity, in which are no distinctions.

---

*John 1:14.
†Psalm 36:9.
‡Mystical neologism; see Introduction, p. xx.

Jesus also reveals Himself in unmeasured sweetness and fullness, which flows from the powerhead of the Holy Spirit, overflowing its unsearchable riches and sweetness into hearts which are sensitive to it. And thus, when Jesus does unite with the soul, the tide moves back again into its own, out of itself, over itself, above all things, with grace and power back to its prime origin. Then the outward man is obedient to the inner man until death and he has constant peace in the service of God for all time. That Jesus may also come into us and drive out all hindrances of body and soul, and that we may be one with Him, here on Earth as in Heaven, may God help us all! Amen.

16. *Being is more than life*

In occisione gladii mortui sunt.
— Hebrews 11:37

We read of the holy martyrs, whom we are to remember today, that "they were slain with the sword." Our Lord said to His disciples: "Blessed are ye ... when ye shall suffer ... for my name's sake."*
According to the Scripture, the martyrs suffered death for Christ's sake, being put to the sword.

We learn three things of them. The first is that they are dead. Whatever one may suffer in this world, there is an end to it. St. Augustine says: "All the pain and trouble of this world have an end but God's reward for it is eternal." Moreover, we ought to keep in mind that since this life is mortal, we need not fear all the pain and trouble that could come, because it is going to have an end. In the third place [we learn that] we should be so dead to the world that nothing will affect us, whether we like it or not.

One authority says: "Nothing can affect heaven," and by this he means the heavenly person who is moved by nothing that happens. Another asks: "If creatures amount to so little, how does it happen that they so easily turn a person from God — when the soul at its worst is better than creatures and heaven to boot?" He says that this comes of paying too little attention to God. If a man paid as much attention to God as he should, it would be well-nigh impossible

*Matthew 5:11.

for him to fall. This is good doctrine. In this world, people should behave as though they were dead. As St. Gregory says: "No one can have as much of God as he who is dead to this world."

But the fourth lesson is best. It says that they are dead but that death gives them Being. An authority says that nature never destroys anything without putting something better in its place. When air turns to fire, that is something better, but when air turns to water, there is destruction, something gone wrong. If, then, nature does so well, how much better may God do! He never destroys without giving something better in return. The martyrs are dead. They have lost their lives but they have received Being. There is an authority who teaches that "Being, life, and knowledge rank highest but knowledge is higher than life and Being, because whoever has knowledge necessarily has both the others." According to that, life would rank ahead of Being as, for example, a tree has life, while a stone has only Being. However, if we reach down into Being pure and simple, as it really is, we should find that Being ranks higher than life or knowledge.

I shall say that they have lost a natural life and received Being. One authority says that God is like nothing so much as Being; to the extent anything has Being it is like God. Another says that Being is so high and pure that God cannot be more than Being. God sees nothing else, knows nothing else, for Being is His arena. He loves nothing else, thinks of nothing else than His Being. Now I should say that creatures as a whole have only one Being. However, one authority says that "Certain creatures are so near to God and so instinct with divine light that they give Being to others." That is not true, because Being is so superior in rank and purity and so much God's own that no one can give it but He — as He gives Himself. Being is the property of God.

One authority says that one creature might well give another life but that whatever really is exists in Being. Being is a name above all names. To be defective is to show a decline in Being. All our lives should reveal Being and therefore, to the extent that life is Being, it is of God. As far as it is included in Being, it is related to God. Let a man's life be ever so mean, if he takes it as Being, it will rank higher than anything else life might be. I am very sure that, if a soul knew the least of what Being is, its attention would never be diverted from it even for an instant. The least one knows of God as, for example, to see a flower get its Being from Him, is more perfect knowledge than any other. To know the least of creatures as one of God's Beings is better than knowing an angel.

When an angel turns its attention to creatures, night falls. St. Augustine says that when angels attend to creatures apart from God, then it is twilight. So it is with the soul. If the soul knows God in creatures, night falls. If it sees how they have their being in God, morning breaks. But if it sees the Being that is in God Himself alone, it is high noon! See! This is what one ought to desire with mad fervor — that all his life should become Being.

There is nothing so mean that to some degree it does not long for Being. Even caterpillars, when they fall off a tree, go at once to climb a wall, to regain their Being. Thus we say that it is good to die in God so that He may give us instead that Being which is better than life, a Being in which our life subsists even now. One ought to be glad to give up to dying and death, so that better Being may be his portion.

I once said that wood is better than gold, which is a fantastic thing to say, and yet a stone, to the extent it has Being, would be better than even God and the Godhead without Being. (Supposing that God could be abstracted from Being.) That must be a strong life in which lifeless things are made to live, in which even death is changed to life. There is no death in God, for in Him everything is made alive. "They are dead," says the Scripture of the martyrs, "and are transformed to life eternal," that is, to a life in which life is Being.

We are to be so dead that neither good nor evil affects us. What we know must be known to its roots, for we shall never know anything until we know its causes. There can be no knowledge until knowing reaches the hidden reasons. Thus, too, life cannot be perfected until it has returned to its secret source, where life is Being, a life the soul receives when it dies even down to its roots, so that we may live that life yonder which itself is Being. One scholar points out what it is that hinders us from that: We are hindered by cleaving to time. Whatever cleaves to time is mortal.

An authority says: "The course of heaven is eternal, and yet it may well be that time comes from heaven by reason of a defection."*

*Plato, *Timaeus* 37.

Heaven itself is eternal in its course and knows nothing about time. That means that the soul, too, consists of pure Being — but then, too, there are opposites in the soul. What are opposites? Good and evil, white and black are such opposites, which, however, are not part of Being.

One authority says that the soul is put in the body to be purified. If it is separated from the body, it has neither intelligence nor will. It is then One and cannot send forth agents through which it might turn to God. Nevertheless, the agents are present [in germ] in the soul's core, which is to say, in its roots rather than its activities.* The soul is purified in the body through its function in gathering together [all the body's] disparate elements. When [the forces] expressed through the five senses are gathered again into the soul, then the soul is one agent by means of which everything is unified.

In the second place, the soul is purified in the practice of virtues by which we climb to a life of unity. That is the way the soul is made pure — by being purged of much divided life and by entering upon a life that is [focused to] unity. The whole scattered world of lower things is gathered up to oneness when the soul climbs up to that life in which there are no opposites. Entering the life of reason, opposites are forgotten, but where this light does not fall, things fall away to death and destruction.

In the third place, the purity of the soul consists in never turning aside to anything [at which it does not ultimately aim]. To turn aside is to die and finally not to be.†

Let us pray our dear Lord God that He help us to mount from life divided to a life unified. Amen.

18. *Justice is even*

Justi autem in perpetuum vivent et apud Dominum est merces eorum.

— Wisdom of Solomon 5:15

"The just shall live forever and their reward is with God." Let us look with care at this dictum. Even though it sounds trite and commonplace, it is nevertheless noteworthy and very good.

---

*Aquinas, *Summa Theologica* I, quest. 77, art. 6.
†It is clear that this sermon is abbreviated considerably. (Blakney)

"The just shall live!" Who are the just? A Scripture says: "He is just who gives to each what belongs to him."* Thus, they are just who give to God what is His, to the angels what is theirs, and to their fellow men what is theirs.

Honor belongs to God. Who are they that do honor to him? Those who become selfless, caring nothing for their own rights in anything, whatever it may be, great or small, who expect nothing beneath themselves or yet above or beside themselves, who think not at all about goods, or comfort, or pleasure, or profit, or spirituality, or saintliness, or reward, or heaven. The just have finished with all these and everything else that belongs to themselves. It is such people who honor God and give Him what is His own.

To the saints and angels, give joy. O Wonder of Wonders! Can one who is still in this life give joy to those in eternity? Certainly, he can. No mouth can tell nor can any mind conceive how great is the joy and pleasure of every single saint in each good work done with good will or in each high desire. How is that? They love God so without measure, they hold Him so dear, that they prefer His honor to their own blessedness.

And not only the saints and angels: even God Himself takes pleasure in these things, just as if, blessing Him, they were vital to Him and His own pleasure and satisfaction depended on them. Ah! — but now look! If we are to serve God for no other reason than the joy it gives to those who are in eternity, still we might well do it by preference and with all diligence. So, too, we should give help to those in hell-fire and betterment to the living.

The person who does these things is just to some degree and to another degree, they are just who take everything from God evenly, just as it comes, great and small, desirable and undesirable, one thing like another, all the same, and none more or less. If one thing means more than another to you, you are unjust. You must always put your own will aside.

There is something that has been much on my mind in recent days: If God does not want what I want, then I must want what He wants. Many people want their own way in everything, and that is bad. That way evil comes. There are others — a little better — who

---

*A translation of the *Institutes of Justinian*, I:1: "Justitia est constans et perpetua voluntas uis suum cuique tribuens."

approve of God's will and who would do nothing contrary to His will but who, when they are sick, wish it were God's will for them to be healthy. These people would have God's will conform to their own rather than theirs to His. This is to be condoned but it is still wrong. The just have no will at all: whatever God wants, it is all one to them, however great the discomfort of it may be.

The just man is so in earnest for justice that, if God Himself were not just, he would not care in the least for God. Indeed, the just are so firmly devoted to justice and so wholly selfless that, whatever they do, they regard neither the pains of Hell nor the joys of Heaven. Indeed, not all the pains of Hell, whether human or fiendish, nor all the pains ever suffered on Earth, or to be suffered, were they heaped upon the just, would influence them one bit, so firmly established are they in God and justice. To the just person, nothing is so hard to bear or so painful as anything opposed to justice, that is to say, as not feeling impartially the same about everything that happens.

How so? If one thing makes them happy and another depressed, they are not just. What is more, if at one time they rejoice more and another time less, that, too, is wrong. He who loves justice is so firmly attached to it that, loving it, it is his Being. Nothing can draw him away from it and he is concerned with nothing else. St. Augustine says: "The soul is more real in what it loves than it is in what it gives life to." Our text sounds ordinary and commonplace, but very few people understand what it really means and how deep a truth it is. Those who understand clearly about justice and the just will understand all I say.

"The just shall live." There is nothing in all the world so dear or desirable as life. Thus, no life is so bad or difficult that a person could not elect to remain alive. A Scripture says: "The nearer death comes, the more painful it is" — and yet, however bad life is, still there is the desire to live. Why do you eat? Why sleep? So that you may live. Why do you desire goods or honors? You know very well why. But why live? For the sake of living — and yet you do not know why you live. Life is so desirable in itself that one wants it for its own sake. Even those who are in the eternal pains of Hell still do not want to part with their lives, whether souls or fiends, because life is so precious, flowing immediately out of God into the soul. That is why they want to live.

What is life? God's Being is my life, but if it is so, then what is

God's must be mine and what is mine God's. God's is-ness is my is-ness, and neither more nor less. The just live eternally with God, on a par with God, neither deeper nor higher. All their work is done by God and God's by them. Thus St. John says: "The Word was with God" — it is completely like Him and immediately with Him — neither deeper nor higher, but only like Him.

When God made people, he made woman from the man's side, so that she might be equal to him. He did not make her from the head or the foot, to be neither man nor woman, but to be like Him. Thus the just soul is to be like God, by the side of God, exactly His equal and neither above nor beneath.

Who, then, are they that are like God? It is they who are like nothing else, save God alone. There is nothing like the divine Being, for in Him there is neither idea nor form. Therefore, those souls that are like God are the ones to whom God has given Himself evenly, withholding nothing. All the Father can give, He gives to them evenly, when they hold to the evenness of justice and do not consider themselves as being more than others and are no more dear to themselves than others are. They shall not consider their own honor or profit, or whatever, more urgent than a stranger's. Personal rights, whether bad or good, they hold to be harmful, foreign, and alien. All the love of this world is based on self-love.

In eternity, the Father begets the Son in His own likeness. "The Word was with God and the Word was God." Like God, it had His nature. Furthermore, I say that God has begotten Him in my soul. Not only is the soul like Him and He like it, but He is in it, for the Father begets His Son in the soul exactly as He does in eternity and not otherwise. He must do so whether He will or not. The Father ceaselessly begets His son and, what is more, He begets me as His Son — the selfsame Son! Indeed, I assert that He begets me not only as His Son but as Himself and Himself as myself, begetting me in His own nature, His own Being. At that inmost Source, I spring from the Holy Spirit and there is one life, one Being, one action. All God's works are one and therefore He begets me as He does His Son and without distinction. My physical father is not my real Father, except for some small bit of his nature. For I am cut off from Him. He may be dead and yet I alive. Therefore the heavenly Father is my true Father and I am His Son and have all that I have from Him. I am identically His Son and no other, because the Father does only one kind of thing, making no distinctions. Thus it is that I am His only begotten Son.

St. Paul says: "We are always being transformed into God and changed."* Consider the simile: The bread of the sacrament is changed into the body of our Lord and, however much it may still seem like bread, it is nevertheless the body of Christ. Similarly, if all the bread were to be changed into my finger, it would still be no more than one finger. Suppose, however, that my finger were changed back into bread, there would still be the same amount of bread as ever, for whatever is changed into something else becomes identical with it. If, therefore, I am changed into God and He makes me one with Himself, then, by the living God, there is no distinction between us. The Father ceaselessly begets His Son. Once the Son is born, He takes nothing more from the Father, for He has it all. Only while He is being born does He take anything from the Father.

The point is that we ought not ask anything from God as we would of a stranger. Our Lord said to His disciples: "I have not called you servants, but friends." Whoever asks something of another is his servant and he who grants is Master. Recently I have been wondering if I could receive or desire anything from God. I must earnestly consider this matter, for if I should take anything from God then I should be His servant and He would be like a master in the act of giving. In life eternal, however, it shall not be so.

I once said, in this place (and it is true): When a man goes beyond himself to fetch or get anything, he is doing wrong. I shall not find God nor even imagine Him apart from myself, but as my own and belonging to me. Neither shall I do anything or serve in any way, neither for God, nor to glorify Him, nor for any cause extraneous to Himself, but only for that which is His own being and the life that is in Him.

Some simple people imagine that they are going to see God as if He were standing yonder and they here, but it is not to be so. God and I: we are one. By knowing God I take Him to myself. By loving God I penetrate Him. Some people say that blessedness lies in willing rather than knowing, but they are wrong. If it were merely a matter of willing, there would never be this unity.

Action and becoming are one. If the carpenter does no work, the

*2 Corinthians 3:18.

house is not built. When his broadax stops, the structure stops. God and I are one in process. He acts and I become, just as fire changes anything that is thrown into the fire, so that it takes the nature of fire. Wood does not change fire into wood but the fire does change wood.*

Thus, if we are to be changed into God, we must know Him as He is,[†] says St. Paul. This, then, is to be our knowledge, that I know Him as He knows me, neither more nor less, but always the same, as our text has it: "The just shall live forever and their reward is with God."

That we shall love justice for its own sake and love God without any reason for loving, may God help us all! Amen.

23. *Distinctions are lost in God*

Qui audit me, non confundetur.
— Ecclesiasticus 24:22

The eternal wisdom of the Father says: "He that heareth me is not ashamed. (If he is ashamed, it is of his shame.) He who acts in me sins not. He that reveals me and fears me shall have eternal life." There is matter enough for one sermon in any of these three statements.

I shall discuss the first — that the eternal wisdom says: "He that heareth me is not ashamed." To hear the wisdom of the Father, one must be "in," at home, and alone.[‡]

Three things there are that hinder one from hearing the eternal Word. The first is corporeality, the second, number, and the third, time. If a person has overcome these three, he dwells in eternity, is alive spiritually and remains in the unity, the desert of solitude, and there he hears the eternal word. Our Lord says: "No man heareth my word or teaching until he hath forsaken selfhood."[§] The hearing of God's Word requires complete self-surrender. He who hears and that which is heard are identical constituents of the eternal Word. What the eternal Father teaches is His own Being, Nature, and Godhead —

*Cf. Plato. *Timaeus* 57, from which this simile is probably drawn. (Blakney)
[†]2 Corinthians 3:18; 1 John 3:2.
[‡]Cf. Matthew 6:6.
[§]Cf. Luke 14:26.

which He is always revealing through His only begotten Son. He teaches that we are to be identical with Him.

To deny one's self is to be the only begotten Son of God and one who does so has for himself all the properties of that Son. All God's acts are performed and His teachings conveyed through the Son, to the point that we should be His only begotten Son. And when this is accomplished in God's sight, He is so fond of us and so fervent that He acts as if His divine Being might be shattered and He Himself annihilated if the whole foundations of His Godhead were not revealed to us, together with His nature and Being. God makes haste to do this, so that it may be ours as it is His. It is here that God finds joy and rapture in fulfillment and the person who is thus within God's knowing and love becomes just what God Himself is.

If you love yourself, you love everybody else as you do yourself. As long as you love another person less than you love yourself, you will not really succeed in loving yourself but if you love all alike, including yourself, you will love them as one person and that person is both God and man. Thus he is a just and righteous person who, loving himself, loves all others equally.

Some people say: "I prefer my friends who are good to me to other people" — but they are wrong and this is not the perfect way. Nevertheless, we have to make the best of it, just as people do who have to sail over the sea with a cross wind and yet manage to get over. Well, it is like this with one who has his preferences in people, as naturally one will. If I care for other people as I do for myself, then what happens to them, whether for better or for worse, let it mean life or death, I should be glad to take it on myself.

That is true friendship. Speaking to this point, St. Paul says: "I could wish to be cut off eternally from God for my friends' sake and for God's sake."* To be cut off from God for an instant is to be cut off from Him forever, and to be cut off from God at all is the pain of Hell. What, then, does St. Paul mean by saying that he could wish to be cut off from God? The authorities question whether or not St. Paul, when he made this remark, was already perfect or only on the road to perfection. I say that he was already quite perfect, for otherwise he would not have said it and now I shall explain why St. Paul could say that he could wish to be cut off from God.

*Romans 9:3.

Man's last and highest parting occurs when, for God's sake, he takes leave of god.* St. Paul took leave of god for God's sake and gave up all that he might get from god, as well as all he might give — together with every idea of god. In parting with these, he parted with god for God's sake and yet God remained to him as God is in His own nature — not as He is conceived by anyone to be — nor yet as something yet to be achieved — but more as an "is-ness," as God really is.† Then he neither gave to God nor received anything from Him, for he and God were a unit, that is, pure unity. Thus one becomes that real person, for whom there can be no suffering, any more than the divine essence can suffer. As I have often said, there is something in the soul so closely akin to God that it is already one with Him and need never be united with Him. It is unique and has nothing in common with anything else. It has no significance [for this world?] whatsoever — none! Anything created is nothing but that Something is apart from and strange to all creation. If one were wholly this, he would be both uncreated and unlike any creature. If any corporeal thing or anything fragile were included in that unity, it, too, would be like the essence of that unity. If I should find myself in this essence, even for a moment, I should regard my earthly selfhood as of no more importance than a manure worm.

God gives to all things alike and as they proceed from God they are alike. Angels, men, and creatures all flow out of God in whom their prime origin is. Take them as they first emanate from Him and you will find them all alike but, if they are alike in this temporal sphere, in eternity and in God they are the much more so. A flea, to the extent that it is in God, ranks above the highest angel in his own right. Thus, in God, all things are equal and are God Himself.

In this likeness or identity God takes such delight that He pours His whole nature and being into it. His pleasure is as great, to take a simile, as that of a horse, let loose to run over a green heath where the ground is level and smooth, to gallop as a horse will, as fast as he can over the greensward — for this is a horse's pleasure and expresses his nature. It is so with God. It is His pleasure and rapture

---

*The lower-case "*god*" means a human conception of God which Eckhart did not explicate and which his contemporaries understood as blasphemous, counter to his intention. (Blakney)

†Cf. Exodus 3:14: "I am what I am."

to discover identity, because He can always put His whole nature into it — for He is this identity itself.

A question is raised about those angels who live with us, serving and guarding us, as to whether or not they have less joy in identity than the angels in Heaven have and whether they are hindered at all in their [proper] activities by serving and guarding us. No! Not at all! Their joy is not diminished, nor their equality, because the angel's work is to do the will of God and the will of God is the angel's work. If God told an angel to go to a tree and pick off the caterpillars, the angel would be glad to do it and it would be bliss to him because it *is* God's will.

Always to be ready to do God's will is to be ready for nothing else than what God is and wills. Such a person, being ill, would not wish to be well. Pain would be a pleasure to him and all the manifold of things would be an empty unity to him who is ready to do God's will. Indeed if the pains of Hell should follow, they would be joy and bliss — for he would be empty, having denied himself, and whatever might happen would not touch him. If my eye is to distinguish colors, it must first be free from any color impressions. If I see blue or white, the seeing of my eyes is identical with what is seen. The eye by which I see God is the same as the eye by which God sees me. My eye and God's eye are one and the same — one in seeing, one in knowing, and one in loving.

To love as God loves, one must be dead to self and all created things, and have as little regard for self as for one who is a thousand miles away. His life is an identity and a unity and there is no distinction in him. This person must have denied himself and the whole world. If anyone owned the whole world and gave it up as freely as he received it, God would give it back to him and eternal life to boot.

And if there were another person who had nothing but good will and he thought: "Lord, if this whole world were mine and two more with it, [or as many more as you please] I would give them up and myself too as completely as it was before I received them" — then God would return to him as much as he had given away with his own hands. There is still another person, who has nothing whatever, material or spiritual, to give away or forsake; he has given away and forsaken most of all. To him who even for one instant completely denies himself shall all things be given, but if a person were to deny himself for twenty years and then return to selfishness even for a moment, it would be as if he had never denied himself at all. One who has denied himself and keeps denying himself and never even casts a glance on what he has given up and remains steady, immovably and unchangeably what he is — he alone has really denied himself.

That we too may remain steady and unchangeable in the eternal Father, may God help us and the eternal wisdom too. Amen.

24. *God enters a free soul*

Intravit Iesus in quoddam castellum et mulier quaedam excepit illum....

— Luke 10:38

I have read a text from the Gospel, first in Latin, which means in English: "Our Lord Jesus Christ went into a little castle and was received by a virgin who was a wife."*

But notice this text with care! It must necessarily be that the person who received Jesus was a virgin. A virgin, in other words, is a person who is free of irrelevant ideas, as free as he was before he existed. Yet see — someone might ask: How can a person, once born and launched into rational life, be as devoid of ideas as if he did not exist? How can he be free?

Listen to the analysis I shall now make. If I were sufficiently intelligent to comprehend all the ideas ever conceived by man or God Himself, and if I were detached from them, so that I did not regard them as mine to take or leave, in either past or future, and if I were free and empty of them in this Now-moment, the present, as it is the blessed will of God for me to be, and if I were perpetually doing God's will, then I would be a virgin in reality, as exempt from idea-handicaps as I was before I was born.

Nevertheless, I assert that being a virgin will not deprive a man of the results of his efforts. Rather, he will be virgin and detached from them and none of them will keep him back from the highest truth — if he, like Jesus, is free and pure and himself virgin. As the

---

*Admittedly, a cavalier rendering of the text in both English and German. (Blakney)

authorities say, "like to like"* is the condition of unity, so that one must be innocent and virgin if he is to receive the innocent Jesus.

Now stop, look, and listen in earnest. To remain virgin forever is never to bear fruit. To be fruitful, it is necessary to be a wife. "Wife" is the optimum term that may be applied to the soul. It is even above "virgin." That within himself, a man should receive God is good; and receiving God, the man is still virgin. Nevertheless, it is better that God should be fruitful through him, for fruitfulness alone is real gratitude for God's gift and in fruitfulness the soul is a wife, with newborn gratitude, when it bears Jesus back again into the Father's heart.

Many good gifts, received in virginity, are not brought to birth in wifely fruitfulness by which God is gratefully pleased. The gifts decay and come to nothing, so that the man is never blessed or bettered by them. The virgin in him is useless when it does not ripen into the wife who is fruitful. Here is the mischief! It is against this that I have said: "Jesus entered a little castle and was received by a virgin who was a wife." This must needs be so, as I have shown.

Married people seldom bear fruit more than once a year, but now I shall speak to another kind of married persons — those who are married to prayers, fasts, vigils, and all sorts of external disciplines and chastisements. Any devotion to any practice that limits your freedom to wait upon God in this present moment and to follow Him into the light, by which He may show you what to do and what not to do — how to be as new and free with each moment as if you had never had, or wanted, or could have another — any such commitment or premeditated practice that limits your freedom — I now call "married life." In it, your soul will bring forth no fruit other than the discipline to which you are so anxiously committed and you will trust neither God nor yourself, until you are finished with it. In other words, you will find no peace, for no one can be fruitful until he is done with his own work. I put this down as an interval [of effort] from which the yield is small, because it has to come out of self-designed bondage and not out of freedom. I call them married who live in this voluntary bondage. They seldom bear fruit and before God there is little profit in them, as I have explained.

*The Aristotelian rule was "like is known by like." See *On the Soul* I, 404b. See also III, 431b: "the soul is in a way all existing things." (Blakney)

A virgin who is a wife, free and unfettered in affections, is equally near both to God and to self. She brings forth much fruit and is big withal, no less and no more than God Himself is. This virgin who is a wife accomplishes this birth, bears fruit every day a hundred- or a thousandfold — yes, she gives birth times without number and bears fruit from the most fertile of soils. To speak plainly, she bears fruit out of the ground in which the Father begets His eternal Word. She is thus fruitful and parturient. For Jesus is the light and shine of the paternal heart (as St. Paul puts it, He is the glory and reflection of the Father's heart — the power shining through). This Jesus is united with her [the virgin soul] and she with Him. She is illumined and radiates Him as the One and only pure, clear light of the Father.

I have often said before that there is an agent in the soul, un- touched by time and flesh, which proceeds out of the Spirit and which remains forever in the Spirit and is completely spiritual. In this agent, God is perpetually verdant and flowering with all the joy and glory that is in Him. Here is joy so hearty, such inconceivably great joy that no one can ever fully tell it, for in this agent the eter- nal Father is ceaselessly begetting His eternal Son and the agent is parturient with God's offspring and is itself the Son, by the Father's unique power.

For this reason, if a person had a whole kingdom or all this world's goods and left it all solely for God's sake, to become the poorest man who ever lived on Earth, and if then God gave him as much to suffer as he ever gave any man, and if this person suffered it out until he was dead, and if then, even for the space of a moment, God once let him see what He is in this agent of the soul, all his suffering and poverty would seem like a very little thing beside the joy of it, so great in that moment. Indeed, if afterwards God never gave him the Kingdom of Heaven at all, he would feel sufficiently repaid for all he had suffered, for God Himself is in that agent of the soul in that eternal Now-moment.

If the spirit were only always united with God in this agent, a man could never grow old. For the Now-moment, in which God made the first man and the Now-moment in which the last man will disappear, and the Now-moment in which I am speaking are all one in God, in whom there is only one Now. Look! The person who lives in the light of God is conscious neither of time past nor of time to come but only of the one eternity. In fact, he is bereft of wonder, for all things are intrinsic in him. Therefore he gets nothing new out of future events, nor from chance, for he lives in the Now-moment that is, unfailingly, "in verdure newly clad." Such is the divine glory of this agent in the soul.

There is, however, still another agent, which also is not incarnate but which proceeds out of the spirit, yet remains in it and is always only spiritual. In this second agent, God glows and burns without ceasing, in all His fullness, sweetness, and rapture. Truly, it holds joy so great and rapture so unmeasured that no one can tell it or reveal it. Yet I say that if there were one person who could look into it for a moment and still keep his right mind, all he had ever suffered or that God wished him to suffer would be a very little thing indeed, nothing at all. Nay — I go even further — suffering would be to him always a joy and pleasure.

If you wish to know rightly whether your suffering is yours or of God, you can tell in the following way. If you are suffering because of yourself, whatever the manner, that suffering hurts and is hard to bear. If you suffer for God's sake and for God alone, that suffering does not hurt and is not hard to bear, for God takes the burden of it. If a hundredweight were loaded on my neck and then someone else took it at once on his neck, I had just as lief it were a hundred as one. It would not then be heavy to me and would not hurt me. To make a long story short, what one suffers through God and for God alone is made sweet and easy.

As I said in the first place, at the beginning of the sermon, "Jesus went into a little castle and was received by a virgin who was a wife." Why? It must needs be that she was a virgin and a wife and I have told you how He was received, but I have not yet told you what the little castle was and that I shall now do.

I have said that there is one agent alone in the soul that is free. Sometimes I have called it the tabernacle of the Spirit. Other times I have called it the Light of the Spirit and again, a spark. Now I say that it is neither this nor that. It is something higher than this or that, as the sky is higher than the earth and I shall call it by a more aristocratic name than I have ever used before, even though it disowns my adulation and my name, being far beyond both. It is free of all names and unconscious of any kind of forms. It is at once pure and free, as God Himself is, and like Him is perfect unity and uniformity, so that there is no possible way to spell it out.

God blossoms and is verdant in this agent of which I speak, with all the Godhead and spirit of God and here He begets His only begotten Son as truly as if it were in Himself. For He lives really in this agent, the Spirit together with the Father giving Birth to the Son and in that light, He is the Son and the Truth. If you can only see with my heart, you may well understand what I am saying, for it is true and the Truth itself bespeaks my word.

Look and see: this little castle in the soul is exalted so high above every road [of approach], with such simplicity and uniformity, that the aristocratic agent of which I have been telling you is not worthy to look into it, even once for a moment. No, nor are the other agents, of which I have also spoken, ever able to peek in to where God glows and burns like a fire with all His abundance and rapture. So altogether one and uniform is this little castle, so high above all ways and agencies, that none can ever lead to it — indeed — not even God Himself.

It is the truth as God lives. God Himself cannot even peek into it for a moment — or steal into it — in so far as He has particular selfhood and the properties of a person. This is a good point to notice, for the onefold One has neither a manner nor properties. And therefore, if God is to steal into it [the little castle in the soul] it [the adventure] will cost Him all His divine names and personlike properties; He would have to forgo all these if He is to gain entrance. Except as He is the onefold One, without ways or properties — neither the Father nor the Holy Spirit in this [personal] sense, yet something that is neither this nor that — See! — it is only as He is One and onefold that he may enter into that One which I have called the Little Castle of the soul. Otherwise He cannot get in by any means or be at home there, for in part the soul is like God — otherwise it would not be possible.

What I have been saying to you is true, as I call on Truth to bear witness and my soul to be the pledge. That we, too, may be castles into which Jesus may enter and be received and abide eternally with us in the manner I have described, may God help us! Amen.

Translated by Raymond Bernard Blakney

"Granum Sinapis"

The anonymous song "Granum Sinapis," usually assigned to the circle of Meister Eckhart, dates from around 1300. Of Thuringian origin, it generated two medieval commentaries — one Latin, one German — which formed part of its literary transmission; its full title ("Granum sinapis de divinitate pulcherrima," "A Grain of Mustard Seed of the Most Beautiful Divinity") derives from the first of these. True to the Biblical simile sounded here, the unknown author deftly combines in his poem a formal simplicity, even minimalism, with a message of maximal spiritual potentiality. In the repertory of images he draws on (e.g., the circle of the Trinity, the Godhead as desert) and in his rhetorical technique (use of oxymoron, *via negativa*), he clearly reveals his indebtedness to Neoplatonic tradition, especially to the thought of Pseudo-Dionysius. A small masterwork of medieval religious writing, his "Granum Sinapis" exemplifies the speculative direction of German mysticism reduced to its most succinct possible terms.

Granum Sinapis

In the beginning
high above comprehension
is the word, eternally.
O rich treasure,
where the beginning eternally bore the beginning!
O paternal bosom,
out of which, in bliss,
the word flowed forth eternally.
Yet the womb still
held fast to the word, truly.

Of the two, one flowing forth,
ember of love,
binding both,
known to both,
so flows the sweetest spirit
in complete symmetry,
inseparable.
The three are one:
do you know, what? No,
it alone knows itself completely.

The enmeshment of the three
harbors deep terror.
No reason has ever
comprehended this circle:
here is a depth without bottom.
Check and mate
to time, to shapes, to space!
The circle of mysteries
is a source of everything;
its point of origin rests, completely immutable, in itself.

Leave your doings
and climb, insight,

the mountain of this point!
The way leads you
into a wondrous desert
which extends wide
and immeasurably far.
The desert knows
neither time nor space.
Its nature is unique.

Never has a foot
crossed the domain of the desert,
created reason
has never attained it.
It is, and yet no one knows what.
It is here, there,
far, near,
deep, high,
so that
it is neither the one nor the other.

Light, clear,
completely dark,
nameless,
unknown,
without beginning and also without end,
it rests in itself,
unveiled, without disguise.
Who knows what its dwelling is?
Let him come forth
and tell us of what shape it is.

Become as a child,
become deaf, become blind!
Your own substance
must become nothingness;
drive all substance, all nothingness far from you!
Leave space, leave time,
eschew also all physical representation.
Go without a way

the narrow foot-path,
then you will succeed in finding the desert.

O my soul,
go out, let God in!
Sink, my entire being,
into God's nothingness,
sink into the bottomless flood!
If I flee from you,
you come to me,
if I lose myself,
I find you:
O goodness extending over all being.

Translated by Karen J. Campbell

Heinrich Seuse

Although he is often identified with his teacher, Meister Eckhart, Heinrich Seuse (c. 1295–1366) less neatly fits the mold of the speculative mystic. The son of patrician parents, he was born in Constance and entered the Dominican monastery there at the age of thirteen. Five years later he experienced a dramatic "conversion" which determined his future religious course. Though he dedicated himself to a strict ascetic regimen early on, he distanced himself from it in later years. In 1324 he became a student of Meister Eckhart in Cologne, and his first work, the *Little Book of Truth* (1326/28), reflects this influence in particular. Reestablished in Constance, Seuse spent most of his adult life as spiritual advisor to Dominican nuns in Switzerland and the Upper Rhine and in association with the mystically minded "Friends of God." Often the object of controversy (doctrinal as well as personal), he was frequently on the move. In addition to the *Little Book of Truth*, his most notable German works were the autobiographical *Vita*, written in collaboration with the nun Elsbeth Stagel (d. 1360), and the *Little Book of Eternal Wisdom* (1328?), excerpted here. Varying the traditional male/female roles of the love dialogue, it conveys the distinctive personal approach to mystical union and the courtly style for which Seuse is especially noted.

From the Little Book of Eternal Wisdom

Prologue

O nce a Preacher stood after Matins in front of a crucifix, and complained feelingly to God that he could not meditate on His Passion and His sufferings, and that this was a source of grief to him, for hitherto he had had very great difficulty in so doing. And, as he was thus lamenting, he fell into an ecstasy, and a voice spoke swiftly and clearly within him thus: "Thou shouldst make one hundred *venias,* and each *venia** should be accompanied by a special meditation of My sufferings, and each meditation should go with a request, and each suffering should be spiritually impressed upon thee in such a way that thou wilt suffer it again for My sake, as far as is possible for thee." And as he stood there in the light,[†] and attempted to count them, he could only think of ninety.

So he asked God: "Beloved Lord, Thou didst speak of a hundred but I cannot find more than ninety." Then ten more were revealed to him, which he had previously received in the chapter house, before walking, as was his custom, in imitation of Christ's sorrowful path to death, and coming to the crucifix. And then he found that the hundred meditations included His bitter death from beginning to end, very precisely. And when he began to practice them as they had been revealed to him, his grief was transformed into lovely sweetness.

Now he desired, if perchance anyone else had the same difficulty, feeling, as he did, pain and bitterness while meditating on the lovable sufferings on which all salvation rests, that such a person might be helped, and that he might practice it, and not desist until he also was

---

*A complete prostration on the right side, as practiced by the Dominicans. (Clark)
†Of the Deity.

healed. And therefore he wrote down the meditations and he did so in German, since they were revealed to him by God in that language.

Afterwards he had many a bright inpouring of Divine truth, of which they* were the cause, and a conversation with Eternal Wisdom began within him. But it was not carried on by means of physical speech or with imaginary answers. It was only carried on by means of meditation in the light of the Holy Scriptures, the answers of which cannot deceive. Thus, the words are taken either from the mouth of Eternal Wisdom, who spoke them Himself in the Gospels, or from the most learned teachers, and they contain either the same words, or the same sense, or the selfsame truth, which is expressed in the sense of the Holy Scriptures, through which Eternal Wisdom spoke. Nor did the visions that are here described take place in physical form; they are only a parable. The words of *Our Lady's Lament* he took from the tenor of the words of St. Bernard.

And he presents the doctrine in dialogue form, so that it may be more attractive; not that he is the one to whom it refers, or who himself spoke the words. He only intends to give therein some simple teaching, so that both he and all other men might find something in it, each according to his needs.

As teachers should, he plays the part of all kinds of persons. At one time he speaks in the role of a sinner, then in that of a perfect man, sometimes in the image of the living soul, then, according to the matter, in the semblance of a servant who speaks to Eternal Wisdom.

Nearly everything is expounded in a figurative manner. Much is in the form of instruction, which a diligent man can choose for himself for devotional prayers. The ideas here expressed are simple, and the words are even simpler, for they proceed from a simple soul, and are meant for simple persons who still have failings to overcome.

When this friar had begun to write on the three subjects: the sufferings,† the imitation, and all the rest that is in the book, and had come to the passage about contrition, it chanced that he found it difficult to proceed in his work. Now, once at noon he had sat down on his chair, and in a trance he seemed to see very clearly two guilty men in conventual garb sitting before him; and he scolded them very

---

*The hundred meditations.
†Of Christ.

severely because they were sitting idle and were not doing anything. Then it was given to him to understand that he was to thread them a needle that was put into his hand. Now the thread was threefold,* and two parts were short, but the third was a little longer. And as he tried to twist the three strands together, he could not succeed in doing it. Then he saw on his right hand beside him, our dear Lord standing, as He was when He was taken away from the pillar,† standing in front of him as kindly and paternally as if He were his father. Then he noticed that His tender body had a natural color. It was not exactly white; it was grain-colored, that is, white and red well mixed together, and that is the most natural color. And he noticed that His whole body was pierced with wounds, and the wounds were fresh and bleeding; and some were round, and some angular; some were very long, where the scourge had torn Him. As He stood there so lovingly before him, and looked at him so kindly, the Preacher raised his hands, and passed them to and fro over His bleeding wounds, and then he took the three strands of thread and quickly joined them together. And then strength was given him, and he understood that he had to complete it,‡ and that God would clothe in eternal beauty, in a garment wonderfully woven from His wounds, those who spend their life here in so doing.

This should be known: it is one thing to hear for oneself a sweet lute, sweetly played, and quite another thing merely to hear about it. In the same way there is a great difference between hearing words received in pure grace flowing from a living heart through a living mouth, and reading the same words when they are written on dead parchment, and especially in the German language. For then they wither somehow, and fade like roses that are plucked, for the joyful melody which above all things moves a human heart then dies away, and they are received in the dryness of parched hearts. No string was ever so sweet that it would not become silent if it was strung on a dried-up stick. A loveless heart can understand a loving tongue as little as a German understands an Italian. And hence a diligent man should hasten to the outflowing source of this sweet doctrine, that he may learn to consider them in their origin, in which they were in their living source, in their wonderful beauty. And that

*The *Little Book of Wisdom* consists of three parts. (Clark)
†After the scourging.
‡The unfinished book.

was the inpouring of actual grace, in which they could even have revived dead hearts. And whoever contemplates them in this way can indeed scarcely ever read through this without his heart being deeply moved, either to fervent love, or to new light, or to longing for God and hatred of sin, or to some other spiritual desire, in which the soul is renewed in grace.

Here ends the prologue, that is, the introduction, of this little book.

1. *How some men are drawn to God, unknown to them*

Hanc amavi et exquisivi a iuventute mea, et quaesivi mihi sponsam assumere.

— Wisdom of Solomon 8:2

These words are written in the Book of Wisdom and are spoken by the fair lovely Eternal Wisdom, and the meaning is: "I have loved her and sought her from my youth, and have chosen her as my bride."

In his early youth, an impetuous soul strayed into the paths of error. Then, in spiritual imaginings, Eternal Wisdom met him, and led him through rough and smooth ways till she brought him to the right path of Divine truth. And when he recalled the wonderful guidance he had received, he spoke to God thus: "Beloved, gentle Lord, since the days of my childhood, my heart has sought for something with an ardent thirst. Lord, what that is I cannot yet fully understand. Lord, I have pursued it for many a year eagerly, and I have never yet succeeded, because I do not rightly know what it is, and yet it is something that draws my heart and soul toward itself, and without which I can never find true peace. Lord, in the first days of my youth I tried to find it in the creatures, as I saw others do; but the more I sought, the less I found it, and the nearer I went to it, the further off it was. For of every image that appeared to me, before I had fully tested it, or abandoned myself to peace in it, an inner voice said to me: 'This is not what thou seekest.' And I have always had this revulsion from things. Lord, my heart now yearns for it, for it would gladly possess it, and it has often experienced what it is not; but what it is, my heart has not discovered. Alas, beloved Lord of Heaven, what is it, or of what nature is it, that it should so mysteriously make itself felt within me?"

Reply of ETERNAL WISDOM: Dost thou not recognize it. Has she* not lovingly embraced thee, and often helped thee on thy way, until she has now won thee for herself?

THE SERVANT: Lord, I have never perceived nor heard of it; I know not what it is.

Reply of ETERNAL WISDOM: That is not surprising, for thy familiarity with the creatures and her strangeness have caused that. But now open thy eyes and see who I am. It is I, Eternal Wisdom, who have chosen thee for Herself from all eternity with the embrace of My eternal providence. I have supported thee so often on the way; thou wouldst have been separated from Me so many times if I had forsaken thee. Thou foundest always in every creature something that repelled, and that is the truest sign of My elect, that I wish to have them for Myself.

THE SERVANT: Gentle, lovely Eternal Wisdom, and art Thou that which I have for so very long sought after? Art Thou the one for whom my soul ever strove? Alas, my God, why didst Thou not show Thyself to me for this long time? How very long Thou hast postponed it! How many toilsome ways I have struggled through!

Reply of ETERNAL WISDOM: Had I done so then, thou wouldst not have recognized my goodness so clearly as thou hast done now.

THE SERVANT: Ah, immeasurable Goodness, how sweetly Thou hast now revealed Thy loving kindness in me! When I did not exist, Thou gavest me my being. When I had departed from Thee, Thou wouldst not leave me. When I wished to escape Thee, Thou didst so sweetly hold me captive! Ah, Eternal Wisdom, if now my heart could break into a thousand pieces, and embrace Thee, the joy of my heart, and spend all my days with Thee in steadfast love and perfect praise, that would be my heart's desire! For truly that man is blessed whose desires Thou dost so affectionately anticipate, by never allowing him true rest until he seeks his rest in Thee alone.

Ah, rare, lovely Wisdom, since I now have found in Thee the one whom my soul loves, despise not Thy poor creature. See, how completely my heart is silent toward all this world in joy and sorrow! Lord, must my heart be forever silent toward Thee? Grant, O grant,

---

*In German, *wisdom* is of the feminine gender. (Clark)

beloved Lord, that my wretched soul may speak a word to Thee, for my full heart can bear it no longer alone. In this wide world it has no one in whom it can confide, save Thee, gentle, rare, beloved Lord and Brother! Lord, Thou alone seest and knowest the nature of a loving heart, and knowest that no one can love what he can in no wise understand. Therefore, since I must now love Thee alone, grant that I may know Thee better, that I may then love Thee entirely.

Reply of ETERNAL WISDOM: According to the natural order, we take the highest emanation of all beings from their first origin through the noblest beings down to the lowest. But the return to the origin takes place through the lowest to the highest. Therefore, if thou wouldst see Me in My uncreated Divinity, thou shouldst learn to know Me in My suffering humanity, for that is the swiftest way to eternal bliss.

THE SERVANT: Then, Lord, I will remind Thee today of the boundless love through which Thou didst descend from Thy high throne, from the royal seat of the Father's heart, down to thirty-three years of exile and contempt, and of the love that Thou hadst for me and for all men, which Thou didst reveal most of all in the most bitter pangs of Thy terrible death. Lord, remember that Thou didst reveal Thyself to my soul in spiritual fashion in the most lovable form to which Thy boundless love has ever brought Thee.

Reply of ETERNAL WISDOM: The more I am worn out, and the nearer to death from love, the more lovely am I to a properly ordered mind. My boundless love reveals itself in the whole bitterness of My sufferings, as the sun in its beams, as the fair rose in its fragrance, and as the strong fire in its burning heat. Therefore, hear with devotion how profoundly I suffered for thy sake.

3. *How He felt on the Cross as regards the inner man*

ETERNAL WISDOM: When I was suspended on the high branch of the Cross with boundless love, for the sake of thee and of all men, My whole form was most wretchedly disfigured, My clear eyes were dimmed and lost their luster; My Divine ears were filled with mockery and insult, My noble sense of smell was assailed by an evil stench, My sweet mouth with a bitter draught, My gentle sense of touch with hard blows. Then I could not find a place of rest in the whole world, for My Divine head was bowed down by pain and torment; My joyful throat was rudely bruised; My pure countenance was defiled with spittle; the clear color of My cheeks turned wan and pallid. Look, My fair form was then disfigured, as though I were a leper, and had never been fair Wisdom.

THE SERVANT: O Thou most charming Mirror of all grace, on whom the heavenly spirits feast their eyes, as on the beauty of the spring, would that I might have seen Thy beloved countenance in Thy dying hour, until I had covered it with my heartfelt tears, and gazed my fill on Thy fair eyes and Thy bright cheeks, so that I might relieve my heart's grief with profound lamentation.

Ah, beloved Lord, Thy sufferings affect some persons deeply, they can lament feelingly, and weep for Thee sincerely. Ah, Lord, would that I could lament as the spokesman of all loving hearts, that I could shed the bright tears of all eyes, and utter the lamentations of all tongues: then I would show Thee today how deeply the anguish of Thy Passion affects me!

Reply of ETERNAL WISDOM: None can better show how much My Passion affects them than those who share it with Me by the testimony of their works. I would rather have a free heart, untroubled by ephemeral love, which with steadfast diligence follows that which is highest, imitating the example of My life, than that thou shouldst forever lament for Me, and shed as many tears weeping over My martyrdom as ever drops of rain fell from the sky. For I suffered the pangs of death in order that I might be irritated, however lovable are the tears, and however acceptable to Me.

THE SERVANT: Alas, gentle Lord, inasmuch as a beautiful imitation of Thy gentle life and of Thy loving Passion is so very dear to Thee, I will in future strive rather after a loving imitation than a tearful lamentation, although according to Thy words, I should do both. And therefore teach me how to resemble Thee in this suffering.

Reply of ETERNAL WISDOM: Break thy pleasure in frivolous seeing and idle hearing; let love taste good to thee, and take pleasure in what has been distasteful to thee; give up for My sake all bodily luxury. Thou shalt seek all thy rest in Me; love bodily discomfort, suffer evil willingly, desire contempt, renounce thy desires, and die to all thy lusts. That is the beginning of the school of Wisdom, which is to be read in the open and wounded book of My crucified body.

And look, even if man does all that is in his power, can anyone in the whole world do for Me what I have done for him?

7. *How lovable God is*

THE SERVANT: Lord, I consider Thy loving invitation, when Thou speakest of Thyself in the Book of Wisdom: *Transite ad me omnes,* etc. Come to Me all ye that desire Me; by My fruits ye shall be filled.... I am the mother of fair love.... My spirit is sweeter than honey, and My inheritance above honey and the honeycomb.... Noble wine and sweet music rejoice the heart, but the love of wisdom is above them both.*

Gentle Lord, Thou canst offer Thyself with such love and tenderness that all hearts should desire Thee, and have an ardent longing for Thy love. The words of love flow so full of life from Thy sweet mouth that they have wounded many hearts in the flower of their youth so deeply that all transient love was completely extinguished in them. Ah, gentle Lord, my heart longs, my mind yearns; I should gladly hear Thee speak of it. Speak, then, my only chosen comfort, one little word to my soul, Thy poor handmaid, for under Thy shadow I have sweetly fallen asleep, but my heart is wakeful.

ETERNAL WISDOM: Hearken, my daughter,† and see; incline thine ear; withdraw wholeheartedly within thyself, forgetting thyself and all things.

I am in Myself the incomprehensible Good, who has forever been and always will be, who has never been expressed in words, nor ever will be. I can indeed make Myself felt within the hearts, but no tongue can properly express Me. And yet, since I give Myself, the supernatural, immutable Good, to every creature according to its power, in the manner in which it is receptive of Me, I will wind the sun's radiance in a cloth, and give thee the spiritual meaning in human words concerning Myself and My sweet love, thus:

I present Myself tenderly before the eyes of thy heart; now embellish Me and clothe Me spiritually, and array Me to thy heart's desire. Adorn Me with everything that can move thy heart to special

*Ecclesiasticus 24:18–20; 40:20.

†As Seuse's works were chiefly read by nuns, this form of addressing the soul was not inappropriate. (Clark)

love, and abundant delight. Behold, everything, indeed everything, that thou and all men could conceive of form, beauty, or grace, is still more lovely in Me than one would express. It is through words of this nature that I make Myself known.

Now hear Me: I am of noble birth, of high lineage. I am the lovable Word of the Father's heart, whose eyes take blissful pleasure in the profound, loving fellowship of My natural Sonship, and His pure Fatherhood, and the sweet, ardent ascending love of the Holy Spirit. I am the throne of heavenly bliss, the crown of joy and happiness. My eyes are so clear, My mouth so gentle, My cheeks are so bright and rosy, and all My person so fair and lovely and altogether perfect, that if, until the Last Day, a man were to remain in a fiery furnace for the sake of a mere glimpse of Me, he would still not have deserved it.

See, I am so charmingly adorned in bright raiment, so beautifully surrounded with the variegated hues of living flowers, of red roses, white lilies, fair violets, and flowers of every kind, that all the lovely blossoms of the month of May, the green foliage of all bright meadows, the gentle flowerlets of all fair pastures are like a rough thistle as compared with My adornment.

In the Godhead I play a game of joy; it gives the angel host of happiness the most. A thousand years do seem to them a fleeting dream. All the heavenly hosts fix their eyes on Me with a new wonder, and gaze upon Me. Their eyes are fastened on Mine; their hearts are inclined toward Me; and their soul is bowed down to Me without intermission. Blessed be he who dances the dance of joy and heavenly bliss by My side, who in complete security will pace, holding My fair hand, for all eternity! One little word, that sounds so clear from My sweet mouth, surpasses all the songs of angels, the melody of all harps, and of all sweet instruments. Ah, look, I am so dear to love, so lovely to embrace and so tender for the loving soul to kiss, that all hearts should be fit to break with longing for Me. I am gentle and companionable, and present at all times to the pure soul. I am secretly present at table, in bed, in the path and on the road. I turn hither and thither. There is nothing in Me that could displease; in Me there is every thing that is well pleasing, the heart's desire and the soul's wish. See, I am completely the pure Good. If anyone in this life obtains one tiny drop of Me, all the joys and pleasures of this world become bitterness to him, all riches and honor become dung and an object of contempt. The dear ones are surrounded by My sweet love, and are swept into the only One, in a love without images or spoken words; they are swept away into the Good, from whom they emanated.

My love can also relieve the hearts of beginners of the heavy burden of sin, and give them a free, clean heart, and create in them a pure and blameless conscience. Tell Me, what is there in this world which could outweigh this alone? The whole world could not outweigh such a heart, for the person who gives his heart to Me alone lives happily, and dies safely; he has Heaven here and hereafter forever.

Now look, I have said many words to thee, and stand in My lovely beauty unaffected by all of them as is the firmament by thy little finger, for eye never beheld it, and ear never heard it, and it could never come into any heart. But let this rough sketch serve thee as a distinction between My sweet love and false, transient love.

THE SERVANT: Ah, Thou gentle, lovely flower of the field, Thou dearly beloved of my heart, in the embrace of the arms of the loving soul, how well known is this to him who has ever experienced Thee truly, and how strange it is to the man to whom Thou art unknown, whose heart and soul are still earthly!

Ah, beloved, incomprehensible Good, this is a beautiful hour, this is a sweet moment, in which I must disclose to Thee a hidden wound that my heart still bears from Thy sweet love. Lord, sharing in love is like water in fire; beloved Lord, Thou knowest that real fervent love cannot endure any duality. Ah, gentle, only Lord of my heart and soul, this is why my heart so fondly desires that Thou shouldst have particular love and affection for me, and that Thy Divine eyes should take particular pleasure in me. Alas, Lord, Thou hast so many loving hearts, which love Thee dearly, and have much influence with Thee, alas, gentle, dear Lord, where am I in this regard?

ETERNAL WISDOM: I am a lover of such a nature that I am not compressed by unity, nor scattered by a number. I am at all times fully concerned and occupied with thee, and endear Myself to thee alone, and accomplish all that affects thee, as if I were free of all other ties.

THE SERVANT: *Anima mea liquefacta est, ut dilectus locutus est.**

---

*Song of Songs 5:6: "My soul failed me when my beloved spoke."

Ah, whither have I been led away? How completely have I been captivated! How completely has my soul been melted away by the friendly, sweet words of the beloved One! Ah, turn Thy bright eyes away from me, for they have altogether overcome me.

Where was there ever a heart so hard, a soul so cold and luke-warm, that it would not be softened and warmed by Thy sweet love on hearing Thy sweet, living, loving words, which are so extremely ardent? Alas, wonder of wonders, that he who could look at Thee with the eyes of his heart should not wholly melt away with love! Ah, how blessed is the lover who is called Thy lover and is so in reality! What sweet consolation and hidden love he may receive from Thee!

Ah, sweet gentle maiden, St. Agnes, the lover of Eternal Wisdom, how well thou couldst praise thy dear lover, when thou didst say: "His blood has adorned my cheeks with the color of roses."* Ah, gentle Lord, if I were but worthy, if my soul could but be called Thy lover! See, if it were possible that all the pleasure, all the joy and love that this world can give were combined in one person, I would freely give him up for this. Ah, blessed be he in God, who is called, and is, Thy lover! If one man had a thousand lives, he should risk them for the chance of winning Thee. O all ye Friends of God, all the hosts of heaven, and thou, dear virgin St. Agnes, help me in my prayers to Him, for I have never truly known what His love is! Ah, my heart, discard, abandon all idleness, and see whether before thy death thou canst come to experience His sweet love! How idly and slothfully hast thou lived hitherto!

Alas, gentle, fair, beloved Wisdom, Thou knowest full well how to be a delightful love above all the loves of this world! How different is Thy love from that of the creatures! How deceitful is everything that seems lovely in this world, and thinks it is anything, when once one begins to know it rightly and close at hand. Lord, wheresoever I turned my eyes, I found always a *nisi* and an *unless*; for, if there were a fair form, it lacked grace; if it were beautiful and lovely, it was devoid of good breeding; or if it had that also, I always found, either without or within, something that repelled all the feelings

---

*From the second antiphon of the second nocturne of the Office of the Feast of St. Agnes. (Clark)

of my heart. On close acquaintance I found that it had an inner dissatisfaction with itself.

Ah, but Thou, Thou beauty with boundless loving-kindness, grace with perfection of form, words and melody, nobility with virtue, riches with power, freedom within and clarity without, and a quality that I never found in the world, namely, a true recompense and satisfaction in knowledge and power for the longing desires of a truly loving heart. The better one knows Thee, the more one loves Thee, the more intimate one is with Thee, and the more lovely one finds Thee. Indeed, what an inexhaustible, complete, pure Good Thou art! Look, all ye hearts, how deluded are those who place their love in aught else! Ah, ye false lovers, flee far from me, never again approach me, for I have chosen the only love of my heart, in whom alone heart, soul, desire and all my powers are satisfied with spiritual love that never dies away! Alas, Lord, if I could but write Thee upon my heart, if I could but engrave Thee in the very depths of my heart and soul in golden letters, so that Thou wouldst never be erased in me! Alas, to my sorrow and misfortune I have not always occupied my heart with Him! What have I gained from all my lovers but lost time, wasted words, an empty hand, few good works, and a conscience burdened with sin!

Reply of ETERNAL WISDOM: I anticipate those that seek Me, and receive with lovely joy those that desire My love. All of My sweet love that thou canst experience in this world is only a drop in the ocean, as compared with the love of eternity.

8. An answer to three points which might above all repel a lover with regard to God. The first is: How can He appear so angry, although He is so lovable?

THE SERVANT: Ah, gentle Lord, I am deeply perplexed about three things. The first is this: that Thou art so extremely lovable in Thyself, and yet so very severe a judge of sin. Lord, when I consider Thy terrible justice, my heart cries out with a yearning voice: "Woe, woe to all those who have ever sinned, for if they knew the strict judgment that Thou dost silently enforce, without any contradiction, for each and every sin, even from Thy dearest friends, they ought rather to tear out their own teeth and their hair than ever to make Thee angry."

Alas, Thy wrathful countenance is so terrible, Thy indignant rejection is so unbearable; woe is me, and Thy hostile words are so very fiery, that they pierce right through the heart and the soul. Alas, Lord, protect me from Thy angry countenance, and do not save up Thy wrath against me till the world to come. See, if I have but a suspicion that Thou hast turned away Thy face in indignation from my guilty errors, it is so unbearable for me that nothing in this wide world is so very bitter for me.

Ah, Lord, and my faithful Father, how then could my heart ever bear Thy terrible countenance? Ah, when I think aright of Thy face distorted by wrath, my soul is so completely terrified, my whole strength is so shattered, that I can compare nothing with it, except the sky, when it begins to darken and grow black, and the lightning rages in the clouds, and a heavy peal of thunder tears the clouds asunder, shaking the earth and then shooting fiery arrows at a man. Lord, let no one trust Thy silence, for indeed Thy quiet silence gives place at last to a grim thunder-clap. Lord, Thy wrathful countenance, Thy fatherly anger, is indeed a Hell above all Hells to a man who fears to anger Thee and to lose Thee, to say nothing of the terrible countenance that the wicked must behold, in the sorrow of their hearts, at the Last Day. Woe, and ever woe, to those who have to encounter this great grief! Lord, this causes great perplexity in my heart; and yet Thou sayest that Thou art so lovable!

Reply of ETERNAL WISDOM: I am the unchangeable Good; I am, and remain the same. But if I seem unequal, that is due to the inequality in those who see Me unequally, with sin and without sin. I am lovable by My nature, and yet a terrible judge of sin. I will have from My children childlike fear and affectionate love, in order that the fear may at all times preserve them from sin, and the love may unite them with Me in true fidelity.

9. The second: Why He so often withdraws Himself from His friends, as He thinks fit, and how one may recognize His real presence

THE SERVANT: Lord, everything is all that the heart could wish for, except one thing: Truly, Lord, when a soul is faint with longing for Thee, and for the sweet, loving converse of Thy presence, Lord, then Thou art silent, and speakest not a single word that one can hear. Alas, my Lord, is it not painful when Thou, gentle Lord, art the only chosen love of their heart and yet dost behave like a stranger, and keep silence so completely?

Reply of ETERNAL WISDOM: Do not all creatures proclaim that it is I?*

THE SERVANT: Ah, Lord, this is not enough for a longing heart.

Reply of ETERNAL WISDOM: Yet every word that is spoken of Me is a messenger of love to their hearts, and every word of Holy Scripture that was written of Me is a sweet love letter, as if I Myself had written it. Should not this suffice for them?

THE SERVANT: Ah, gentle, fair Beloved, Thou knowest full well that to a loving heart nothing is sufficient save its only love, its sole consolation. Lord, Thou art altogether such a dear, beloved, unfathomable Love. Lo, and even if all the tongues of angels spoke of Thee to me, unbounded love still struggles and strives for the One that it desires. A loving soul would rather have Thee than Heaven, for Thou art its Heaven. Ah, Lord, if I durst say so, Thou shouldst be a little more affectionate to the poor loving hearts that languish and long for Thee, that heave so many deep, unfathomable sighs for Thee, their only Love, that look up to Thee so wretchedly, saying with a voice full of feeling: *Revertere, revertere,*† talking to themselves and saying: "Alas, dost thou think that thou hast angered Him, and that He will abandon thee? Dost thou think that He will ever again grant thee His loving presence, so that thou canst embrace Him with the arms of thy heart, and press Him to thy heart, so that all thy sorrow may disappear? Lord, Thou hearest all this, and Thou art silent!"

WISDOM asks: Now answer Me a question, after this searching

---

*That I exist.
†"Return, return" (Song of Songs 6:13).

for hidden things, what is it that, among all things, tastes best to the highest spirit?

THE SERVANT: Alas, Lord, I should like to know this from Thee; for the question is too high for me.

Reply of ETERNAL WISDOM: Then I will tell thee. Nothing tastes better to the highest angel than to fulfill My will in all things. And if he knew that My glory depended on rooting out nettles or other weeds, that would be to him the most desirable thing to accomplish.

THE SERVANT: Ah, Lord, how dost Thou strike at me with this question! For Thou meanest that I should keep myself free and self-abandoned in all desires, and seek only Thy glory in hardships, as also in sweetness.

Reply of ETERNAL WISDOM: An abandonment above all abandonment is to be abandoned in abandonment.

THE SERVANT: Alas, Lord, it is so very painful.

Reply of ETERNAL WISDOM: Where does virtue better prove its worth than in adversity? But know that I often come and ask to be admitted into thy house, yet I am refused. Often I am received as a pilgrim, and am unworthily treated and swiftly cast out. But I come to My beloved Myself, and have loving converse with her. Yet that takes place so secretly that it is completely hidden from all men, except only those who are so fully detached and who take heed of My ways, who are on the lookout how to satisfy My grace. For I am, according to My Divinity, a pure essential spirit, and am received spiritually by pure spirits.

THE SERVANT: Gentle Lord, methinks Thou art withal a secret lover; therefore I pray Thee to give me some signs of Thy true presence.

Reply of ETERNAL WISDOM: Thou canst recognize My true presence in no better way than this: when I conceal Myself, and withdraw what is Mine from the soul, then thou wilt for the first time perceive who I am, and who thou art. I am the eternal Good; without this Good no one has anything good; and for this reason, when I, the eternal Good, pour Myself out so kindly and graciously, then everything to which I come is made good. By this means can My presence be recognized, as the sun is ˙recognized by its brilliance, which, nevertheless, one cannot see in its substance. If thou hast ever felt Me, enter into thyself, and learn to distinguish roses from thorns, and to pick flowers out of the grass.

THE SERVANT: Lord, truly, I seek and find in myself a very great inequality. When I am abandoned, my soul is like a sick man to whom nothing tastes good, to whom everything is repugnant; my body is weary; my mind is heavy; inwardly there is hardness, outwardly sorrow. At such times I am vexed by everything I see or hear, however good it is; for all sense of fitness deserts me. I am inclined to error, weak to resist my enemies, cold and apathetic toward all that is good. Whoever comes to me finds an empty house, for the host is not at home who gives good counsel, and by whom the whole household is made cheerful.

But Lord, when the bright morning star rises in the midst of my soul, then all sorrow vanishes, all darkness disappears, and bright clarity arises. Lord, my heart rejoices, my mind is glad, my soul is cheerful; I have a gay, festive feeling, and all that is in me and is mine joins in Thy praise. Whatever had been hard, toilsome, or even impossible, now becomes most easy and sweet. Fasting, watching, praying, suffering, abstinence, and all kinds of austerities are become as nothing in Thy presence. Then I obtain great courage, which, however, deserts me in abandonment.

My soul is transfused with clarity, truth, and sweetness, so that it forgets all its troubles. My heart can sweetly meditate, my tongue can speak of lofty things, my body can attack every task with ease, and, if anyone but asks, he can obtain all the lofty counsel he desires. I feel then as if I have passed beyond the bounds of time and space and stand in the antechamber of eternal bliss. Ah, Lord, who will grant that it may last for long! For suddenly, in a moment, it flashes away, and then am I naked and forsaken; sometimes almost as if I had never enjoyed it, until after sore misery it comes back again. Ah, Lord, is it Thou, or is it I, or what is it?

Reply of ETERNAL WISDOM: Thou art, and hast of thyself, naught but failings. It is I, and this is the play of love.

THE SERVANT: Lord, what is the play of love?

Reply of ETERNAL WISDOM: As long as the lover is with his beloved, he knows not how dear love is, but when the lover parts from his beloved, love feels how dear love was.

THE SERVANT: Lord, a laborious task. Ah, Lord, are no men spared these vicissitudes in this world?

Reply of ETERNAL WISDOM: Very few men, for freedom from changeableness belongs to eternity.

THE SERVANT: Who are these men?

Reply of ETERNAL WISDOM: The purest of all, and those nearest to eternity.

THE SERVANT: Lord, who are they?

Reply of ETERNAL WISDOM: They are the men who have the most zealously put away all obstacles.

THE SERVANT: Gentle Lord, teach me how to bear myself in this respect, imperfect as I am.

Reply of ETERNAL WISDOM: In the good days thou shouldst consider the evil ones; and in the evil days forget not the good ones; then neither elation in the presence [of God], nor depression in abandonment can injure thee. If on account of thy limitations thou canst not renounce Me joyfully, then wait patiently and seek lovingly.

THE SERVANT: Ah, Lord, long waiting is painful.

Reply of ETERNAL WISDOM: He who will have a love in this world must endure joy and sorrow. It is not enough to give Me part of the day; he must constantly remain in meditation who would feel God within, and hear His secret words, and understand His hidden thoughts.

Ah, how thou dost let thine eyes and thy heart rove around so carelessly, when thou hast before thee the lovable and eternal image that never turns away from thee for a moment. How thou dost let thine ears fail thee, while I say so many loving words to thee! How thou dost forget thyself so manifestly, when thou art so closely surrounded by the presence of the Eternal Good! What does the soul seek in anything external, when it carries the Kingdom of Heaven hidden within itself?

THE SERVANT: Lord, what is the Kingdom of Heaven that is in the soul?

Reply of ETERNAL WISDOM: That is justice and peace and joy in the Holy Spirit.

THE SERVANT: Lord, I recognize from these words that Thou dost often act in the soul in mysterious ways, in ways that are quite concealed from it, and that Thou dost draw the soul in secret, and lead to love and knowledge of Thy high Divinity the soul, which was once only concerned with Thy sweet humanity.

10. *Thirdly: Why God permits His friends to suffer so much in this world*

THE SERVANT: Lord, there is a question in my heart. Dare I say it to Thee? Ah, sweet Lord, if only I durst dispute with Thee concerning Thy judgments, as the holy Jeremiah did!* Gentle Lord, be not angry with me, and listen to me patiently! Lord, they say: However deep and sweet are Thy love and friendship, Thou dost sometimes allow Thy friends to undergo many grievous and bitter sufferings, with the scorn of the whole world, and many tribulations, both outward and inward. For, when a man begins to enter into Thy friendship, the first step he has to take is to prepare himself for suffering, and to summon his resolution. Lord, I ask Thee by Thy goodness, what joy can they have in this, or why dost Thou permit Thy friends to suffer all this? Or wilt Thou not deign to let me know?

Reply of ETERNAL WISDOM: As My Father loves Me, even so do I love My friends; I act toward My friends now as I have always done, from the beginning of the world until the present day.

THE SERVANT: Lord, it is just that of which men complain, and they say the reason why Thou hast so few friends is because Thou dost permit them to have such an ill life in this world. Lord, for this reason there are many of them who, when they obtain Thy friendship, and are about to be tested by suffering, forsake Thee, and, alas, I must say it with deep sorrow and heartfelt tears, they then relapse into the ways they had abandoned for Thy sake.

Reply of ETERNAL WISDOM: This is the complaint of men who are weak in faith, and poor in works, lukewarm in life, and of an undisciplined spirit. But thou, beloved, be of good cheer, rise out of the mud and the deep mire of worldly pleasure. Unlock thy inner senses, open thy spiritual eyes, and behold. Observe what thou art, and where thou dost belong. See, and then wilt thou comprehend that I act toward My friends in the most loving manner.

In thy natural being thou art a mirror of the Deity, thou art an image of the Trinity,† and a type of eternity. And just as I, in My eternal uncreatedness, am the Good that is infinite, in the same way

---

*Jeremiah 12:1.

†The higher faculties of man: will, memory, and thought, form a trinity (St. Augustine, *De Trinitate,* ix, 3). St. Thomas speaks of memory, intelligence, and will. (Clark)

thou art boundless in thy desires; and, just as a tiny raindrop can add but little to the vast depth of the ocean, all that the world can offer would be even so ineffective for the realization of thy desires.

Thou art in this wretched vale of tears, wherein are mingled joy and sorrow, laughter and tears, gladness and sadness, and wherein no heart ever realized complete happiness; for it cheats and deceives us, as I will tell thee; it promises much and fulfils little; it is short, inconstant and changeable. Much joy today, but sorrow fills the heart tomorrow: That is the way of the world.

11. *Of the never-ending pangs of Hell*

Ah, my chosen One, look now from the depths of thy heart at this lamentable and mournful sight. Where are now all those who hitherto have settled down in rest and pleasure in this world, in luxury and bodily ease? Ah, alas, what avails them all the joy in the world, which will pass by so quickly in the short time, as if it had never been? How swiftly the pleasure is over, the pain of which must last forever and ever! O stupid fools, where are now the words you spoke so gaily: "Come, friends, let us be merry. Let us take our leave of sadness, and give ourselves to joy and gladness"? What do all the joys you ever had avail you now? Well might you cry out with a lamentable voice: "Woe, woe and woe forever to us, that we were ever born into this world! How the short time has deluded us, how death has pounced on us unawares!

"Alas, has anyone else on earth been deceived as we poor wretches have been? Or is there anyone who will learn sense from the troubles of others? If a man had the sufferings of all men for a thousand years, that would be like a moment, as compared with this. Alas, how happy is he who never sought joy against God's will, who for His sake never had a happy day in the world. We senseless fools thought that they were forsaken and forgotten by God. Ah, how lovingly has He now embraced them in His eternity, and placed them so high in honor before all the heavenly host! How could they be injured by all the sufferings and scorn that have brought them so great happiness? But how completely all our joy has disappeared!

"Ah, sorrow and misery, it must indeed last forever! Alas, forever and ever: where art thou? Alas, end without end, as, death worse than all deaths, to die every hour and yet never to be able to be dead! Alas, father, mother, and all our dear ones together, farewell forevermore, for we shall never again see you happy; we must indeed be parted from you forevermore! Alas, what a parting, a parting that lasts forever, how painful it is! Alas, the beating of hands, the gnashing of teeth, the sighing and the weeping! Alas, to howl and cry, and never to be heard! Our wretched eyes can never see anything but pain and anguish; our ears hear nothing but lamentation and woe. Alas, all ye hearts, have pity on this eternity of misery, and take it well to heart.

"Alas and alas, O mountains and valleys, why do ye wait, why delay so long, why do ye spare us? Why do you not crush us to hide this miserable sight? Alas, how different are the sufferings of this world from those of the next! Alas, O present, how thou dost blind and deceive! Alas, that we did not foresee this in the beautiful, delightful days, which we so wantonly wasted, which, alas, will never return! Ah, alas, if only we could have one brief hour of all the long lost years that are denied to us by the justice of God, and must forever be denied without any hope of redress!

"Ah, sorrow, and pain, and lamentation, forever and ever, in this forsaken land, where we must be forever bereft of all love, all comfort, and hope! Alas, we could have but one wish: if there were a millstone as large and wide as the whole Earth, and so big that round about it would touch the heavens on all ends, and if a small bird were to come once every hundred thousand years, and bite off a piece of the stone as large as the tenth part of a millet seed, and once again in a hundred thousand years the same amount, so that in a million years as much would have been pecked off the stone as the size of a whole grain of millet — we poor wretches only ask that our eternal tortures would end as soon as the stone would come to an end — and that cannot be!"

See, this is the lamentable song that accompanies those who are the friends of this world.

THE SERVANT: Alas, strict Judge, how profoundly terrified my heart is! How my soul sinks down powerless with grief and compassion for these poor souls! Who is there in the whole world who is so wicked that, hearing this, he would not tremble at this terrible suffering? Alas, and alas, my only Love, do not forsake me! Alas, my only Beloved and my only consolation, do not depart from me thus! Alas, should I ever at any time be thus parted from Thee, my only Love, of the rest I will be silent, alas, sorrow and grief, I had rather be tortured every day a thousand times. At the very thought of the parting, I am like to collapse with anguish. Ah, my Lord, gentle Father, do with me here as Thou wilt, I give Thee leave to do so freely, but spare me the lamentable separation from Thee, for I could not endure it at all.

Reply of ETERNAL WISDOM: Be not afraid! Those who are united in this world, remain undivided in eternity.

THE SERVANT: Ah, Lord, if only all men could hear this, all who still waste their fair days so foolishly, that they might see reason, and improve their lives, before the same fate also befalls them!

12. *Of the boundless joys of Heaven*

ETERNAL WISDOM: Now raise up thine eyes, and see where thou dost belong. Thy home is the celestial paradise; here thou art a strange guest, an exiled pilgrim. And hence, as a pilgrim hastens home again, where his dear and beloved friends await him, and abide his coming with great longing, in the same way shouldst thou hasten to thy fatherland, ah, where they would see thee so gladly, where they long so deeply and sorely for thy cheerful presence, where they would welcome thee lovingly, receive thee tenderly, and invite thee to join their happy society forever! See, and couldst thou but know how they yearn for thee, how they desire that thou shouldst fight bravely in suffering, and bear thyself like a true knight in all the adversities that they have overcome; and how they now with great joy remember the hard years that they had; couldst thou but know all this, all thy sufferings would be the easier. For the more bitterly thou hast suffered, the more nobly wilt thou be received.

Ah, how pleasant is the honor, how joy transfuses the heart and mind, when the soul is so gloriously extolled, lauded, and praised before My Father and all the heavenly host, because it has suffered so much here in this time of struggle, fought so much and conquered so often, which is so strange a thing to many who have been without suffering! How wondrously the crown will shine that has been won so dearly here! How bright and glorious are the wounds and scars which have been received for love of Me! See, thou shalt be so well befriended in thy fatherland that the greatest stranger among the vast number will love thee more affectionately and faithfully than any father or mother ever loved their beloved only child in this world.

THE SERVANT: Alas, Lord, may it please Thy goodness, if I but durst make bold to ask Thee to tell me more of this fatherland, that I may long for it the more, and the better bear all sufferings! Alas, my Lord, what is it like in that land, and what do they do there? And are there perchance many of them, and do they know how things are here, as Thy holy Word informs us?

Reply of ETERNAL WISDOM: Now set out with Me, I will lead thee thither in meditation, and will give thee a distant glimpse, in the form of a rough parable.

See, above the ninth Heaven, which is infinitely more than a hundred thousand times larger than the whole Earth, there is another Heaven, which is called *coelum empyreum,* the Heaven of fire, not because of the fire, but because of the immense shining brightness, immovable and incorruptible, that is its nature. And this is the court of glory, in which the morning stars praise Me together, and all the children of God rejoice. Here are the eternal thrones, surrounded by ineffable light, by which the evil spirits are banished, where dwell the elect. See, the fair city shines with inlaid gold, it glows with noble pearls, set in precious stones, clear as crystal, reflecting red roses, white lilies, and all kinds of living flowers. Now, look thyself at the fair heavenly meadow, ah, the whole joy of summer is there, the fields of bright May, the valley of true happiness! Here one sees the happy glances exchanged by lovers; here are harps and fiddles; here they sing, and leap and dance, and play all joyful games. Here there is abundant joy, gladness without sadness, forever and a day. Now look around thee at the countless multitude, how they drink of the living sparkling fountain to their heart's desire! Look, how they gaze at the pure, clear mirror of the naked Godhead in which all things are made known and revealed!

Pass on farther, and see how the sweet Queen of the celestial country, whom thou so dearly lovest, hovers with dignity and joy above all the heavenly host, bending tenderly down to her Beloved, surrounded by flowers, by roses and lilies of the valley. Look, how her lovely beauty gives bliss and joy and wonder to all the heavenly host. Ah, see a vision now that will rejoice thy heart and soul;

see how the Mother of Mercies has turned her eyes, those mild, merciful eyes, so gently toward thee and toward all sinners, and how powerfully she protects them and reconciles them with her beloved Son.

Now turn with the eyes of pure intelligence, and see also how the high Seraphim and the loving souls of this choir ascend toward Me unceasingly in ardent flames; how the bright Cherubim and their company receive a clear influx and outpouring of My eternal and incomprehensible light; how the high Thrones and their host rest sweetly in Me, and I in them. Then see how the three choirs of the second hierarchy, the Dominions, Virtues, and Powers, in orderly manner, establish the fair, eternal order of the natural universe. See, also, how the third host of angelic spirits carries out My errands and My laws in the various parts of the world. Ah, now observe in what profound beauty and variety the vast host is ordered, and how lovely a sight it is!

Then turn thine eyes, and see how My chosen disciples and My very dearest friends sit in such great peace and honor on the judges' seats of honor, how the martyrs shine in rosy garments, the confessors glow in verdant beauty, how the gentle virgins are resplendent in angelic purity, how all the heavenly host is suffused by Divine sweetness. Ah, what a company, what a happy land! Blessed is he that ever he was born, who is to live here forever!

See, into this country I lead My dear spouse home, on My arm, back from exile, with the great riches of her bounteous dowry. I adorn her inwardly with the fair garment of the light of glory, that raises her up above all her natural strength. She is outwardly clad in the transfigured body, which is seven times as bright as the sun's beams, swift, subtle, and impassible. I place on her head a fair golden crown, and thereon a golden halo.

THE SERVANT: Gentle Lord, what is the dowry, and what is the crown and the bright halo?

Reply of ETERNAL WISDOM: The dowry is a clear view of that which here thou canst only believe, a present grasp of that which here thou dost hope, and a loving, joyful enjoyment of that which here thou dost love. So the fair crown is the essential reward, but the bright halo is the accidental reward.

THE SERVANT: What is that, Lord?

Reply of ETERNAL WISDOM: Accidental reward depends on the

particular joy which the soul obtains from special noble actions, with which it has conquered here, as with the learned doctors, the strong martyrs, and the pure virgins. But essential reward lies in the contemplative union of the soul with the naked Godhead, for it will never rest until it is led above all its powers and strength, and brought into the essential nature of the Persons, and into the simple purity of the Being. And it is in this object that it finds satisfaction and eternal bliss. The more detached the going-out, the more free the ascension; and the more free the ascension, the deeper the penetration into the wild desert and the profound abyss of the pathless Godhead, into which it sinks, is swept away, and united, in such a way that it cannot will anything but what God wills; and that is to be the same as God is; that is, that they are blessed by grace, as He is blessed by nature.

Ah, now lift up thy face joyfully, forget for a while all thy sorrow, cool thy heart in this dark stillness with the dear company that thou dost so mysteriously behold, and see how rosy, how most lovely, the faces look that here were so often red with shame for My sake. Lift up a cheerful heart, and say: "Where is now the bitter shame that penetrated your pure hearts so deeply? Where are the bowed heads, the downcast eyes; where are the suppressed heartfelt sorrows, the deep sighs, and the bitter tears? Where are the pale faces, the great poverty and privation; where is now the miserable voice crying: 'Ah, Lord, alas God, how sad and sorrowful I am!' Where are all those who once despised and persecuted you?"

No longer does one hear the words: "Forward to the fight, on to the struggle, to the battle!" day and night, as do those who fight against the heathen. Where are now the cries that you used to raise in your hearts a thousand times in the presence of grace: "Art thou prepared to stand firm in abandonment?" One hears no more the wretched, lamentable cry that you used to raise: "Alas, Lord, why hast Thou forsaken me?" I hear a loving voice sounding in your ears: "Come to Me, My beloved, and possess the eternal kingdom which was prepared for you from the beginning of the world." Where are all the suffering, pain, and discomfort that you ever had on earth?

Ah, God, how all that has gone by, as swiftly as a dream, as if you had never had any sorrow. Ah, gentle God, how Thy judgments are hidden from the world! Ah, ye chosen ones, there is no need now to steal into corners, and hide from the senseless raging of others. Alas, if all hearts were one heart, they could not realize the great honor, the immense dignity, the praise, the glory, that you are to have forever and ever! O ye princes of heaven, ye noble kings and emperors, ye eternal children of God, how lovely are your faces, how happy your hearts, how joyful your souls, how cheerfully your voices resound in the song: "Ah, ah, thanks and praise, salvation and blessing, grace and bliss and everlasting honor from the bottom of our hearts be to Him through whose grace we have possessed all this, ever and eternally!" See, here is your country, here is perfect peace, here is heartfelt jubilation, here is boundless, everlasting praise!

THE SERVANT: Ah, wonder above all wonders, ah, unfathomable Good, what art Thou? Ah, tender, fair, loving Lord, how good it is to be here! Ah, my only Love, let us remain here!

Reply of ETERNAL WISDOM: The time has not yet come to remain here. Thou must first fight many a bold fight. This glimpse is only granted thee so that thou canst swiftly turn to it in all thy sufferings — see, thou canst never lose heart again now — and forget all thy pain, and as an answer to the complaints of men without understanding who say that I deal unkindly with My friends. Now look, what a difference there is between My friendship and that of the world, and indeed how passing well I treat My friends — I will say nothing of the great grief, the toil, and of many severe sufferings, in which they swim and watch day and night, but they are so blinded that they do not understand it. For it is My eternal decree that a disorderly mind should be a torture to itself and a severe punishment. My friends have bodily discomfort, and yet they have also peace of mind; but the friends of this world seek bodily comfort and obtain discomfort of heart, soul, and mind.

THE SERVANT: Lord, they are foolish and mad, who, because Thou hast few friends, always compare Thy true friendship with that of the false world — for that is the fault of their great blindness — and who are forever complaining of some suffering or other. Ah, how loving Thy paternal rod is in very truth! Blessed is he whom Thou hast never spared with it! Lord, I now see full well that suffering is not due to harshness; it comes from loving tenderness. Let no one say again that Thou hast forgotten

Thy friends! Thou hast forgotten those — for Thou hast despaired of them — whom Thou hast spared suffering here. Lord, they should never again have good days, or joy, or comfort here, whom Thou wilt save hereafter from eternal distress, and to whom Thou wilt give everlasting joy. Ah, Lord, grant that these two visions may never leave the eyes of my heart, and that I may never lose Thy friendship.

Translated by James M. Clark

Johannes Tauler

Next to Meister Eckhart, Johannes Tauler was the most celebrated preacher in the flowering of fourteenth-century German mysticism. Born into a wealthy Strasbourg family around 1300, he entered the local Dominican monastery in his early teens and came under the influence of Eckhart's ideas as a young man, though it is unclear whether he ever came to know him personally. With the exception of a number of years spent in Basle, beginning in 1339 (exact dates are sketchy), Tauler spent most of his mature life in his native Strasbourg. Like Seuse, he was actively involved with the "Friends of God," and like him, he was entrusted with the spiritual education of religious women. His preaching won him a wide following among clerics as well as laymen; some eighty of his sermons survive. As the sampling offered here suggests, Tauler's brand of mysticism echoes certain central Eckhartian themes (such as the birth of Christ into the soul, in the first sermon given), but its greater focus on the purgation of the soul, as well as its exceptional practical orientation, have often been named as its distinctive features. Tauler died in 1361.

Selected Sermons

Sermon 1
(Christmas)

Puer natus est nobis et filius datus est nobis
A child is born to us, a son is given to us
— Isaiah 9:6

Today Holy Christendom commemorates a threefold birth, which should so gladden and delight the heart that, enraptured with joyful love and jubilation, we should soar upward with sheer gratitude and bliss. And whoever cannot experience this ought to be quite distressed.

The first birth, and the most sublime, is that in which the Heavenly Father begets His only Son within the divine Essence, yet distinct in Person. The second birth we commemorate is that of maternal fruitfulness brought about in virginal chastity and true purity. The third birth is effected when God is born within a just soul every day and every hour truly and spiritually, by grace and out of love. These are the three births observed in today's three Holy Masses.

The first we celebrate in the darkness of night, and it begins with the words: "The Lord has said to me: you are my Son, this day have I begotten You." This Mass points to the hidden birth which happens within the secrecy of the unknown Godhead. The second Mass starts with the words: "This day shall a light shine upon us." And here is meant the radiance of human nature divinized. This Mass begins in the darkness of night, and ends in the brightness of day, for it was partly known and partly unknown.

The third Mass is solemnized in the brightness of noon, and it commences thus: "A child is born to us, a Son is given to us." It signifies that very sweet birth which should and does occur every day and every moment within every just and holy soul if only it directs its attention lovingly toward that goal. For if it is to experience such a birth, it must turn inward and reverse all its faculties. Then God will give Himself in such a high measure, and surrender Himself so utterly that this gift will exceed anything the soul may ever have possessed.

We read in Holy Scripture that a child is born to us, and a Son is given to us, which is to say that He is ours, He belongs to us in a special way, above all ways; that He is begotten in us always, without ceasing. It is of this very sweet birth, referred to in the last of the three Masses, that we wish to speak first.

In order to attain to this wondrous birth, so that it may bear noble and rich fruit, we should consider the first — the paternal — birth, by which the Father begets His Son in eternity; for the superabundance of the Father's divine goodness is such that it transcends all human ways. It keeps back nothing, and this causes an eternal outpouring and communicating. For this reason Boethius and St. Augustine say that it is God's nature and character to pour Himself out and to communicate; and thus the Father pours Himself forth in the Processions of the divine Persons and then on into creatures. St. Augustine says further: "Because God is good, we are; and any good that creatures possess derives alone from the essential goodness of God."

What, then, should we observe about the paternal generation, and how should we perceive it? Note that the Father, distinct as Father, turns inward to Himself with His divine Intellect and penetrates in clear self-beholding the essential abyss of His eternal Being. In this act of pure self-comprehension He utters Himself completely by a Word; and the Word is His Son. And the act whereby He knows Himself is the generation of the Son in eternity. Thus He rests within Himself in the unity of essence, and He flows out in the distinction of Persons.

And so He turns inward, comprehending Himself, and He flows outward in the generation of His Image (that of His Son), which He has known and comprehended. And again He returns to Himself in perfect self-delight. And this delight streams forth as ineffable love, and that ineffable love is the Holy Spirit. Thus God turns inward, goes outward, and returns to Himself again. And these Processions happen for the sake of their return. Hence the celestial orbit is the noblest and most perfect, for it constantly returns to the origin and source from which it emerged. And for the same reason the human circuit, in its essential meaning, is the noblest and most perfect when it returns again to its source.

Now the specific character which the Heavenly Father possesses in this divine circulation should also be adopted by us if we are to attain spiritual motherhood in our soul. We, too, must completely turn inward in order to go out again. How, then, can this be accomplished?

The soul has three faculties, and in these it is the true image of the Blessed Trinity — memory, understanding, and free will. With their aid the soul is able to grasp God and to partake of Him, so that it becomes capable of receiving all that God is and can bestow. They enable the soul to contemplate eternity, for the soul is created between time and eternity. With its highest part it touches eternity, whereas with its lower part — that of the sensible and animal powers — it is bound up with time. Now because of the way these two powers are intertwined (due to the fall), the soul has turned toward time and temporal things. Accordingly, transitory things come easily to the soul, and it tends to love itself in them, thus turning to time and away from eternity.

We can see now that a reversal must necessarily take place if such a birth is to occur. There must be a definite introversion, a gathering up, an inward recollection of faculties without any dispersal, for in unity lies strength. So a marksman who wishes to hit his target more accurately shuts one eye to focus with greater precision. Whoever wishes to comprehend something clearly applies all his senses and concentrates them in the soul from which they have arisen. For just as all the branches of a tree spring from one trunk, so also must all powers of the soul be gathered up within its ground. And this is the introversion we are speaking of.

Moreover, should a going forth, an elevation beyond and above ourselves ever come about, then we must renounce our own will, desire, and worldly activity, so that we can orient ourselves single-mindedly toward God, and meet Him only in complete abandonment of self. What should remain is a pure cleaving to God alone, a making room for Him, who is the highest and the nearest, so that His work can prosper, and His birth can be accomplished without hindrance. For if two are to become one, one must be passive whereas the other must act. If, for instance, my eye is to receive an image of the wall, or anything whatever, it must first be free from other images; for if there remained an image of color, it could not receive another. The same is true of the ear: If it already perceived a sound, it cannot hear another. In short, whatever should receive must first be empty, passive, and free.

In regard to this St. Augustine said: "Pour out that you may be filled, go out of yourself, so that you may enter." And in another passage he comments: "Noble soul, sublime creature, why are you seeking Him outside yourself when He dwells wholly, truly, and purely within you? Why do you, a partaker of divine nature, busy yourself with what is creaturely?" If the ground in the depth of the soul has been prepared by man, then, without doubt, God must fill it wholly, or sooner the heavens would burst and fill the void. Still less does God leave anything empty, so contrary is this to His nature and to His ordinance.

And therefore you should observe silence! In that manner the Word can be uttered and heard within. For surely, if you choose to speak, God must fall silent. There is no better way of serving the Word than by silence and by listening. If you go out of yourself, you may be certain that God will enter and fill you wholly: the greater the void, the greater the divine influx.

This exodus is elucidated by a parable from the First Book of Moses.* God commanded Abraham to go out of his land and leave his kin, so that He might show him all good. "All good" signifies the divine birth, which contains all good within itself. Land and earth He bade him to leave stand for the body with its worldly gratifications and disorders. By kin we understand the inclinations of our sensual nature and all they entail. They, too, fascinate us and slow down the soul's progress, causing love and grief, pleasure and sorrow, desire and fear, anxiety and frivolity. These inclinations are indeed our close kin, and for that reason we ought to watch them carefully, so that we can turn our back on them completely should the highest good, the divine birth be effected in us.

A proverb says that a child kept too much at home remains uncouth abroad. That holds true of those people who have never left the house of their natural inclinations, who have not gone beyond their nature or beyond all those messages they have received from seeing and hearing, from emotions and excitements. Such people,

*Genesis.

who have never moved away from sensible things and have never risen above them, will indeed be uncouth when brought face-to-face with divine things. Their interior ground resembles an iron mountain never touched by a ray of light. Once their momentary mood and external circumstances change, such people are at their wits' end. They have never overcome their natural selves and so cannot experience this noble birth. Christ had them in mind when He said: "Whoever leaves father and mother and all possessions for my sake shall receive a hundredfold and eternal life."

Until now we have spoken of the first and the last birth, and how the first should teach us about the last. But now we would like also to refer to the second birth, when God's Son was born on this night of the Mother and has become our brother. In eternity He was born without a mother, and in time He was born without a father. "Mary," so St. Augustine tells us, "was more blessed because God was born spiritually in her soul than because He was born from her in the flesh." Now whoever wishes this birth to occur in his soul as nobly and as spiritually as it did in Mary's should reflect on the qualities which made her a mother both in spirit and in the flesh. She was a pure maiden, a virgin; she was betrothed, given in marriage; and she was turned inward, secluded from exterior things, when the Angel came to her. And these are the qualities a spiritual mother ought to possess, should God be born in her soul.

First, the soul should be a pure and chaste virgin. And if it ever lost its purity, it should reverse its ways and become pure and virginal again. It should be a virgin, bringing forth no outward fruit (in the eyes of the world), but much fruit within. This also means shutting out external concerns, not paying too much attention to them, not expecting much reward from them. Mary's heart was fixed solely on the divine. Inwardly a virgin should bear much fruit, for "all the splendor of the King's daughter is within." Thus she should live detached from the exterior world and from the senses. Her conduct, her thoughts, her manner, should all be interiorized. In this way she brings forth great and rich fruit. And this fruit is God Himself, His Son and Word, He who embraces and contains all that is.

Secondly, Mary was betrothed; and so should we be, according to St. Paul's teaching. We should immerse our mutable will into the divine, immutable one, so that our weakness may be turned into strength.

Thirdly, Mary was also turned inward, and if God is to be truly born in us, we must imitate her in this as well and live secluded from the world. This does not come about by merely avoiding temporal distractions which may appear harmful, but, above all, by interiorizing all our acts of virtue. What is truly needful is the creation of inner stillness and peace, a retreat protecting us from our senses, a refuge of tranquillity and inward repose.

This will be the subject of next Sunday's Mass when we sing the Entrance Hymn: "While all things were in quiet silence, and the night was in the midst of its course, Your almighty Word, O Lord, came down from Heaven, out of Your royal throne." And in this nocturnal silence, in which all things remain hushed and in perfect stillness, God's Word is heard in truth, for, should God speak, you must be silent; should He enter, created things must give way.

When Our Lord entered Egypt, all the idols crashed to the ground; those are our false gods, everything that hinders the immediate generation of the divine Word in the soul, however good and holy it may seem. Our Lord tells us that He had come to bring a sword to cut off all that clings to man, even mother, sister, and brother. For that with which you keep intimate company [without God], that is hostile to you. The multiplicity of images conceals the divine Word and prevents its birth in you, although the inner stillness may not be entirely removed. Though it may sometimes desert you, it should nevertheless become a fertile ground for the divine birth. Cherish this deep silence within, nourish it frequently, so that it may become a habit, and by becoming a habit, a mighty possession. For what seems quite impossible to an unpracticed person becomes easy to a practiced one. It is habit which creates skill.

May God help us to prepare a dwelling place for this noble birth, so that we may all attain spiritual motherhood.

AMEN.

Sermon 2
(Eve of Epiphany)

Accipe puerum et matrem eius et vade in terram Israel. ...
Take the Child and His mother, and go into the land of Israel
— Matthew 2:20

No matter how often one may read the glorious works of the Holy Gospels, preach from them, or meditate on them, one will always be struck by a new truth that went unnoticed before. "Take the Child and His mother, and go into the land of Israel, for they are dead that sought the life of the Child."

As soon as some people feel an aspiration for a renewal of their interior life, their enthusiasm carries them away. They become so impetuous about the newness of it all that they never stop to wonder if they perhaps take on more than they can manage, or if God's grace in them is such that they can carry it through. One should always consider the end before one hastily embarks on a new devotion. The first thing is to have recourse to God and commend to Him one's new spiritual fervor and impetus. But this is not the way some people choose; they want to rush off by themselves and start all kinds of new practices, and in their rashness they come to grief, because they rely on their strength alone.

When Joseph had fled into Egypt with the child and His mother, and an Angel had told him in his dream that Herod was dead, he greatly feared that the Child would be killed, because he learned that Herod's son Archelaus was now on the throne. Herod, who wanted to persecute the Child and kill Him, signifies the world, which would doubtless kill the Child, and we must certainly flee from it if we wish to retain the Child within us. But even when we have fled the world, in an exterior sense, and have retired into our cells and cloisters, there will always be an Archelaus reigning in the soul. A whole world will rise up in us which we will never overcome without constant practice and effort and the help of God. There are strong and fierce foes which will assail us, and to vanquish them is exceedingly hard.

First there is worldliness and spiritual pride. You wish to be seen and noticed and highly thought of; you want to impress others with your appearance and grand manner; you desire to be known for your brilliant talk, your worldly ways, your friends, family, wealth, rank, and all the rest. The second enemy is your own flesh, which attacks you with spiritual impurity; for a person is guilty of this whenever he indulges in sensual satisfactions, no matter of what kind they may be. Everybody has different temptations against impurity and he should guard carefully against them. Some people have a tendency toward infatuations of one kind or another, and they cherish them willfully in their hearts, day in and day out. For just as your bodily nature can lead your body to impurity, so your inward impurity takes away the noble purity of the spirit; and since your spirit is far nobler than your flesh, the sins of the spirit are also graver and more grievous. Your third enemy is malice, resentment, suspiciousness, rash judgment, feelings of hatred and spite. "Do you know what this person has done? And what he has said about me?" you say, and your bitter gestures, words, and actions make it clear that you will pay back the offender in any possible way. You may be convinced that all this is the work of the devil.

If you wish to be pleasing to God, you must renounce all this sort of thing, for it is the veritable work of Archelaus. Beware of this enemy, for it is he who can kill the Child for you.

But Joseph was constantly on his guard against anyone who might seek to kill the Child. In the same way, even when all the enemies are overcome, there are still a thousand ties to break. Only if you turn inward and look into your heart can you tell what they are. "Joseph" means a constant growth in the interior life and an active progress in spiritual things. They are indeed the best guard for the Child and His Mother.

Joseph was warned by the Angel and called back by him to the land of Israel. Now, Israel means land of vision. At this point many spiritual-minded people go astray, for they want to free themselves from their innumerable ties without waiting for God to set them free by the sending of His Angel. Thus they fall into grievous error. They want to free themselves with the aid of their cleverness and their ability to hold forth about such lofty matters as the Blessed Trinity. It is a great pity to think what harm and misunderstanding this has caused, and still causes every day. Such people refuse to endure the chains of captivity in the darkness which is Egypt, for Egypt means darkness. One thing you may be sure of: No creature God has ever called into life can free you or help you. God alone can do it. Run about as you will, search the whole world, you will never find the help except in God. If God wishes to avail Himself of an instrument, man or Angel, to achieve His purpose, He may do so, but nonetheless it is He who does the work. Therefore you should look into the depth of your soul, and give up all the running and outward searching; patiently endure, surrender yourself to God, and remain in the darkness of Egypt until the Angel comes to call you.

Joseph was asleep when the warning came. A person asleep does not sin, even if some evil thought comes to him, provided he has not caused it previously. In the same manner we should be asleep to all exterior sufferings and temptations which may assail us. We should accept them with calm endurance, humbly submitting ourselves to God, as if we were asleep and cared for nothing. This attitude of self-surrender to the End is the best safeguard against sin. In this sleep, in that true passivity, you will hear the calling of the voice.

Such guardians the prelates of the Church should be: Pope and bishops, abbots, priors and prioresses, and father confessors, too. They should all be guardians of the young, each one guarding them in the way that will benefit them most. All of us have many guardians, many superiors. I have a prior, a provincial, a master-general, a Pope, a bishop. All of these are my superiors. And if they all turned upon me as ferociously as wolves, I should submit, I hope, with true humility. If they were benevolent and kind, I should accept that, too. And if they wanted to do me harm, and if there were a hundred times as many of them as there are now, I ought to suffer it all with equal resignation.

Note that Joseph was in constant fear, although the Angel announced that those who sought the Child's life were dead; he diligently inquired who reigned in the land of Israel. There are those who want to live free from all fear. This is wrong, for as long as you live on this earth you will never be free from fear. *"Timor sanctus permanet in saeculum saeculi"* — "the fear of the Lord shall remain until the end of the world." Even if an Angel came and spoke to you, you should still be afraid and inquire diligently who is really reigning in you. Somewhere Archelaus may still be in power.

Joseph took the Child and His mother. By the Child we should understand a spotless purity. We should remain unstained by transitory things, and small like a child in submission and humility. By the mother we should understand a true love of God, for love is the mother of true humility; it is love which makes our self-will decrease so that we become childlike in pure submission to God's will. While man is still young he should not stray into the land of vision at will; he may do so to ask pardon, but then he must return to Egypt again. Let him stay there till he has grown to full manhood, steeled by the weapons of Our Lord Jesus Christ. He has taught us everything by His example; anything we are not told explicitly may be learned from His life. When He was twelve years old, He came to Jerusalem, but He did not remain there; He withdrew because He had not reached full manhood. He withdrew till He reached the age of thirty, He was there every day, rebuking and admonishing the Jews and teaching the truth as a master. He preached and instructed them, dwelling in the countryside, going wherever He wished, to Capernaum and Galilee and Nazareth, and all through Judea. He was a mighty teacher, working signs and wonders.

In this manner we, too, should act: As long as we are children and imperfect, we should not settle in that noble land, the land of the Lord; we may go there from time to time for a fleeting visit and then return again. But when we have reached full manhood we may come and live in the land of Judea. "Juda" means "to confess God." We can teach and admonish now, in the true peace, which is Jerusalem, and then cross over to Galilee; it is indeed a crossing over. For here all things have been overcome, and by this transcending Nazareth is reached, the sweet flower-garden where the blossoms of eternal life abound and where we experience a true foretaste of it. Here is utter security, inexpressible peace, tranquillity, and joy. We arrive there only by waiting in patience and submission for God to lead us forth. Those who have thus surrendered their will shall enter this peace, this blossoming of Nazareth, and here we shall find what will be our everlasting joy.

May God in His loving bounty grant us to share in this.

AMEN.

Sermon 24
(Monday before Pentecost)

Estote prudentes et vigilate in orationibus
Live wisely, and keep your senses awake to greet
the hours of prayer
— 1 Peter 4:7

St. Peter said in his letter: "Live wisely, and keep your senses awake to greet the hours of prayer." And since we are now approaching the lovely feast of the Holy Spirit, we should prepare ourselves with all our strength to receive Him with a heart abounding in holy desire. As we said yesterday, we must search, in a spirit of discernment, whether there is perhaps anything in our actions and in our lives that is not of God. We mentioned that this preparation falls into four parts: detachment, abandonment, inwardness, and single-mindedness. Furthermore it is necessary that the outer man be at peace and well versed in the natural virtues, the lower faculties governed by the moral virtues, after which the Holy Spirit will adorn the higher faculties with infused virtues. All this must, of course, be ordered and directed by true discernment and applied to our lives by the light of reason. Let everyone examine, first, whether his life is wholly directed toward God, and should he discover anything in his actions that is not, let him correct it.

In all this we should proceed precisely like a farmer who in March sets out to prepare his ground; when he sees the sun climbing higher, he trims and prunes his trees, he pulls up the weeds, and turns over the ground, digging diligently. In the same manner we should work deeply into our ground, examine it, and turn it over thoroughly. Now it is time to prune the trees — our exterior senses and faculties — and see that the weeds be pulled out completely. We ought to begin by clipping away the seven Deadly Sins thoroughly and boldly. We should get rid of all pride in its exterior and interior form; do away with avarice, anger, hatred, and envy, and all impurity and covetousness in body, heart, senses, and mind. This applies to the natural as well as to the spiritual level. We must also look for false and hidden motives and any tendency toward self-indulgence. All this should be cut off and eradicated entirely.

At this point, however, the soil is still dry and hard. Though the sun is beginning to ascend, its rays have not yet penetrated the wintry earth. Still, it is climbing higher now, swiftly, and the summer is rapidly approaching. Now it is time for the divine sun to shine upon the well-prepared ground. As soon as the outer man has prepared his lower and higher faculties, the whole of him becomes receptive, and the tender, divine sun begins to send its bright rays into his noble ground; and now a joyous summer commences, a downright May-blossoming is about to unfold. The gracious, eternal God permits the spirit to green and bloom and bring forth the most marvelous fruit, surpassing anything a tongue can express and a heart can conceive. Such is the rapture that arises within the spirit.

As soon as the Holy Spirit can come with His presence and freely flood the depth of the soul with His wondrous radiance and divine light, then He, who is rightly called the Comforter, is able to exercise His sweet comfort there — oh, what a blissful rapture is now to occur! There is holiday feasting everywhere, and the kitchen abounds in sweet fragrances of rich and rare dishes. What savory and delicious fare is being prepared there, and how it draws us by its scent! May has arrived and stands in full bloom. These aromatic sweets reach far out into poor human nature, which now has a fair share in these joys. The ecstasy which the Holy Spirit so richly and generously bestows as a gift upon the well-prepared soul, oh, could one savor just a single drop, it would exceed and extinguish any taste for all the sweetness that created things can offer in any way known or imagined.

Now, as soon as some people discover and experience this rare comfort, they would like to immerse themselves and fall asleep in it, rest forever in its bliss, just as St. Peter, tasting one drop of this joy, wished to build three tents and remain there forever. But this was not Our Lord's wish; for the goal to which He would guide and lead him was still far off. And as it was with St. Peter, who exclaimed, "It is good for us to be here," so it is with us: As soon as we become aware of this bliss, we believe ourselves in possession of the entire sun, and we would like to bask in its radiance and stretch out under its warmth. Those who act thus will always remain in the same place; nothing will come of them, they have missed the point.

Others, again, fall into a different trap by wishing to find a false freedom in this sweetness. In this state of emotional joy, nature cleverly turns back upon itself and takes possession; and this is what human nature is most inclined to do, it likes to rely upon emotions. The effect is as bad as with some people who take too many medicines: as soon as nature grows accustomed to them, it becomes dependent, relents, turns lazy, and thinks that it has a good crutch there, and would not work as hard as it would otherwise. If, however, it is left without any assurance of such help, it becomes active again and helps itself. Just observe, Beloved, how sly and treacherous this nature of ours is, and how it invariably seeks its own comfort and convenience. And this is true to a much higher degree in spiritual matters. For, as soon as a man experiences this pleasure and feels this extraordinary well-being, he thinks he can rely upon it. He leans on it and does not work with the same zeal and fidelity as before. He becomes self-indulgent and pampered, imagining that he cannot suffer and work as he used to, and must keep himself in a state of repose. As soon as the devil sees a man in such a condition, he invests it with a false sweetness in order to keep him in his state of treacherous tranquillity.

How, then, should we conduct ourselves in such a case? Shun this sweetness and reject it? Certainly not. It is with immense gratitude that we should receive it, and then humbly offer it back to God, giving Him great thanks and praise and confessing our own unworthiness. We should conduct ourselves like a young man who sets out on a journey: He is poor, hungry, and thirsty and still has a long stretch of road ahead of him. "If I only walk four more miles," he says to himself, "I will get a square meal and then I shall be satisfied and refreshed." At this thought his cheerfulness and strength return, and he can happily walk another ten miles. That is precisely the way in which we should act when God strengthens and feeds us with sweet comfort and spiritual joys; everything should increase: our love, our gratitude, our praise, our intention to live according to His will. We should stretch toward God in sweet longing and ardent love and be so consumed in this service that God would rightfully multiply His gifts of comfort and spiritual delectation.

This could also be compared to a man who wished to see the Pope to make him a gift of one single florin and the Pope came out to meet him and gave him a hundred thousand pounds of gold in return, and he would repeat this over and over again, each time the man offered a florin; this is the way God deals with us when we turn to Him with gratitude, making an offering of ourselves with love and thankfulness. Each time, God hastens toward us with more and more gifts and graces, more sweet comfort at every single moment. In this manner [the gift of] spiritual consolation turns into a help, and a means to God and thus to a higher good. We should avail ourselves of such comfort, but not for its own sake, just as a man who travels in a carriage enjoys it not for its own sake but for its usefulness. So, too, it is with God's gifts: They are to be used, but God alone is to be enjoyed.

St. Peter tells us to beware of this harm, and he admonishes us to live wisely, and to keep our senses awake; he warns us not to fall asleep cradled by this comfort, for a sleeping man is as it were half dead and unable to act on his own accord. We should keep our senses awake and be brave and sober. A sober person performs his work cheerfully, courageously, and intelligently. That is why St. Peter says: "Brethren, be sober and watchful; the devil who is your adversary goes about roaring like a lion, to find his prey, but you, grounded in faith, must face him boldly." Beloved! Be not drowsy and indolent, and do not persevere in anything that is not entirely of God. Glance watchfully around you and, guided by your reason, attend to yourselves and to God within you in loving desire.

For not even the loving disciples of Our Lord himself were granted to remain in the joy of His Presence, should they become partakers of the Holy Spirit. "If I should not go from you," said the Lord, "the Spirit, the Comforter, cannot come to you!" So filled were the holy disciples, inwardly and outwardly, by the joyful presence of Our Lord Jesus Christ, so saturated were their hearts, souls, minds, and faculties, that every trace of the attachment had to be taken from them, to make room for the true, spiritual, interior consolation. This plenitude of exterior comfort had to leave them, however bitter it might have seemed at the time, if they were ever to progress and not remain on the lowest level, that of the senses. Once, however, man transcends the senses, he enters the realm of the higher faculties, those of the intellect, and here this comfort is received in a manner more lofty and sublime; from here we attain the interior ground, the sanctuary of the spirit, and this is the proper dwelling-place of such joy; here it is received in essence and in reality; here, in all sobriety, we partake of the fullness of life.

Now St. Peter says: "Be watchful in prayer, for the adversary goes about like a roaring lion." What kind of prayer does St. Peter have in mind? Is it the prayer of the mouth, practiced by people who reel off the Psalter that way? No, that is not what he meant. He rather meant the prayer which our Lord called true prayer, when He called true worshipers those who pray in spirit and in truth. The saints and spiritual masters tell us that prayer is an ascent of the mind to God; reading and vocal prayer can occasionally help us to achieve this, and to that extent they may be useful. Just as my cloak and my clothes are not myself and yet serve me, so also vocal prayer serves and leads occasionally to true prayer, although it falls short of being that by itself. For true prayer is a direct raising of the mind and heart to God, without intermediary. This and nothing else is the essence of prayer.

This loving ascent to God, in profound longing and humble surrender, that one is true prayer; nevertheless, the clergy, religious, and those who receive benefices are bound to the recitation of the canonical hours and to vocal prayer; but no external prayer is as devout and as deserving of our love as is the sacred Our Father. The greatest of all the masters taught it to us and said it Himself. More than any other, it leads to essential prayer; indeed it is a heavenly prayer. This true prayer is said and contemplated in Heaven without ceasing: It is a genuine ascent to God, a lifting of the spirit upward, so that God may in reality enter the purest, most inward, noblest part of the soul — its deepest ground — where alone there is undifferentiated unity.

In regard to this St. Augustine says that the soul has a hidden abyss, untouched by time and space, which is far superior to anything that gives life and movement to the body. Into this noble and wondrous ground, this secret realm, there descends that bliss of which we have spoken. Here the soul has its eternal abode. Here a man becomes so still and essential, so single-minded and withdrawn, so raised up in purity, and more and more removed from all things, for God Himself is present in this noble realm, and works and reigns and dwells therein. This state of the soul cannot be compared to what it has been before, for now it is granted to share in the divine life itself. The spirit meets wholly with God and enflames itself in all things, and is drawn into the hot fire of love, which is God in essence and in nature.

And from this height such men descend again into all the needs of Christendom, and in holy prayer and desire address themselves to everything God wills to be prayed for. They pray for their friends, for sinners, for the souls in purgatory; their charity embraces every man's need in holy Christendom. Not that they petition God for each person's selfish desires; their prayer is simple and wise. Just as I see you all sitting before me at one glance, so they draw all into their embrace in this same abyss, in this fire of love, as in a divine contemplation. Then they turn their gaze back to this loving abyss, to this fire of love, and there they rest; and after plunging into it, they descend to all who are in want until they return to the loving, dark, silent rest of the abyss.

Thus they go in and out, and yet remain at all times within, in the sweet, silent ground in which they have their substance and life, in which they move and have their being. Wherever one finds such men, one finds nothing but divine life. Their conduct, their actions, their whole manner of life is divinized. They are noble souls, and the whole of Christendom draws profit from them. To all they give sustenance, to God glory, and to mankind consolation. They dwell in God, and God in them. Wherever they are, they should be praised.

May God grant that we, too, may have a share in this.

AMEN.

Sermon 29
(Feast of the Blessed Trinity II)

Quod scimus loquimur, et quod vidimus testamur
We speak of what we know,
and we bear witness to what we have seen
— John 3:11

Our dear Lord said: "We speak of what we know, and we bear witness to what we have seen; and our witness you do not receive. If I have spoken of earthly things to you, and you do not believe, how will you believe if I shall speak to you of heavenly things?" These words are taken from the Gospel of the exalted feast of the sublime, lofty, and most glorious Trinity. And all the feasts we have observed throughout the year, whatever they commemorated, have led up to this one feast and found their consummation in it, just as the course which creatures run, especially rational creatures, has its goal and end in the Holy Trinity, for in a sense it is both beginning and end. When we come to speak of the Most Blessed Trinity, we are at a loss for words, and yet words must be used to say something of this sublime and ineffable Trinity. To express it adequately is as impossible as touching the sky with one's head. For everything we can say or think can no more approach the reality than the smallest point of a needle can contain Heaven and earth; indeed, a hundred, a thousand times, and immeasurably less than that.

It is utterly impossible for our intellect to understand how the lofty, essential Unity can be single in essence and yet threefold in Persons; how the Persons are distinct from each other; how the Father begets the Son; how the Son proceeds from the Father and yet remains within Him (by comprehending Himself the Father utters His Eternal Word); how from this comprehension that proceeds from Him, there streams forth an ineffable love, which is the Holy Spirit; and how these wondrous Processions stream back again in essential unity, in ineffable self-delight and self-enjoyment; how the Son is equal to the Father in power, wisdom, and love; how the Son and the Holy Spirit are also one. And yet there is an inexpressibly vast distinction between the Persons, although they proceed in an ineffable way in unity of nature. On this subject a staggering amount of things could be said, and yet nothing would have been said to convey how the supreme, superabundant Unity unfolds into Trinity.

To experience the working of the Trinity is better than to talk about it. In fact one shies away from a busy scrutiny of this mystery, especially as the words are borrowed from the world as we know it, and also because of the disproportion between the subject and our intelligence to which all this is unutterably high and hidden. For this subject even surpasses the understanding of the Angels. So let us leave the learned discourses to the scholars: They have to engage in them in order to safeguard the Faith. And they have written weighty volumes on the subject. It is for us to believe in simplicity.

St. Thomas says: "No one should go beyond what those doctors affirmed, who have experienced and pursued these truths at the source, where they have received them from the Holy Spirit." And though there is no subject more joyous and sweet to the taste, there is also nothing more grievous than falling into error concerning it. Therefore stop your disputations on that mystery, and believe it in simplicity, entrusting yourselves wholly to God. Even for the great scholars there is no better way than this, and yet they have never been more subtle in their reasoning than now. You, however, should allow the Holy Trinity to be born in the center of your soul, not by the use of human reason, but in essence and in truth; not in words, but in reality. It is the divine mystery we should seek, and how we are truly its Image; for this divine Image certainly dwells in our souls by nature, actually, truly, and distinctly, though of course not in as lofty a manner as it is in Itself.

Above all, cherish this very sweet Image which dwells in you in such a blessed and unique manner. Nobody can express adequately its nobility, for God is in this Image, indeed He is the Image, in a way which surpasses all our powers of comprehension.

Scholars discuss this Image a great deal, trying to express in various natural ways its nature and essence. They all assert that it belongs to the highest faculties of our soul, which are memory, intellect, and will; that these faculties enable us to receive and enjoy the Blessed Trinity. This is indeed true, but it is the lowest degree of perception, leaving the mystery in the natural order. St. Thomas says that the perfection of the Image lies in its activity, in the exercise of the faculties; that is, in the active memory, in the active intellect, and in the active will. Further than that St. Thomas will not go.

Other theologians, however, state — and here we have something of far greater significance — that the Image of the Blessed Trinity rests in the most intimate, hidden, and inmost ground of the soul, where God is present essentially, actively, and substantially. Here God acts and exists and rejoices in Himself, and to separate God from this inmost ground would be as impossible as separating Him from Himself. This is God's eternal decree; He has ordained that He cannot and will not separate Himself. And thus in the depth of this ground the soul possesses everything by grace which God possesses by nature. In the measure in which man surrenders himself and turns to that inmost ground, grace is born in the highest way.

A pagan master, Proclus,* has this to say on the subject: "As long as man is occupied with images inferior to himself, and as long as he does not go beyond them, it is unlikely that he will ever reach this depth. It will appear an illusion to really believe that this ground exists within us; we doubt that it can actually exist in us. Therefore,"

*Fifth-century Greek Neoplatonist philosopher.

he continues, "if you wish to experience its existence, you must abandon all multiplicity and concentrate your attention on this one thing with the eyes of your intellect; and if you wish to rise higher, you must put aside all rational methods, for reason is now beneath you, and then you may become united with the One." And he calls this state a divine darkness: still, silent, at rest, and above all sense perception.

Beloved, it is a disgraceful thing that a pagan philosopher understood and attained this truth, while we are so far from both. Our Lord expressed the same truth when he said: "The kingdom of God is within us." It is to be found in the inmost depth, beyond the activity of our faculties. And so we read in today's Gospel: "We speak of what we know, and we bear witness to what we have seen; and our witness you do not receive." Indeed, how could a person who lives merely by his senses receive this witness? To those who subscribe to such a way of life, that which is beyond the senses appears as an illusion. As Our Lord says: "As the heavens are exalted above the earth, so are my ways exalted above your ways, and my thoughts above your thoughts." And Our Lord says the same thing today: "If I have spoken to you of earthly things and you believe not, how will you believe if I shall speak to you of heavenly things?" Recently I spoke to you about wounded love, and you said that you could not understand me, and yet we were dealing only with earthly things. How can you then expect to understand things spiritual and divine?

You are concerned with so many external affairs, always busy with one thing or another; this is not the witness of which Our Lord said: "We bear witness to what we have seen." This witness is to be found in your inmost ground, beyond sensual images; within this ground the Heavenly Father begat His only-begotten Son, swifter a million times than the twinkling of an eye. And this happens in the swiftness of eternity that is forever new, in the inexplicable splendor of His own Being. Whoever wishes to experience this must turn inward, far beyond his exterior and interior faculties, beyond all that the imagination has ever acquired from outside, so that he may sink and melt into that ground. Then the power of the Father will come and call the soul into Himself through His only-begotten Son, and as the Son is born of the Father and returns into Him, so man is born of the Father in the Son, and flows back into the Father through the Son, becoming one with Him. Thus Our Lord says: "You will call me Father and will not cease to walk after me. This day have I begotten you, through and in my Son." And now the Holy Spirit pours Himself out in inexpressible and overflowing love and joy, flooding and saturating the ground of the soul with His wondrous gifts.

Two of these may be called active gifts, namely, piety and knowledge. They make man kind and gentle. And the gift of knowledge allows him to discern what way is best for him. But the corresponding virtues must have preceded these gifts, for the gifts now bestowed lead man into a state beyond the exercise of virtues.

Next come the passive gifts, and they go hand in hand: fortitude and counsel. The third gift, fear, faces inward, for it protects and strengthens what the Holy Spirit has worked. Finally come the two highest gifts, understanding, and the wisdom that is a taste of God. Beloved, the devil lays snares for such people, they are tempted by those demons who are the craftiest and most subtle. Therefore such men are in great need of the gift of discerning knowledge. To remain in that state of interior union for just one second is worth more than all exterior works and rules; and it is in the depth of this ground that we should pray for our friends, living or dead. That would be far more efficacious than reciting a hundred thousand Psalters.

This, then, is the true witness: "The Holy Spirit, testifying to our spirit that we are the children of God." And thus we receive this testimony in our hearts, as it says in today's Gospel. In Heaven, that means in the heaven within our soul, there are three who bear witness: the Father, the Word, and the Spirit. They are your witnesses who give the true testimony that you are a child of God. They illuminate the depth of your ground, and thus your own ground becomes your witness. And this witness also testifies against you and against all the disorders within you; and this testimony enlightens your reason, whether you like it or not, and reveals your whole life to you, if you will only listen. Listen carefully to this testimony and live accordingly if you wish to be saved at the Day of Judgment. If you reject it by your words and deeds and by your whole life, the same witness will condemn you at the last day and that will be your fault and not God's. Beloved, always listen to this witness within, and you will never regret it.

You have sailed down the Rhine in order to take up a life of poverty. But if you fail to reach this ground within you, no amount of traveling will get you there. Do not waste your energy! Shed all outward attachments, turn inward, and seek the deepest ground of your soul; exterior precepts and techniques will be of no avail. In the lives of the Fathers we read of a good husband who fled into the forest to avoid these obstacles; he had as many as two thousand brethren under his care, all seeking this same interior ground. And his wife had a community of many under her care. This ground, however, is a single, hidden solitude, utterly sublime, a darkness forever accessible to your free will. No path of the senses will ever lead you there. And then you will say: "I love spiritual people and would like nothing better than helping those who have felt God's touch and have received interior illumination." Whoever draws such people away from the higher graces, enforcing exterior practices upon them, prepares a terrible judgment for himself. Trying to force such souls into pious exercises puts more obstacles in their way than did the pagans and the Jews. And so I warn you, who are so ready to judge with cutting remarks and disdainful gestures, to be indeed careful in dealing with such spiritual people.

And now, if you wish to contemplate the Holy Trinity within you, keep these three points in mind. First, keep God alone before your eyes, His honor, and not your own. Secondly, in all your works and exterior activities keep a close watch over yourself; be constantly mindful of your utter nothingness, and observe carefully what occupies you most. Thirdly, ignore what goes on around you: If it is not your business, do not pay attention to it; it will take care of itself. If things are good, let them be so; if they seem bad, do not criticize and ask questions. Turn into the depth of your ground and remain there, so that you may hear the voice of the Father who calls you. He calls you to Himself and endows you with such riches that, if it were necessary, you could answer all the questions of the entire clergy in the Church; of such clarity and brilliance are the gifts God bestows upon His lovers.

And should you forget everything that has been said here, keep in mind these two little points: First, be truly humble, throughout your whole being, not only in mind and in outward conduct; think lowly of yourself, and see yourself honestly for what you are. And secondly, let the love you bear God be a true one; not just what is usually understood by the term, which refers only to emotions, but a love that embraces God most ardently. Such love is a far cry from what is usually meant by religious feeling, which is situated in the senses. What I mean here transcends all sensible experience; it is a gazing upon God with one's entire spirit, a being drawn by love, just as a runner is drawn, or an archer, who has a single goal before his eyes

May the Blessed Trinity grant us to arrive at this inmost ground where its true image dwells.

AMEN.

Sermon 44
(Feast of the Nativity of John the Baptist)

Hic venit ut testimonium perhiberet de lumine
He came to bear witness to the light
— John 1:7

"He came to bear witness to the light." This week our mother, Holy Church, celebrates the Feast of the Nativity of the great and honorable St. John the Baptist. There is little we can contribute with our praise, since his honor and greatness were praised by Our Lord Jesus Christ Himself, who said no one born of woman has been of such greatness as he.

Our Lord also said: "What did you go to see? A prophet? This man is greater than a prophet. What did you go out for? To see a man clothed in soft garments? Or a reed shaken to and fro by the wind? No, there is nothing of the kind here." John said of himself that he was a voice crying in the wilderness: "Prepare the way of the Lord, make straight this path." Also, in our Office we sing this week that he was a burning and a shining lantern. John the Evangelist referred to him as a witness to the light. It is about these last words that I want to talk to you today.

Is there any higher praise we could give to this saint? He is called "a witness to the light." His light of which he was a witness was a real light, transcendent, beyond all our comprehension. This light illuminates the innermost core, the deepest ground of the soul. And when this light and this witness is brought to bear on us, instead of receiving it where it shines, we turn away from the depth of our soul and run in the opposite direction, turning everything the wrong way around. We fail to receive the witness because we are so immersed in external activities. There are others, too, who will not accept the light because they are opposed to it. "He came to His own," says the Evangelist, "and His own received Him not." These are the people with worldly dispositions, resembling the Pharisees, whom St. John called descendants of vipers, though they called themselves descendants of Abraham. They stand in opposition to all who love the light, and they are in a most grievous and precarious state. They cling to the light of the Faith by a single thread.

Now, we must bear in mind that human nature is weak and seriously flawed. That is why our merciful God has come to its rescue with supernatural aid and supernatural power. This is the light of grace. It is a created light, but it lifts nature high above itself and brings with it all the nourishment which it will require for a new life. Beyond that there is an uncreated light, the light of glory, which is God Himself. If we ever are to know God, it must be through Him, with Him, and in Him: God through God; as the Prophet says: "Lord in Your light we shall see the light." This is an overflowing light, enlightening every man who comes into the world. It shines upon everyone, the bad as well as the good, just as the sun shines upon all creatures. If they are blind to it, so much the worse for them. If a man finds himself in a darkened house, he needs only sufficient light to find a window. Then he can open it and put his head out and he is in the light. Such a man becomes a witness to the light.

Now let us see how we should act initially, when we are about to receive this witness. We must detach ourselves from everything that is temporal and transitory, for this witness is to be received by the lower and higher faculties within us. The lowest faculty is our appetite for pleasure and the irascible appetite. Hence it is the faculty for pleasure which will first receive this witness, and therefore we must cut ourselves off from all those natural pleasures we find most gratifying, society, fashion, in short anything which satisfies the senses, though God permits us to satisfy our needs. It is indeed a wilderness into which God is taking us: a life of detachment in which we shed our desires, spiritual and natural, in our interior and exterior life.

Secondly, this witness comes to our irascible appetite, teaching us perseverance and strength. When we have received this testimony, we become immovable, like an iron mountain, instead of being swayed to and fro like a reed. When Our Lord said of St. John that he was not clothed in soft garments, he was alluding to people who seek bodily pleasures for their comfort. But there are many who despise those, and yet are like reeds. They are moved by what people say; a sarcastic or severe word can throw them completely off balance. How foolish! What harm can such words do? Then along comes the devil with his insinuating voices, making them feel now high and then low. They are indeed reeds shaken by the wind.

But this testimony is given to our higher faculties as well: to our reason, will, and love. In our reason, it is a prophet; prophet means "one who sees far, *videns*." Reason is far-seeing, it amazes one how far it sees. If an enlightened man who had not yet attained this degree were to hear things mysterious to him, his reason would bear witness in the depths of his soul and say: "Yes, this is true." But our Lord said: "He is more than a prophet." That is, in this depth, which reason cannot penetrate, we behold light within light. We now move within this inward light, the light of grace: and thus we behold and perceive, by means of the created light, the divine, uncreated One.

All this comes to us first in a veiled manner, for our faculties cannot come within a thousand miles of this depth of the soul. The breadth which opens up here has neither form nor image nor any other mode or manner; nor are there any concepts of space. For it is an unfathomable abyss, poised in itself, unplumbed, ebbing and flowing like the sea. As one is immersed in it, it seems still and void; yet in an instant it wells up as if it would engulf all things. One sinks into this abyss, and in it is God's own dwelling-place, more real than in heaven and in all His creatures. Whoever finds his way there would truly find God, and himself one with God, for God would never part from it again. God would be present to him, and here eternity would be tasted and savored, for there exists no past or future.

No created light can touch this ground and illumine it, for it is truly God's home and dwelling-place. The whole of creation would not fill or plumb this void, nothing created could ever penetrate it or fulfill its yearnings. God alone can fill it with His divine immensity. This abyss of the soul belongs to the divine abyss, to nothing less. As it is said: "Deep calls on deep." And if we are carefully attentive, this ground sheds light upon our faculties, drawing and leading the higher and lower ones back to their source and their origin. If only we would adhere closely to this depth, we would perceive the lovely, divine accents of that voice which calls us into the wilderness, into the ground, drawing us ever deeper.

No one can imagine the solitude which reigns in this wilderness, no one at all. No thought can enter here, not a word of all the learned treatises on the Holy Trinity with which people busy themselves so much. Not a single word. So inward is it, so infinitely remote, and so untouched by time and space. This ground is simple and without differentiation, and when one enters here, it will seem as if one has been here from all eternity, and as if united with God, be it only for an instant. This experience sheds light and bears witness that man was everlasting in God, before his creation in time. When he was in Him, he was God in God.

St. John writes: "Everything that has been made was one life in Him." What man now is in his createdness, he was from the beginning in God's uncreatedness, one with Him in essence. And until he returns to that imageless state which was his when he issued from the origin, from uncreatedness to createdness, he will never find his way back into God. Every natural inclination, every adherence to creatures, every trace of complacency must be left far behind. And along with it, all possessiveness which may stain the depth of the soul, all the inordinate pleasures of soul or body freely consented to, they all must vanish. Unless they are utterly eradicated, unless man is as he was when he first emerged from God, he will never attain to the Source.

Nor is this liberation from human images and forms sufficient: Our human spirit must first be clothed with the divine form by the light of grace. If we give ourselves to this reforming in the form of God, if we withdraw into this ground and remain there in perfect order, we might well be granted in the present life a glimpse of this divine transformation, although no one can enter into God or comprehend Him except in the uncreated light which is God Himself: *"Domine, in lumine tuo videbimus lumen."* A person who often turns to this inmost ground and is at home there will be granted many a lofty glimpse, though of brief duration. He will then behold God more clearly and more distinctly than he can behold the sun with his bodily eyes.

This ground of the soul was already known by the pagan philosophers. As they searched its depth, the knowledge of it caused them to think poorly of transitory things. Such great masters as Proclus and Plato gave a lucid account of it, in order to guide those who could not find the way by themselves. St. Augustine says that Plato had already fully foreseen the first part of St. John's Gospel, "In the beginning was the Word" up to "there was a man sent from God." The expression of this knowledge was still inchoate, although the Holy Trinity was already prefigured in their thought. This understanding, my Beloved, arose from their inmost ground, for which they lived and which they cherished.

Is it not shameful and a great scandal that we poor latecomers, we Christians, aided by grace, the Faith, and the sacraments, should be running about like blind hens, ignorant of our own self and of the depth within us? The reason is that we are so fragmented, so scattered all over the lot. We put great emphasis on what appeals to the senses, on our activities and various projects. The number of vigils and psalms and other pious practices occupy us to such an extent that we cannot find the way to our inmost ground.

My dear Sisters, if we cannot fill our casks with the noble wine of Cyprus, then let us fill them with stones and ashes, so as not to provide space for the devil by leaving them entirely empty. This would be preferable to reeling off one's beads in a mindless manner.

There is still another witness in our higher faculties; it is in the faculty which enables us to love and to will. We have sung about it this week: *"Lucerna lucens et ardens,"* a shining and burning lantern. This lantern gives light and heat. Your hand can feel the heat, but you cannot see the flame unless you look down on it, where you can see the light glimmering through the panes. If you only paid attention to this comparison, you would be more receptive to its light and heat! It is the wounding love which will lead you into this ground. And as long as you feel it within yourself, it must drive you on, so that you can bend the bow to the utmost in order to hit the supreme target.

But once you have come into that hidden abyss, into captive love, you must let love have its way. No longer do you have any command over yourself, over your thoughts, your practices, or even your works of virtue. If, when in this state, you are left enough liberty and space for thought, you will fall back again into wounding love. But if this happens, summon all your strength, raise yourself up, storm ahead with your love, compel it to rush forward aided by all the desire and prayer you are capable of. Even if you cannot speak, let your desires and thoughts speak, as St. Augustine said: "Lord, you have ordained that I should love you; grant what you have ordained. You have ordained that I should love you with all my heart, with all my soul, with all my strength, with all my spirit. Grant me, O Lord, that I may love you above all else." And if you cannot conceptualize all this at the moment, say it out aloud. Do not be like the people who just sit and wait: They will never experience that love.

After this comes agonizing love, and finally in the fourth place enraptured love. Alas, my dear Sisters, how much has this love decreased nowadays, and how much has natural reason increased! People have never used their reason more cunningly than when it comes to buying and selling. Enraptured love can be compared to our lantern. Whoever loves with this love knows its heat. It makes him impetuous in all his faculties; he longs and yearns for this love, not knowing that he possesses it. It consumes his very flesh and blood. Now is the moment to do yourself harm with external practices and devotions. If love is to do its work, you must do nothing to withdraw from it, but follow it through all its tempests. There are some who want to take shelter from this storm for fear of perishing, saying it is not for them. My beloved! When enraptured love comes upon us, all merely human activities must give way. It is our Lord Himself who comes and speaks through us: He speaks one Word that is nobler and more telling than are a hundred thousand spoken by men.

St. Dionysius* said: "When the Eternal Word is uttered in the ground of the soul, and the ground is so prepared that it can receive that Word in its unutterable immensity and fruitfulness, not in part but fully, the ground and the Word become one." The ground becomes one with the Word not in essence, for the soul retains its created nature in this union. Our Lord bore witness to this when He said: "Father, let them be one as We are one"; and again when He said to Augustine: "You must be changed into me." No one can attain this stage except through this degree of love. When St. John the Baptist said: "I am the voice of one crying in

*Sixth-century mystic and Neoplatonist philosopher.

the wilderness, make straight the way of the Lord," he refers to the path of the virtues. This path is very straight. And again he says that he is to prepare the Lord's paths. Footpaths reach the goal faster than public roads. The shortcut across the fields is indeed rougher and may lead one astray; and yet it is more direct than the open road.

Beloved! Whoever would discover the paths leading to the ground, he would take the shortest and most direct way, keeping all his energies to himself so as to be very attentive. For these paths are rugged, dark, and alien to our nature, and only those who are sufficiently skilled can take them. If they are aware of this, they will not be put off by hurdles and hindrances or any other human anguish. Quite the opposite: Everything will point to the ground, beckon, and draw them there.

In the same manner we should straighten the paths within ourselves, the paths which lead our spirit to God and God to us. These relations also require skill, and their difficulties are of a hidden nature. At this point many give up and begin to run after exterior devotions and activities. They are like people starting for Rome and taking the road to Holland. The more they advance, the farther they get away from their destination. And when they return, they are old and spent and no longer up to the tempestuous work of love.

Beloved, when we find ourselves in the tempests of love, we should not dwell on our sins and failings. Our only concern should be that love's work be accomplished. We can be overcome by this tempest even when our hearts appear cold, disinterested and hard. Now more than ever we must adhere to love, clinging to it in perfect faith, freed and stripped of everything that is not love. Constantly long for it, put your whole trust in it, cleave to it, and your experience will be as powerful and overwhelming as is possible in this life. If your faith in love is imperfect, your desire will fade away. Love will be extinguished, and nothing will come of it all.

This may seem very hard to you. The devil will allow you all the marks of a spiritual life, but he will do everything in his power to deprive you of love's true witness. He will leave you with all kinds of treacherous love which many will mistake for the real thing. If they looked deeply into their ground, they would see whether their love was true or false. The one thing necessary is to have access to the ground in order to be able to enter its depth. There you would find that grace which would incessantly raise you up. But man often resists that voice until he makes himself unworthy to ever receive it again. This is due to complacency. If only he would respond to the glance of grace, it would lead him to find such union with God that he would experience in time the joy that will be his in eternity, as some have done before him.

May God grant that we may all experience this.

AMEN.

Translated by Maria Shrady

Theologia Germanica

This anonymous late-fourteenth-century devotional tract owes its name, "A German Theology," to its most influential admirer, Martin Luther, who undertook to edit it himself: first in 1516, then again in 1518, after a more complete version of the work had come into his hands. The actual author, known only as "the Frankfurter," served as priest and warden in the House of the Teutonic Order in Frankfurt, according to the foreword to one early (pre-Lutheran) manuscript. Here he identified himself with the so-called "Friends of God," a mystically oriented group of clergy and laymen active in the Rhineland and elsewhere. His immediate purpose in writing the tract was to distinguish this spiritual community from the extremist and libertine Brethren of the Free Spirit, a contemporary heretical movement. While the Christ-centered "theology" he presents in support of his position breaks little new ground conceptually — it stands squarely in the tradition of Eckhart and Tauler — its very accessibility makes it stand out among early German mystical texts. This relative simplicity, expressly commended by Luther in his preface, may help to account for the vast popularity it enjoyed in the sixteenth century and beyond, especially among Anabaptists and Pietists.

From Theologia Germanica

Preface

We read that St. Paul, in spite of his lowly and despised status, wrote mighty and fearless letters* and testified that his speech was not embellished with ornate and flowery words,† yet it proved to be full of treasures of knowledge and wisdom.‡

This is the manner of God's wonders. Look at these wonders and you will find that pompous and vainglorious preachers are never chosen to proclaim God's words. Rather, as it is written, *ex ore infantium,* that is to say, out of the mouths of babes You have most fittingly brought forth Your praise.§ Again, God's wisdom loosens the tongues of the slow of speech so that they speak most eloquently.**

On the other hand, He punishes conceited folk who are offended and irritated by the simple.††

Consilium inopis, and so forth. You have shown disrespect for good counsel and teaching because it was conveyed by poor and lowly persons, and so forth.‡‡

I point to the above because I want to alert each and every reader of this little book to the danger of harming himself by becoming irritated with its imperfect German and its unembroidered and ungarlanded words.

For this noble little book, poor and unadorned as it is as far as

---

*The reference is presumably to 2 Corinthians 10:10. Luther often quoted from memory. (Hoffman)

†The reference is presumably to 1 Corinthians 1:17. (Hoffman)

‡The reference is presumably to Colossians 2:3-4. (Hoffman)

§The reference is presumably to Psalm 8:2. (Hoffman)

**Luther may refer to Proverbs 10:20: "The tongue of the righteous is choice silver"; or to Isaiah 35:6: "The tongue of the dumb shall sing for joy." (Hoffman)

††Luther may refer to Proverbs 3:34. (Hoffman)

‡‡See Psalm 14:6.

wording and purely human wisdom are concerned, is all the richer and abundantly precious in true knowledge and divine wisdom. And, if I may speak with Biblical foolishness: Next to the Bible and St. Augustine no other book has come to my attention from which I have learned — and desired to learn — more concerning God, Christ, man, and what all things are.

It is now brought home to me how false it is when many learned people speak disparagingly about us Wittenberg theologians, alleging that we are disseminating novelties. They speak as though there would not have been people in the past and in other places who said what we say.

Indeed, there have been such people. But God's wrath, evoked by our sin, has prevented us from recognizing or hearing them. We were not considered worthy.

For instance, it is clear that their message has not for a long time been treated at our universities. It has gone so far that God's holy word has not only been shoved under the workbench but in fact almost moldered away there, gathering dust and assailed by moths.

Read this booklet, anyone, and determine for yourself whether the theology as we do it in Wittenberg is newfangled or in a solid tradition. This book is certainly not new.

Now, some will perhaps say, as they have done before, that we are German theologians. This is quite all right with us. I thank God that I can hear and find my God in the German tongue, the way I do here, in a manner in which I and the German theologians with me so far did not find Him even in Latin, Greek, or Hebrew.

God grant that this little book may become increasingly known. It will then be confirmed that the German theologians are no doubt the best theologians.

Doctor Martinus Luther
Augustinian at Wittenberg

Chapter 1

St. Paul says that, when that which is perfect comes, then that which is imperfect and partial is done away with. Note now what the perfect and the partial are. The Perfect is a Being who has comprised and embraced in Himself and in His Being all that is. Without this Being and outside of it there is no true being and in it all things have their being since it is the core of all things.*

This ultimate Being is in Himself unchangeable and immovable, yet changes and moves everything else.†

But the incomplete and partial originates from or emerges out of total perfection — just as the sun or a light emits radiance and beams — and becomes manifest in one form or another.

None of these parts is perfect. Thus the Perfect is not identifiable with any of its parts.

Creatures that are partial and imperfect can be comprehended, known, and described in words. But the Creator, the Perfect, cannot be comprehended, known, and described in the same manner by creatures, on account of their creatureliness.

The Perfect must consequently be nameless because it is not any created thing.

The creature as created is incapable of discerning, comprehending, naming, or formulating in thought that which is perfect.

Now, when that which is perfect comes, the imperfect will be rejected.

When does it come, then? I say, when it is known and felt and tasted in the soul to the extent possible.

Now one might ask: Since no creatures can know or apprehend the Perfect and since the soul is creaturely, how then can the Perfect be known in the soul?

Answer: That is why we speak of the soul as creature; that is to say, it is impossible for the creature to know on the basis of its creatureliness, createdness, and I-related-ness. For in whichever creature this perfect life is to be known, creatureliness, createdness, selfishness, must be abandoned and destroyed.

This is what St. Paul's words mean when he writes that when the Perfect comes — that is when it is known in the heart — then that which only exists in part — creatureliness, createdness, selfishness, impulse-ridden desire — will be spurned and considered nought.

As long as one holds to these things and is cemented to them, the Perfect remains unknown.

---

*See 1 Corinthians 13:10.
†The reference is apparently to Acts 17:28. (Hoffman)

Someone might also say: You maintain that there is nothing outside this wholeness, this complete being, or extraneous to it. Yet you also say that something flows out of the Perfect Being; what thus flows out of Him is outside of Him, is it not?

I answer: That is why we say that there is no *true* being outside or without Him. What has flowed out is not true being and has no being except inside the Perfect. It is accidental or a radiance and a beam, which is "being" only in the sense in which a fire, the sun, or a candle light emits radiance.

Chapter 2

The Scriptures, the Truth, and the Faith proclaim that sin is nothing but a turning away on the part of the creature from the unchangeable Good toward the changeable.

This is to say that the creature turns from the Perfect to the imperfect, to separateness, to the partial, and preeminently to itself.

Note that when the creature assumes for itself some good thing, like being, life, knowledge, power — briefly, everything one might term good — as though the creature *were* indeed one of these goods, or as though the Good *belongs* to the creature — in such situations the creature is turning away from God.

Was that not what the devil did? What else did his apostasy and fall consist of but that he assumed for himself that he, too, was something, and that something was his and that something was his own property.

This assumption and his "I" and his "Me" and his "Mine" — that was his apostasy and his fall. And this is still the case.

Chapter 3

What else did Adam do but precisely this thing?

We are used to saying that Adam was lost and fell because he ate that apple.

I say it was because of his presumption and because of his I and his Mine, his Me and the like.

He could have eaten seven apples, yet had this not been connected with his presumption, he would not have fallen.

But he fell at the moment his presumption occurred and that could have happened even if he had not bitten into a single apple.

But listen — I have fallen a hundred times deeper than Adam and strayed a hundred times further. No humans in the world could make amends for or undo Adam's fall and apostasy.

How, then, shall the fall be redeemed? It must be amended like Adam's fall and by the same one who amended Adam's fall, and in the same manner.

By whom or in what manner did this healing take place?

Man could not do it without God and God has not deigned to do it without man. Hence God assumed human nature or humanity. He became humanized and man became divinized. That is the way the amends were made.

My fall must be amended in the same way. I cannot do it without God and God does not command or will it without me. For if it is to happen, God must become humanized in me. This means that God takes unto Himself everything that is in me, from within and from without, so that there is nothing in me that resists God or obstructs His work.

Even if God would take to Himself all humans in the world and become humanized in them and they would become divinized in Him and this did not happen in me, my fall and my apostasy would never be amended. No, it must also occur in me.

In this return and healing I can, may, or shall do nothing from myself but simply let it happen. This means that God alone works and I suffer His work and His will to take place.

When I do not suffer this to occur but let my I and my Me rule, I hinder God from working alone without obstruction.

Hence my fall and my apostasy remain unredeemed. Lo, my presumption brings all this about.

Chapter 5

Not a few argue that man before God should become free from rules, will, love, knowledge, and so on.

However, this cannot mean that there is no knowledge in man or that God does not become known in man or loved in man, or willed, desired, and praised in man. That would be a great deficiency in God's economy. Then man would be just like cattle, yes indeed like a dumb beast.

No, this way of talking — the voiding of rule, will, and so forth — actually means that acknowledging God becomes so clear and perfect that this knowledge is not man's knowledge or any creature's knowledge but the knowledge of the Eternal, which is to say the eternal Word.

And thus man — or the creature — sets out on a new quest, claiming nothing for his own self. The less he assumes on his own behalf the more perfect and whole he becomes.

Will, love, and desire reflect this change. For the less one claims these powers to oneself the more transparent and divine they become and the more one ascribes them to oneself the baser and more contaminated and imperfect they become.

It is therefore best to rid oneself of those grosser contaminations, that is to say, the false claims. To the extent that we do so we begin to have the noblest, clearest knowledge that can ever dwell in man, and also the noblest and purest love and desire. For these powers are then all of God. It is better and nobler that they are of God than of the creature.

That I ascribe some good to myself stems from the illusion that the Good is mine or that I am It. If I had inner knowledge I would indeed know that I am not the Good, that It is not mine, that It does not emanate from me, and so forth. The false assumption would fall off by such knowledge.

It is better that God and things divine be known, loved, and praised even if the worshiper should vainly think that *he* produces the love and the praise — as though God would otherwise remain unpraised, unloved, unhonored, and unknown.

For when the illusion and the ignorance turn into a realization of the Truth, the assumption that the Good comes from us will disappear of its own.

Man will then say, "Look, I poor fool imagined that it was I but, in truth, it is and was God!"

Chapter 7

Remember how it is written that the soul of Christ has two eyes, a right eye and a left eye. In the beginning, when these were created, Christ's soul turned its right eye toward eternity and the Godhead and therefore immovably beheld and participated in divine Being and divine Wholeness. This vision continued unmoved and unhampered by all vicissitudes, travail, agitation, suffering, torment, agony — tribulations surpassing anything ever experienced in a person's outer life.

But at the same time the left eye of Christ's soul, His other spiritual vision, penetrated the world of created beings and there discerned distinctions among us, saw which ones were better and which ones were less good, nobler or less noble. Christ's outward being was structured in accordance with such inner discrimination.

Thus Christ's inner being, its vision through the soul's right eye, always participated in full measure in the divine nature, in complete bliss and joy.

But the outer man, the left eye of His soul, was involved in a full measure of suffering, distress, and travail. Yet this took place in such a way that the inner, right eye remained unmoved, unimpeded, untouched by all the travail, suffering, and torment that the outer man had to deal with.

It has been said that Christ, when bound to the pillar and beaten and when hanging on the cross, experienced all this in His outer man, while the inner man, the soul in its function as the right eye, rested in the same bliss and joy as it did after the Ascension or as it does at this very moment.

By the same token Christ's outer man, the soul in its function as the left eye, was never impeded or weakened in its discharge of external duties. The one does not wait for the other.

Now, the created soul of man also has two eyes. One represents the power to peer into the eternal. The other gazes into time and the created world, enabling us to distinguish between the lofty and the less lofty, as I said above.

But these two eyes, which are parts of man's soul, cannot carry out their functions simultaneously. If the soul is looking into eternity through its right eye, the left eye must cease all its undertakings and act as if it were dead. If the left eye were to concentrate on things of this outer world (that is to say, be absorbed by time and created beings), it would hinder the musing of the right eye.

Chapter 8

People ask: While still in the body could the soul possibly attain some insight into eternity and thereby have a foretaste of eternal life and eternal bliss?

The answer given is generally no. In one sense this is a proper answer. For as long as the soul has its gaze on bodily and temporal things, on created objects, and is consequently filled with images of this varied world, eternal life cannot be grasped.

If the soul is to gaze or look into eternity, it must become chastened and empty of images and detached from all created things and, above all, from the claims of self.

This is the reason some hold that eternity cannot possibly be grasped in a temporal existence.

However, St. Dionysius considers it possible. This conclusion can be drawn from his words to Timothy: "As far as beholding a divine mystery is concerned, you have to be detached from the sensual and from sensuality and all that the senses can grasp and reason may comprehend and know, including both created and uncreated things. Then you rise in a going-out of yourself, unconscious of the sense-bound and the reason-founded and move into union with that which is above all human existence and knowledge."*

Now, if he did not regard such a movement as possible in our temporal existence, why should he have taught it and accordingly given advice to a co-pilgrim on earth?

---

*The reference is to Pseudo-Dionysius, the sixth-century Neoplatonist philosopher who spuriously identified himself as a contemporary of Paul (and thus also of Timothy).

Besides, you should note that a master speaks about this work of Dionysius's to the effect that the experience is indeed possible and that it may well occur so often in a person's life that he becomes accustomed to looking into and seeing eternity whenever he so desires.

And the glance is like no other. It is nobler, dearer to God, and worthier than anything that the creature can do as creature.

Chapter 10

Mark this: Illumined people, living in the true light, perceive that everything they might desire or elect is nothing compared to that which has always been desired or elected by all creatures in the depth of their being.

This realization leads them to let go of all desire and reliance on worldly things, surrendering themselves and all to the eternal Good.

Yet there remains in them a desire to advance toward and to get closer to the eternal Good, by a deeper knowledge, a more burning love, a greater preparedness and more complete surrender, and a fuller obedience — and this in such a manner that each illumined person would say: "Would that I were united with the eternal Good as the hand is part of the body."

The illumined always fear that they are not up to the task. They also wish blessedness for all. But they are not bound to this desire and they do not count it as their achievement. They know full well that their desire does not issue from man but from the eternal Good.

No one should claim for himself, as his own, anything that is good, seeing that it belongs only to the eternal Good.

The illumined ones live in freedom. This means that they are free from fear of pain or hell. They have abandoned hope of reward or heaven. They live in pure surrender and obedience to the eternal Good, in love that frees.

This mind dwelled in Christ most perfectly, and it dwells in His disciples, in some more than in others.

It is sad to think that the eternal Good beckons and calls us to the noblest and that we do not want it.

What is nobler than true spiritual poverty? Yet, when it is held up before us we want no part of it.

We wish to be stroked, as it were; there is in us a strong longing for pleasure and sweetness and enjoyment and in the very experience of it we believe that all is well and that we love God.

Yet, when the illusion is withdrawn, we become sore distressed, forget God, and imagine that all is lost.

This is a great breach and a bad sign.

A true lover of God loves Him or the eternal Good equally well in having or not having, in wealth or in want, in sweetness or in bitterness.

May everyone search himself in this regard.

Chapter 14

One speaks of "the old man" and of "the new man." You should know what that language means.

The old man is Adam, disobedience, self, I, and the like.

But the new man is Christ and obedience.

When one speaks of dying and destroying and things like that, one means that the old man should come to nought. And when and where that happens in a true divine light, the new man is born again.

One also says that man should die to himself, that is to say, man's self and his I must die.

St. Paul speaks of the same thing: Put off the old man with its practices and put on the new man whom God has created and formed.*

He who lives in his selfdom and according to the values of the old man is called — and is — Adam's child.

He may be leading the Adamic life on the fringe or be in the thick of it — he is nevertheless the devil's child and brother.

But he who lives in obedience, the life of the new man, is Christ's brother and God's child.

Lo, where the old man dies and the new one is born again, there the second birth takes place about which Christ says: For unless

---

*The paraphrase may refer to Colossians 3:9–10 or to Ephesians 4:22–24. (Hoffman)

you are born again and thus renewed you will not come into the kingdom of God.*

St. Paul also says: "For as in Adam all die, so also in Christ shall all be made alive."

This says as much: All who follow Adam in disobedience are dead and will never come alive except in Christ, that is to say, in obedience.

For this reason, as long as man is Adam, or his child, he exists without God.

Christ says: "He who is not with me is against me."†

Now, he who is against God is dead before God.

It follows that all the children of Adam are dead before God.

But the one who is with Christ, in obedience, is with God and lives.

I have described sin as a turning away of the creature from the Creator. This accords with what we are saying here. For he who is in disobedience is in sin.

And sin can never be atoned for or healed except through a return to obedience.

For so long as man abides in the state of disobedience, sin is never atoned for or amended, do what he may. Yes, note this: Disobedience itself is sin.

But when disobedience turns into true obedience, everything is amended, and atoned for, and forgiven. There is no other way. Mark this.

If the devil would come to true obedience he would turn into an angel and all his sin and wickedness would be amended and atoned for and all at once forgiven.

And if an angel slipped into disobedience, he would right away become a devil even though he did not add hurt to injury.

Would it be possible for a human to live, as a whole and entirely cleansed being, without attachment to his lower self, in renunciation of the entire objective world, in full true obedience? Could a person in that way be without sin and one with Christ?

By means of grace this human being would thus become what Christ is by means of nature.

*See John 3:3.
†See Matthew 12:30.

One contends this cannot be. In the same vein we are reminded: No one is without sin.*

Be that as it may, it is in any case a fact that the closer one comes to this obedience, the less is the power of sin; and the farther away one is, the stronger is the hold of sin.

In a word, whether man is good, better, or best of all, whether he is bad, worse, or worst of all, sinful or saved before God, all of this hangs on the matter of obedience and disobedience.

Against this background it has been written: The more of self and I, the more sin and wickedness; the less of self and I, the less of sin. It has also been written: The more Mine and I, that is to say I-attachment and selfishness, recede, the more God's I, that is God Himself, increases in me.

If all mankind lived in obedience we would have no pain, no suffering — except of course more bearable bodily suffering of which we should not complain.

If this were the case, all people would be at one, no one would cause his neighbor pain, or suffering. No one would lead his life or do any deed contrary to God. Under those circumstances, from where would pain and suffering come?

But, alas, all humans, the whole world, live in disobedience.

If someone were genuinely and wholly obedient (as we believe that Christ was, else he would not be Christ), all human disobedience around him would be a source of inner, bitter suffering to such a person.

All disobedience is nothing but resistance to God.

Truly, God is not set against any created thing, nor against any works that creatures perform, nor against anything whatever that we can name or think; none of this is contrary to God, it is not displeasing to God. Only one thing is displeasing to God: disobedience and disobedient man.

In short, everything in this earthly life is pleasing to God; He likes it well. Only disobedience and the disobedient please Him not at all. The disobedient person goes wholly against the divine grain and God sorrows much over his disobedience.

The person who experiences in his own suffering and feeling that disobedience is a source of sorrowing for God, and that it is against

---

*A probable reference to 1 John 1:8. (Hoffman)

God, would rather suffer a hundred deaths, vicariously, in order for disobedience to die, even if it were in just one single soul, and for obedience to be born again. I grant you, then, that no one lives totally and purely in this obedience, the way Christ did. It is, however, possible for man to approach and come so close to it that he can be called — and can in fact be — godly and divinized.

And the closer man approaches divine obedience and the more godly and divinized he becomes, the more he will feel the pain over disobedience, sin, and unrighteousness, and the more such waywardness will hurt him and the more keenly he will suffer.

Chapter 17

Let no one believe that he can come to this true Light and this inner knowledge or to the Christ life with the aid of much questioning or secondhand information or by way of reading and studying, or with high skills and academic mastery, or with high natural reasoning.

Moreover, I would say this: As long as a person attaches high regard to something or treats something with preference in his love, opinion, desire, or urge — things of the varied world, that is, his own self or whatever — he will not attain it.

Christ Himself spoke about this. He says: If you want to come to Me, then renounce yourself and follow after Me. And he who does not renounce himself and all and leaves and loses it, he is not worthy of Me, nor may he be My disciple.*

This means: He who does not let go of and relinquish the things of the world can never truly know nor come into My life.

Should this never have been uttered by a human voice, the truth of it speaks nevertheless by its own force, for it is thus in true reality.

But as long as man loves the parts, the fragments, and above all himself, and consorts with them and considers this all-important, he is and will remain so blind as to know nothing about the Good.

For he considers as best and dearest what is most useful, comfortable, and enjoyable to himself and to his own.

*The paraphrased material comes from Matthew 16:24 and Matthew 10:37–38.

Chapter 19

Someone may ask: What is the state of a person who follows the true Light to the best of his ability?

I must tell you frankly that it can never be fully described.

For he who is not on this path is unable to put it in words. And he who is on the path and knows is equally unable to voice it.

Whoever wants to know must wait until he becomes what he knows.

Yet I believe that moral deportment and commands are part of the matter in the following way.

The obligations and rules of this earthly life must be in keeping with and an outflowing of the true Light.

But that which does not represent such a "must" or such an "ought" but rather flows from sheer egotistic desire cannot be in keeping with the true Light.

Man often invents for himself many musts and oughts that are actually false.

When he is driven by his pride, avarice, and other vices and also evils of commission and omission, he declares: "It must be, it ought to be."

When he is driven by the urge for people's approval and friendship, or by his body's desire in this direction or that, he declares: "It must be, it ought to be."

Look, all this is false.

If man had no other must and ought than that which God and the Truth inspire in him, he would often have more truly upbuilding tasks than he has right now.

Chapter 25

Moreover, let us point to the following. When it is said — indeed, Christ Himself says it — that man must forsake and surrender all things, this should not be understood to mean that there is nothing for us to do and to take in hand.*

*See Matthew 19:21.

For man is also meant to be a doer and carry out ordinary tasks as long as he lives. This, however, should not be perceived in such a way that the union with God depends on man's creaturely power, his activity, his repose, and his learning.

What is then this union? Nothing but a truly pure simple repose in the one eternal Will of God. Or — it can also be expressed this way — the union is to be without will so that the created will flows into the eternal Will and ceases to be therein, becomes nought, with the result that the eternal Will alone wills, works, and speaks in us.

Now mark what serves and aids a person toward this end. Neither words, works, rules, nor a single creature's effort, nor the efforts of all created beings can attain the union. Deeds, learning, abilities, activity, cannot attain it. We must let all such designs go, that is to say, we should not entertain the idea that any kind of works, words, rules, wit, or mastery, briefly, any created things at all, can contribute or be of help here.

Rather, one has to let all this go, leave these things for what they are, and proceed into the union with God. But, of course, the outward things are parts of the design; we must live with them in our action and inaction. To be specific: We must sleep and awaken, walk and stand still, talk and keep silent, and many other things that must be as long as we live.

Chapter 30

I will now ask you to think about God from the aspect of the Good. God is Goodness looked upon as Goodness, not this or that particular form of good.

Note this: What exists in a particular spot cannot be in all spots, nor transcend every place where it appeared. What is here today and gone tomorrow does not abide forever, nor does it cover all time. What is particular, a special thing, is not all things, nor does it embrace all things.

You see, if God were a particular thing that we could point to, He would not be all in all and above all — and the latter is of course the case. If He were only in the particular He would not be true Wholeness. Therefore, God is. Yet He is not a special created thing that created beings perceive, name, conceive, or describe in their role as creatures.

So if God-as-Good were a particular good He would not be all Goodness and above all good things. He would not be the One total and perfect Good, which He is.

Now God is also a light and an inner knowing, whose nature is to shed light, to shine and to know, for God is light and knowing; He must emit light and knowing and all this giving and knowing is God, apart from the created world.

It is not there as a manifest activity but as a being or as a beginning. Yet if this being is to express itself as activity, as creative work, this must take place through created beings.

You see, where this inner knowing and this light are at work in a material being, this being recognizes and testifies as to what it is, that it comes from the Good itself, not from this or that particular thing.

Since it is neither this nor that particular thing, its inner knowing and testimony does not spring forth from separate things. Rather, it knows and testifies that there is a true, simple, perfect Good that is not identical with individual good things but is the totality of all good things, that which exceeds separate forms of goodness.

We have said that the Light testifies to the one, simple Good. But what does it say about that one Good?

Mark this: as God is simple goodness, inner knowledge, and light, He is at the same time also one will, love, righteousness, and truth, the innermost of all virtue. Yet, although different, all of these are one being in God and none of the particular goods can ever be realized or practiced in deeds without created beings. For the good in God without creatures is nothing but being and beginning without deeds.

But suppose that the One, who is the All, receives a human being and becomes his strength and brings him to the point of spiritual capability where the One and All can recognize his own in this human life. In that situation will and love, united in the One, are actually proclaimed by Himself in and through the follower, for the One is both light and knowledge. The One, who is the Good, cannot will anything except that which He is.

So, as this person continues on his way, he wills and loves nothing but the good for the sake of the Good, for no other reason but its goodness. He does not will and love because the circumstance is a particular one or because it is good for this or that purpose, pleasure or pain, joy or sorrow, sweetness or bitterness, or similar contrasts. He does not choose to take such questions into consideration, least of all not on behalf of the self or as a self. For in the life now described, all matters of the self and the I and the Me have been surrendered and abandoned. There one does not assert: "I love myself, I love you, I love this or that."

If you were to ask Love, "What do you love?" the answer would be, "I love goodness." "Why?" She replies: 'Because it is good and for the sake of goodness."

It is good, right, and well warranted to love in that sense. If something were better than God it should be loved better than God. Therefore God does not love Himself as Himself but as the Good. If there were something better than God, and God knew thereof, He would love it and not Himself.

Thus the temporal I and the self are totally separated from God. They do not belong to God except as He needs them to reveal personhood.

Now, the descriptions above must become reality in a godly or a truly divinized person, or else he would not be godly or divinized.

Translated by Bengt Hoffman

Jacob Boehme

Jacob Boehme (1575–1624), the shoemaker of Görlitz, was the most influential Protestant mystic of German-speaking Europe. Following a transformative experience of illumination in 1600, he waited twelve years to commit his theosophical vision to writing. The resulting manuscript — *Aurora; or, Day-Dawning* — was secretly copied and circulated by his followers, but it inevitably drew the hostile notice of the local Lutheran minister, who led the campaign to have Boehme branded a dangerous subversive. Though official efforts to silence his "enthusiasm" ultimately failed, Boehme's continual problems with the Silesian authorities, his frail health, and especially his own limited education make the literary output of his later years all the more remarkable. The selections included here, from *Aurora, De Signatura Rerum, Quaestiones Theosophicae,* and *The Way to Christ,* suggest his work's conceptual and formal range, with the third of these in particular illustrating the peculiar alchemical idiom for which he is well known. Eliciting a strong religious resonance far beyond his own time and place (e.g., in the Netherlands and the New World), Boehme's writings also found a warm literary reception among the German Romantics.

From Aurora; or, Day-Dawning

From The Preface of the Author

I compare all of philosophy, astrology and theology, along with their mother, to a precious tree growing in a beautiful pleasure garden.

2. Now the earth in which the tree stands always gives the tree sap, from which the tree receives its vitality; and the tree itself grows from the sap of the earth, and becomes big and spreads out its branches.

3. Now, just as the earth applies its force to the tree, so that it will grow and increase in size; so too does the tree continually apply all its power to its branches, so that it will always produce many good fruits.

5. Now the tree, moreover, has this feature, that the bigger and older it gets, the sweeter the fruit it bears: in its youth it bears few fruits, for that is caused by the rude and wild quality of the soil, and the excessively warm moisture in the tree; and even though it blossoms prettily, its apples most often fall off as they are growing, unless it happens to be standing on a particularly good piece of land.

7. But when the tree gets old, and its branches wither, so that the sap can no longer reach to the top, then many little green shoots appear growing around the trunk, and finally on the roots as well, and they glorify the old tree, just as it too was once a lovely little green shoot and sapling, and has now gotten quite old. For nature or the sap is cut off until the trunk withers completely; then it is chopped down and burned in the fire.

8. Now note what I have alluded to with this parable. The garden of this tree signifies the world. The piece of land, nature; the trunk of the tree, the stars; the branches, the elements; the fruits which grow on the tree signify human beings; the sap in the tree signifies

the clear Godhead. Now human beings were made from nature, the stars and elements: but God the creator rules in everything, just as the sap in the entire tree.

Translated by Karen J. Campbell

From De Signatura Rerum

Chapter 1

How all that is spoken of God without the knowledge of the signature is dumb and without understanding; and that in the mind of man the signature lies very exactly composed according to the essence of all essences.

1. All that is spoken, written, or taught of God without the knowledge of the signature is dumb and void of understanding; for it proceeds only from a historical conjecture, from the mouth of another, wherein the spirit without knowledge is dumb; but if the spirit opens to him the *signature,* then he understands the speech of another; and further, he understands how the spirit has manifested and revealed itself [out of the essence through the principle] in the sound with the voice. For though I see one speak, teach, preach, and write of God, and though I hear and read the same, yet this is not sufficient for me to understand him; but if his sound and spirit out of his signature and similitude enter into my own similitude, and imprint his similitude into mine, then I may understand him really and fundamentally, be it either spoken or written, if he has the hammer that can strike my bell.

2. By this we know that all human properties proceed from one; that they all have but only one root and mother; otherwise one man could not understand another in the sound, for with the sound or speech the form notes and imprints itself into the similitude of another; a like tone or sound catches and moves another, and in the sound the spirit imprints its own similitude, which it has conceived in the essence, and brought to form in the principle.

3. So that in the word may be understood in what the spirit has conceived,* either in good or evil; and with this signature it enters into another man's form, and awakens also in the other such a form in the signature; so that both forms mutually assimilate together in one form, and then there is one comprehension, one will, one spirit, and also one understanding.

4. And then secondly we understand that the signature or form is no spirit, but the receptacle, container, or cabinet of the spirit, wherein it lies; for the signature stands in the essence, and is as a lute that lies still, and is indeed a dumb thing that is neither heard nor understood; but if it be played upon, then its form is understood, in whatever form and tune it stands, and according to whatever pitch it is set. Thus likewise the signature of nature in its form is a dumb essence; it is as a prepared instrument of music, upon which the will's spirit plays; whatever strings it touches, they sound according to their property.

5. In the human mind the signature lies most artificially composed, according to the essence of all essences; and man wants nothing but the wise master that can strike his instrument, which is the true spirit of the high might of eternity; if that be quickened in man, that it stirs and acts in the center of the mind, then it plays on the instrument of the human form, and then the form is uttered† with the sound in the word. As his instrument was set at the time of his incarnation,‡ so it sounds, and so is his knowledge; the inward manifests itself in the sound of the word, for that is the mind's natural knowledge of itself.

6. Man has indeed all the forms of all the three worlds lying in him; for he is a complete image of God, or of the Being of all beings; only the order is placed in him at his incarnation; for there are three

---

*Or, formed itself; or originally put forth itself.
†Proceeds from the mouth.
‡Or conception.

work-masters in him which prepare his form [or signature], viz. the threefold fiat, according to the three worlds; and they are in contest about the form, and the form is figured according to the contest; which of the masters holds the predominant rule, and obtains it in the essence, according to that his instrument is tuned, and the others lie hid, and follow with their sound, as it plainly shows itself.*

7. As soon as man is born into this world, his spirit plays upon his instrument, so that his innate genuine form [or signature] in good or evil is seen by his words and conversation; for as his instrument sounds, accordingly the senses and thoughts proceed from the essence of the mind, and so the external spirit of the will is carried in its behavior, as is to be seen both in men and beasts; thus there is a great difference in the procreation, so that one brother and sister does not as the other.

8. Further we are to know that though one fiat thus keeps the upper hand, and figures the form according to itself, that yet the other two give their sound, if their instrument be but played upon; as it is seen that many a man, and also many a beast, though it is very much inclined either to good or evil, yet is moved either to evil or good by a contrary tune, and often lets its inbred signature [or figure] fall, when the contrary tune is played upon its hidden lute or form: so we see that an evil man is often moved by a good man to repent of and cease from his iniquity, when the good man touches and strikes his hidden instrument with his meek and loving spirit.

9. And thus also it happens to the good man, that when the wicked man strikes his hidden instrument with the spirit of his wrath, that then the form of anger is stirred up also in the good man, and the one is set against the other, so that one might be the cure and healer of the other. For as the vital signature, that is, as the form of life is figured in the time of the fiat at the conception, even so is its natural spirit; for it takes its rise out of the essence of all the three principles, and draws its will from this accordingly.

10. But now the will may be broken; for when one stronger comes, and raises his inward signature with his introduced sound and will's spirit, then its upper dominion loses its power, right, and

*Boehme's conception of a threefold world as the context for (actual and potential) human events assumes the generation of a created world of "spirit" (3), out of the interaction of an original "wrath-fire" principle (1), and the "love-light" principle it posits (2). See Introduction, p. xix.

authority; which we see in the powerful influence of the sun, how by its strength it qualifies a bitter and sour fruit, turning it into a sweetness and pleasantness; in like manner how a good man corrupts among evil company, and also how a good herb cannot sufficiently show its real genuine virtue in a bad soil; for in the good man the hidden evil instrument is awakened, and in the herb a contrary essence is received from the earth; so that often the good is changed into an evil, and the evil into a good.

11. And now observe, as it stands in the power and predominance of the quality, so it is signed and marked externally in its outward form, signature, or figure; man in his speech, will, and behavior, also with the form of the members which he has, and must use to that signature, His inward form is noted in the form of his face;* and thus also is a beast, an herb, and the trees; everything as it is inwardly [in its innate virtue and quality], so it is outwardly signed; and though it happens, that often a thing is changed from evil into good, and from good into evil, yet it has its external character, that the good or evil [that is, the change] may be known.

12. For man is known herein by his daily practice, also by his course and discourse; for the upper instrument, which is most strongly drawn, is always played upon: thus also it is with a beast that is wild, but when it is tamed and brought to another property, it does not easily show its first innate form, unless it be stirred up, and then it breaks forth, and appears above all other forms.

13. So it is likewise with the herbs of the earth; if an herb be transplanted out of a bad soil into a good, then it soon gets a stronger body, and a more pleasant smell and power, and shows the inward essence externally; and there is nothing that is created or born in nature, but it also manifests its internal form externally, for the internal continually labors or works itself forth to manifestation. And we see this in the power and form of this world, how the eternal essence has manifested itself with the external birth in the desire of the similitude, how it has manifested itself in so many forms and shapes, which we see and know in the stars and elements, likewise in the living creatures, and also in the trees and herbs.

14. Therefore the greatest understanding lies in the signature, wherein man (viz. the image of the greatest virtue) may not only

*His look, or physiognomy.

learn to know himself, but therein also he may learn to know the essence of all essences; for by the external form of all creatures, by their instigation, inclination, and desire, also by their sound, voice, and speech which they utter, the hidden spirit is known; for nature has given to everything its language according to its essence and form, for out of the essence the language or sound arises, and the fiat of that essence forms the quality of the essence in the voice or virtue which it sends forth, to the animals in the sound, and to the essentials* in smell, virtue, and form.

15. Everything has its mouth to manifestation; and this is the language of nature, whence everything speaks out of its property, and continually manifests, declares, and sets forth itself for what it is good or profitable; for each thing manifests its mother, which thus gives the essence and the will to the form.

Translator unknown

From Quaestiones Theosophicae

The Third Question

What is God's love and anger? How is He an angry jealous God, seeing that He Himself is unalterable love? How can love and anger be one thing?

ANSWER

1. Though we may here be difficult to be understood by the reader, yet in the Divine power and in calling upon God he may understand all, if real right earnestness be his.

*Plants.

2. The reader is to know that in Yes and No consist all things, be they divine, diabolic, terrestrial, or however they may be named. The One, as the Yes, is pure power and life, and is the truth of God or God Himself. He would in Himself be unknowable, and in Him would be no joy or elevation, nor feeling, without the No. The No is a counterstroke of the Yes or the truth, in order that the truth may be manifest and a something, in which there may be a *contrarium*, in which the eternal love may be moving, feeling, willing, and such as can be loved.

3. And yet it cannot be said that the Yes is separated from the No, and that they are two things side by side with each other. They are only one thing, but they separate themselves into two beginnings or principles, and make two centers, each of which works and wills in itself: as day in relation to night, and night in relation to day, form two centers, and yet are not separated, or separated only in will and desire. For they have two fires in themselves: (1) the day, as opening out the heat, and (2) the night, as shutting in the cold; and yet there is together but one fire, and neither would be manifest or operative without the other. For the cold is the root of the heat, and the heat is the cause of the cold being perceptible. Without these two, which are in continual conflict, all things would be a nothing, and would stand still without movement.

4. The same is to be understood regarding the eternal unity of the Divine power. If the eternal will did not itself emanate from itself and introduce itself into receivability, there would be no form nor distinction, but all powers would be but one power. Neither could there thus be any understanding, for the understanding arises in the differentiation of the manifold, where one property sees, proves, and wills the other.

5. It is likewise the same with joy. But if receivability is to arise, there must be a desire to feel itself, that is, there must be a special will to receivability, which is not identical with nor wills with the one will. For the one will wills only the one good, which itself is; it wills only itself in similarity. But the emanated will wills dissimilarity, in order that it may be distinguished from similarity and be its own something, in order that there may be something which the eternal seeing may see and feel. And from the special individual will arises the No, for it brings itself into ownness, that is, into receptivity of self. It desires to be a something, and does not make itself one with

the unity. For the unity is an emanating Yes, which stands ever thus in the breathing forth of itself, being insentient; for it has nothing in which it can feel itself save in the receptivity of the differing will, as in the No which is a counterstroke of the Yes, in which the Yes is revealed, and in which it has something that it can will.

6. For a one has nothing in itself that it can will, unless it double itself that it may be two; neither can it feel itself in oneness, but in twoness it feels itself.

7. Understand, then, the foundation aright. The separated will has proceeded from the identity of the eternal willing, and has nothing that it can will but itself. But because it is a something as distinguished from the unity (which is as a nothing, and yet is all), it brings itself into a desire for itself, and desires itself and likewise the unity from which it flowed.

8. It desires the unity in order to attain to the felt joy of love, that the unity may be perceptible in it. And it desires itself so as to attain to motion, knowledge, and understanding, in order that there may be a diremption in the unity, that forces may take their rise. And though the power has no ground nor beginning, yet in the receivability distinctions arise, from which distinctions nature springs.

9. This emanated will brings itself into a desire; and the desire is magnetic or intrahent, and the unity is emanant. There is thus a *contrarium*, viz. Yes and No. For the flowing-out has no ground, but the drawing-in makes a ground. The nothing wishes to pass out of itself that it may become manifest, and the something wishes to be in itself that it may be sentient in the nothing, in order that the unity in it may become sentient. Accordingly the out and in would thus be an inequality.

10. And the No is therefore called a No, because it is a desire turned inwards, a shutting-in to negativity. And the Yes is therefore called Yes, because it is an eternal efflux or outgoing and the ground of all beings, that is, truth only. For it has no No before it; but the No first arises in the emanated will of receivability.

11. This emanated desiring will is intrahent, and comprehends itself in itself, and from it come forms and properties.* The first property is Sharpness, from which comes hardness, coldness, dry-

---

*In the following, Boehmean metaphysics meets Boehmean "physics," as the original Yes/No dialectic is developed in relation to seven properties of the natural world.

ness, and darkness. For what is drawn in overshadows itself, and this is the true ground of eternal and temporal darkness. And the hardness and sharpness is the ground of sensibility. The second property is the Movement of attraction, and this is a cause of separation. The third property is true Feeling, as between the hardness and the motion, in which the will feels itself; for it finds itself in a great sharpness, as a great anxiety contrary to the unity, so to speak. The fourth property is Fire, as the flash of brightness. This arises in the conjunction of the great anxious sharpness and the unity. For unity is gentle and still; and the moving hard sharpness is terrible, and is a ground of painfulness.

12. Thus in the conjunction a terror appears; and in this terror [shock] unity is laid hold of, so that it becomes a flash or gleam, an exulting joy. For thus light arises in the midst of the darkness. For the unity becomes a light, and the receptivity of the desiring will in the properties becomes a spirit-fire, which has its source and origin from the sour cold sharpness, in the motion and sensibility in the darkness; and its very nature is a terrible consumingness.

13. And in accordance therewith God is called an angry, jealous God, and a consuming fire; not according to what He is in Himself as independent of all receivability, but in accordance with the eternal principle of fire. And in the darkness is understood the foundation of hell, as an oblivion of the good; which darkness is entirely concealed in the light, like night in the day, as may be read in John 1:5.

14. Thus in the above properties is seen God's anger. The first property of the drawing-in is the No. It does not identify itself with the Yes or the unity, for it makes in itself a darkness, i.e., a losing of the good.

15. Secondly, it makes in itself a sharpness, which is the ground of the eternal dying of the gentleness or the gentle unity. Thirdly, it makes in itself a hardness, which is eternal death or a powerlessness. Fourthly, it makes in itself, in such hardness of death, a continual painful feeling. Fifthly, it makes in itself an anxious source of fire. In these properties God's anger and Hell-fire is understood; and it is called hell or hollowness, because it is a hiddenness or shutting-in. It is likewise called an enmity against God because it is painful, whereas the unity of God is a pure gentleness. And they are opposed to each other, like fire and water; and therefrom fire and water have had their origin in the existence of this world.

16. The fifth property in this kindling of the emanated will is the perceptibility of the unity of God, that is, Love, which in fire becomes mobile and desireful, and makes in the fire (as in pain) another principle, as a great fire of love. For the love is the cause and origin of the light, so that in the fire's essence light arises. It is the power in the light. And thus the unity brings itself into movement and perceptibility, in order that the eternal power may be perceptible, and that there may be a will, desire, and separation in it. Otherwise the unity would be an eternal stillness, and imperceptible.

17. This love and light dwells in the fire, and permeates the fire, so that the fire's essence is transformed into the highest joyfulness, and fierce wrath is no more known, but only a pure love-taste of the Divine perceptibility.

18. For the eternal unity thus superincends itself that it may be a love, and that there may be something which may be loved. For if the love of the unity were not rooted in a fiery burning nature, it would not be operative, and there would be no joy or movement in the unity.

19. Thus in the fire's essence is understood God's wrath, and in the love-perceptibility or perceptible unity is understood the Divine love-fire. These form two centers in one Principle, as two kinds of fire.

20. (1) The wrath-fire in the emanated will of receivability is a principle of the eternal Nature, from which the angels and the souls of men have obtained their ground, and is called *Mysterium magnum*. From this eternal Nature the visible world also sprang and was created, as an objective representation of what is inward.

21. (2) And the center of the love is the Yes as the fire-flaming breath. And it is called God's Word, or the breathing of the unity of God, the foundation of power. And in the efflux of the love-breathing is understood the true Holy Spirit, as the movement or the life of the love. The angelic spirit as well as the soul's spirit is also understood in this efflux, in which God is manifest and dwells.

22. But the ground of souls and angels, in respect of their own nature, is understood in the eternal Nature-fire. For the clear Godhood becomes not creaturely, for it is an eternal unity; but it permeates and pervades nature as a fire heats through iron.

23. And here we understand the possibility of the damnation of angels and souls. If they lose the love-fire, so as to separate them-

selves from the Divine unity and enter into their own desire, then the wrath-fire burns in them, and is their proper life.

24. But if the Divine love-fire burns in their central fire, then their fire-life is a pure joy and gentle pleasing delight, and the fire of God and the fire of Nature subsist in them in a single principle.

25. In this fifth property the Glory and the Majesty of God is revealed as a light of love. Of which the Scripture says (1 Timothy 6:16): God dwelleth in a light that no man can attain; signifying, that no creature was ever born from the central fire of love, for it is the most holy fire and God Himself in His Triad.

26. And from this holy fire has emanated the Yes, as a ray of the perceptible unity. This ray is the precious name Jesus, which had to redeem the poor soul from the fire of wrath; and, in assuming humanity, introduced itself into the soul, into the dissident central wrath-fire of God's anger, and kindled the soul again with the fire of love and united it with God.

27. O ye men, observe this. Understand, then, the right foundation. In God there is no anger, there is pure love alone. But in the foundation, through which the love becomes mobile, is the fire of anger, though in God it is only a cause of joy and of power. On the other hand, in the center of the wrath-fire it is the greatest and most terrible darkness, pain, and torment.

28. These two are in one another like day and night, where neither can take hold upon the other, but one dwells in the other. And they make two principles, as two eternal beginnings.

29. The first beginning is called the kingdom of God in love. And the other beginning is called the kingdom of God's wrath, or the foundation of hell, wherein dwell the expelled spirits.

30. The foundation of the kingdom of God is pure Yes, as powers of the separable Word. And the foundation of the wrath of God is pure No, whence lies have their origin. Therefore Christ said that the devil was a father of lies; for his foundation is pure No, and opposition to the truth as the Yes.

31. The sixth property in the emanated will is Sound, tone, understanding, speech, or distinction, that is, the true understanding; and it has its subsistence in the two central fires at once. In the center of self-receptiveness of the natural fire, without co-operation of the holy fire (in so far as these two fires are separated, as is to be understood in the case of the devils and damned souls), there is

no understanding, but only subtlety or acuteness, as a putting to the proof the foundation of nature; a vain abuse of the forces of nature, whence spring imposture, distrustfulness, folly, and frivolousness.

32. In this sixth property stand the holy names, that is, the Divine powers in the opening of the Unity, in the working and willing. And they stand in the two fires at the same time, viz. in the fire of natural motion and in the fire of the flame of love.

33. And here we have the wonder-working Word in its operation. For the great name of God *TETRAGRAMMATON* (JeHoVaH) is here the center of the wonders of God, and it works in both the central fires. This name the evil spirits, in their transmutation according to the center of the fire's nature, misuse.

34. And the ground of all cabala and magic is contained in this principle, these being the active powers whereby the imperceptible co-works in the perceptible. And here the law of Moses forbids misusing this principle on pain of eternal punishment, as may be seen in the ten commandments. For our fellow-scholars enough has been said, and for the godless a strong bar lies before it.

35. The seventh property of the emanated desireful will is Essential being, where all the powers are contained and are operative in the being, as a basis of all the powers. From this the visible world has arisen, and by the motion of the wonder-working Name has flowed out, and gone into separation and form.

36. Hence in all the beings of this world there are the two central fires, according to God's love and wrath, as may be seen in the creatures.

37. But the holy fire lies hidden. The curse, or the motion of God's wrath, keeps it shut up in sin. As is to be understood by the tincture*; and yet with God's permission there is a possible entrance.

38. This emanated holy fire, when it was yet operative throughout the earth, was Paradise. And it is Paradise still, but man has been expelled from it. And many a one meets his death with seeking in connection with this fire, and yet finds it not unless he has first found it in himself.

39. In this question regarding God's love and anger, two kinds of fire are to be understood. First, a love-fire, where there is light only; and this is called God's love or the perceptible unity. And sec-

---

*See the discussion of "esoteric alchemy," Introduction, p. xviii.

ondly, a wrath-fire derived from the receivability of the emanated will, through which the fire of love becomes manifest. This wrath-fire is a principle of the eternal Nature, and in the center of its inwardness is called an eternal darkness and pain. And yet the two fires form but a single principle, and have been from eternity to eternity, and are unchanging. But they separate into two eternal beginnings, as may be considered of in fire and light.

Translated by John Rolleston Earle

From The Way to Christ

From The First Treatise on True Repentance

How a man must arouse himself in his will and mind, and what his consideration and earnest resolution are to be when he wishes powerfully to repent, and with what kind of a mind he is to come before God when he wishes to request and receive from Him forgiveness of sins.

Together with short formulas for prayer; how a man's soul is to awake itself in the grace of God, and to grasp and hold the same.

Preface of the Author to the God-loving Reader

St. Paul says: Whatever you do, do in the name of the Lord and thank God and the Father in Christ Jesus (Colossians 3:17).

God-loving reader, if you wish to use this little book correctly, and are in earnest, you will truly know its value. However, I wish to warn you if you are not in earnest, leave untouched the precious names of God (in which the highest holiness is named, made known and mightily desired), so that they do not ignite the wrath of God in your soul, for one is not to misuse God's holy Names. This little book belongs only to those who wish eagerly to repent, and who have a desire to begin. They will experience both the words that are in it and the source that gave rise to them. With this receive the eternal goodness and mercy of God.

1. When a man wishes to proceed to repentance, and turn himself to God with his prayers, he is to examine his mind before any prayer, [considering] how it is completely and wholly turned from God; how it has become faithless to God; how it is ordered only in the temporal, fragile, earthly life and directs no correct love to God or to its neighbor; and how it thus lusts and seethes against God's law and seeks only itself in temporal, perishable, fleshly lust.

2. Secondly, he is to consider how all this is an enmity against God that Satan, by his deceit, awoke in our first parents, for which abomination we must die and perish in our bodies.

3. Thirdly, he is to consider the three abominable chains by which our souls are bound fast to the time of this earthly life. The first is God's stern wrath, the abyss and dark world that is the *centrum* and creaturely life of the soul. The second chain is the devil's desire against the soul by which he continually sifts the soul, tempts [it], and constantly wishes to drag it away from God's truth into vanity, as into pride, covetousness, envy, and wrath, and to kindle and continually increase these same evil characteristics by his desire in the soul. Through this the soul's will is turned from God and enters into self. The third and most abominable chain by which the poor soul is bound is the corrupted, and completely vain, earthly, mortal flesh and blood, full of evil desires and inclinations. Here a man is to consider how, with body and soul, he lies captive in the slime of sin, in God's wrath, in the jaws of hell's abyss; how God's wrath burns in him, in soul and body; and how he is a stinking swineherd who has wasted and used up his father's inheritance, God's love and mercy, in earthly pleasure with the devil's fatted pigs; and [how he] has not perceived the precious covenant and reconciliation of the innocent suffering and death of Jesus Christ, which God, out

of pure grace, placed in our humanity, reconciling us in Him; also how he has so completely forgotten the covenant of holy baptism (in which he promised his Savior faith and loyalty), and that, [living] so completely in sin, he has defiled and darkened the righteousness (which God gave him by grace in Christ), so that he now stands in God's presence with the beautiful cloak of the innocence of Christ that he has soiled, as a dirty, tattered and ragged swineherd who has continually eaten the husks of vanity with the devil's pigs, and is not worthy to be called a son of the Father and a member of Christ.

4. Fourthly, he is to consider earnestly that angry death waits for him every hour and moment, and wishes to seize him in this swineherd's cloak, in his sins and abominations, and cast him into the hellish abyss as a perjurer and faith-breaker, to be held in the dark death chamber for God's judgment.

5. Fifthly, he is to consider the earnest and stern judgment of God when he, with his abominations, will be set alive before the judgment; and that before the eyes of Christ and before all holy angels and men, all those whom he has wronged by word or work and caused to do evil so that they sinned by his instigation will come before him and curse him; and how he will stand there in great shame and scorn, as well as in great fright and eternal despair; and how this will make him eternally regret that for so short a time of pleasure he lost such great eternal happiness, and that he did not better perceive that he might be among the community of the saints, and enjoy eternal light and divine power.

6. Sixthly, he is to consider how the godless man loses his noble image (how that God made him to His image) and becomes a formless specter, like a hellish worm or abominable beast since he is then an enemy of God, against heaven and all holy angels and men; and how his community is eternally in horrid darkness among devils and hellish worms.

7. In the seventh place, he is to consider earnestly the eternal punishment and pain of the damned, how in eternal horror they suffer pain in their self-created abominations and do not see the land of the saints in eternity nor receive any revival, as is to be seen with the rich man (Luke 16:22). A man is to consider this earnestly, and think how God created him in such a beautiful and majestic image, in His likeness, in which He Himself wished to dwell; and that He created him to His praise, to His own eternal joy and majesty; that

he might dwell with the holy angels, with God's children, in great joy, power and majesty, in eternal light, in the song and sound of the harmony of the angelic and divine kingdom of joy; that he ought eternally to have enjoyment with the children of God without fear of any end, where no evil thought can disturb him, neither suffering nor grief, neither heat nor cold, where night is unknown, where neither day nor time are any longer, but eternal bliss, where soul and body tremble in joy and rejoice in infinite wonder and power, in beauty of color, in the adornment of the infinite birth, in the wisdom of God on the new crystalline earth that is as transparent glass. And [he is to consider] how he thus wantonly forfeits this for so brief and vile a time, which, in this vanity, in the evil life of the lustful flesh, is full of sorrow, fear, and restlessness, of vain misery; and [how] the godless fare as the pious; how one must die even as the other [does], but [how] the saints' death is an entrance into eternal rest, and the death of the godless man is an entrance into eternal restlessness.

8. Eighthly, he is to consider the course of this world, how every-thing is a plaything by which he spends his time in restlessness; that it happens to the rich and powerful as to the poor; that we all live and move among the four elements; and that the poor man's bite tastes as good in his weariness as the rich man's in his cares; that we all live in one breath, and that the rich man has nothing for his advantage but a connoisseur's palate and a lustful eye. Otherwise everything is for the one as it is the other. Because of this lustful eye man has lost so great a blessedness and leads himself because of this into such great eternal restlessness.

9. In such consideration a man will feel in his heart and mind — especially if he continually pictures his end — that he will have a deep longing to gain God's mercy and [he] will begin to feel sorry for his past sins, and that he has spent his days so evilly and neither perceived nor considered how he stands here in this world, in a field, as a plant [bearing] fruit either in the love of God or in wrath. He will first begin to realize that he has not yet begun to work in Christ's vineyard, and that he is a dry branch on the vine of Christ. In many [a man] whom Christ's spirit stirs to such consideration there mounts up great sorrow and heartache, complaint against oneself, over these days of evil that he has so spent and lost through vanity without effect in Christ's vineyard.

10. He whom Christ's spirit leads to sorrow will have his heart opened so that he can know his sin and be sorry for it. It will be easy to advise him. He need only take the promises of Christ that God does not wish the death of the poor sinner (Ezekiel 33:11) but calls all to come to Him (Matthew 11:28), and that there is great joy in heaven over one sinner who repents (Luke 15:7). Let him only seize Christ's words and wrap himself in Christ's suffering and death.

11. But I wish to speak to those who feel in themselves a desire for repentance but cannot in any way come to knowledge nor to correct true sorrow for past sins, since the flesh always says to the soul, "Now listen, tomorrow is good enough," and then, when tomorrow comes, the flesh says again, "Tomorrow." Since the poor soul groans and stands in weakness, and receives neither true sorrow for past sins nor any comfort, I say to it: "I shall describe a way in which I myself have gone, which he is to do, and what happened to me." If he desires to follow it, he will experience what is hereafter described.

Way of Repentance

12. When through the aforementioned consideration, a man finds within himself a hunger, so that he would eagerly repent, but finds in himself no proper sorrow for his past sins, and yet a hunger for sorrow (as the poor, captured soul ever groans, fears itself, and acknowledges itself as guilty of sins before God's judgment), he can do no better than to gather sense, mind, and all reason together into one and in that hour commence his first consideration; when he feels a desire to repent he is to make a powerful resolution, that in this hour, in this minute, he will enter into repentance, and leave his godless way, give no attention to any worldly power and honor and, if it must be, leave all for true repentance and esteem nothing.

13. And [he] is to make such a firm and stern resolution for himself that he will never again leave [repentance], even if the whole world considers him a fool; and that he will wish to lead his mind obediently away from the beauties and pleasures of this world into the sufferings and death of Christ, under His cross, and order his whole hope to the coming life and enter into Christ's vineyard, in

righteousness and truth to do God's will, and begin and complete all his work in this world in Christ's spirit and will. For the sake of Christ's word and promise by which He promised us heavenly reward, he should eagerly suffer and bear all misfortune and suffering, so that he may be counted among the community of Christ's children, and so that he may be incorporated and united into His humanity by the blood of the lamb of Jesus Christ.

14. He is strongly to consider, and completely wrap his soul [in the idea] that he has made the resolution to gain the love of God in Christ Jesus, and that according to His true promise God will give him the noble pledge of the Holy Spirit as a beginning so that in himself he might be reborn in Christ's humanity, according to the heavenly divine being, and that the spirit of Christ might renew his mind in His love and power, and strengthen his weak faith so that in his soul's desire that continually hungers and thirsts, he might receive the body and blood of Jesus Christ as meat and drink (John 6:55) and in the soul's thirst drink from the sweet fountain, Jesus Christ, the water of eternal life according to Christ's promise and truly firm pledge (John 4:10).

15. He is to consider fully the great love of God, that God does not wish the death of the sinner, but that he be converted and live (Ezekiel 33:11). And he is also to [consider] how Christ, in a friendly manner, calls poor sinners to Himself, since He desires to revive them (Matthew 11:28); and that God sent His son into the world to seek and to make holy that which was lost, the poor, repentant, converted sinner; and how, for the sake of the poor sinner, He gave His life unto death, and for him died in our humanity, taken on [for us].

16. He is to consider strongly also that God in Christ Jesus will more readily hear [him] and receive him into grace than he himself wants to come to Him; and that in the love of Christ, in the very precious Name *Jesus,* God can desire no evil, that there is no glimpse of wrath in this Name, but that He is the highest and deepest love and faithfulness, the great sweetness of the Godhead in the great Name *Jehovah* that He revealed to our dead and corrupted humanity in its heavenly part, which disappeared through sin in Paradise; that [God] therefore was moved in His heart so that He would pour His sweet love into us so that the Father's wrath, which was enflamed in us, might be put out and changed into love. All of this occurred

for the sake of the poor sinner so that he might again gain the open gate of grace.

17. In such a consideration he should firmly imagine that at this hour and moment he stands in the presence of the Holy Trinity, and that God is truly present in him and outside of him, as the Holy Scripture says, Am I not He who fills all things? (Jeremiah 23:23–24). (Again: The word is near you, even in your mouth and in your heart [Romans 10:8].) Again: We will come to you, and make our home in you (John 14:23). Again: I am with you always, until the end of the world (Matthew 28:20). Again: The kingdom of God is within you (Luke 17:21).

18. Thus, he is to know and believe for certain that he stands, with his soul, before the face of Jesus Christ, before the holy God-head, and that his soul has turned from God's face; and that he now, this hour, wishes to turn his soul's eyes and desire to God, and, with the poor, prodigal, and returning son [desires to] come to the Father. With downcast eyes of soul and spirit, in fear and deepest humility, he is to begin to confess his sin and unworthiness as follows.

A Short Form of Confession before the Eyes of God

Each one may change and enlarge this form of confession according to his situation, as the Holy Spirit teaches. I desire to set down only a short guide.

19. O great, unsearchable, holy God, Lord of all being, who in Christ Jesus, out of pure love for us, revealed Your holy being in our humanity, I, a poor, unworthy, sinful man, come before Your revealed face, in the humanity of Jesus Christ, even though I am unworthy to raise my eyes to You, and [I] implore You, and confess to You that I have been faithless and disloyal to Your great love and grace that You have given us. I have forsaken the covenant that You, out of pure grace, made with me in baptism, in which You took me as a child and heir of eternal life. [I] have led my desire into the vanity of this world, and defiled my soul thereby, and made it completely bestial and earthly, so that, because of the mire of the sin, my soul does not know itself, and sees itself wholly as a strange child before Your sight, unworthy to desire Your grace. I lie as deep

as my soul's lips in the mire of sin and in the vanity of my corrupted flesh, and have only a small spark of breath in me that seeks Your grace. In vanity I have thus become dead to myself so that, in this vanity, I dare not raise my eyes to You.

O God in Christ Jesus, who for the sake of poor sinners became man so that You could help them, to You I cry; I still have a spark of refuge for You in my soul. I have not regarded Your purchased inheritance that through Your bitter death You purchased for us, and I have shared the inheritance of vanity in Your Father's wrath, in the curse of the earth, and am trapped by sin and half dead to Your kingdom. I lie in weakness before Your power, and angry death waits for me. The devil has poisoned me so that I do not recognize my Savior. I have become a wild shoot in Your tree and have devoured my inheritance from You with the devil's pigs. What shall I say before You, I who am not worthy of Your grace? I lie in the sleep of death that has trapped me, and I am bound fast with three strong chains. O help me, You Breaker of death. I can and am able to do nothing. I have become dead to myself and have no power before You, and dare not lift my eyes to You because of my great shame. I am a defiled swineherd and have spent my inheritance with the false adulterous whore of vanity, wasting it in the lusts of the flesh. In my own lust I have sought myself and not You. Now I have become a fool in myself and am naked and bare; my shame stands before my eyes; I cannot hide it. Your judgment waits for me. What am I to say to You, You who are the judge of the world? I have nothing more that I can bring to You. Here I stand before You naked and bare, and fall down before Your face, and complain to You of my misery, and cry for Your great mercy. Although I am not worthy, take me into Your death and let me die Your death in my death. Strike down my assumed "I" and destroy by Your death my "I," so that I no longer live, since in myself I only sin. Kill the evil beast full of false cunning and self-desire, and redeem the poor soul from its heavy bondage.

O merciful God, it is because of Your love and patience that I am not already lying in hell. I give myself up with my whole will, thought, and mind to Your grace, and ask for Your mercy. By your death I call out of the small spark of my life surrounded by death and hell, which open their jaws to me, and seek to swallow me up in death. You have promised You will not put out the glimmering wick. I have no other road by which to come to You than [by] Your suffering and death, because You have made our death life by means of Your humanity and have broken the chains of death. Therefore I sink my soul's desire into Your death, into the broken gates of Your death.

O great Fountain of the love of God, let me die to my vanity and sin in the death of my Redeemer Jesus Christ.

O Breath of the great love of God, revive my weak breath in me so that it may begin to hunger and thirst after You. O Jesus, sweet power, in Your fountains of grace give my soul to drink the sweet water of eternal life so that it may wake from death and thirst after You. O how it has become completely exhausted in Your power. O merciful God, convert me; I cannot. O Conqueror of death, help me to strive since the enemy holds me with his three chains and will not let my soul's desire come before You. Come, and take my soul's desire into You. Be my pull to the Father, and redeem me from the devil's bonds. Do not look upon my deformity, that I stand naked before You, and have lost my cloak. Clothe my breath that lives in me and desires Your grace and let me once again see Your salvation.

O deepest Love of all, take my soul's desire into You, and, by Your death, lead it into You out of death's bonds through Your death into Your resurrection. Revive me in Your power so that my desire and will begin to grow anew. O Conqueror of death and God's wrath, conquer my "I" in me. Break its will, and crush my soul so that it is in fear before You, continually falling on the ground before You, and make it ashamed of its own will before Your judgment so that it may become an instrument obedient to You. Bend it in death's bonds; remove its power so that it wills nothing without You.

O God, Holy Spirit, my Savior in Christ, teach me what I ought to do so that I might turn to You. Redirect my will in me to You. Draw me, in Christ, to the Father, and help me so that from now on I might leave sin and vanity and nevermore enter into them. Awake true sorrow for past sins in me. Keep me in Your bonds, and do not let me loose from You so that the devil may not lead me again into the death of deaths. Enlighten my spirit so that I may see the divine way, and continually walk in it. Take me from myself and give me completely to Yourself alone. Do not let me begin, will, think nor do anything without You. O how long, Lord, will I not be worthy of what I desire of You? Let my soul's desire dwell merely in the doorways of Your outer room. Make it a servant to Your servants. Preserve it from the horrible pit in which there is no solace or refreshment.

O God in Christ Jesus, I am blind to myself. I do not know myself because of vanity. In my blindness You are hidden from me, You who are yet close by me. Yet Your anger that my own desire has ignited has made me dark. Take the breath of my soul's desire to Yourself. Test it, Lord, and shatter it, so that my soul may reach Your beam of sweet grace.

I lie before You as a dead man whose life, like a small spark, hovers at his lips. Ignite it, Lord. Direct my soul's breath to You. Lord, I wait on Your promise, for You have said, As I truly live, I have no desire in the death of the sinner, but that he turn and live (Ezekiel 33:11). I sink myself into the death of my Savior Jesus Christ, and wait on You, Your word is truth and life. Amen.

20. In this, or a similar manner, as each one feels in his conscience what sins he led his soul into, may he confess. Although [I say], if his resolution is truly earnest, he needs no formula, for the spirit of God who is soon in the will of the mind will make [one] for Himself, for it is He Himself who in true earnest desire works repentance and represents the soul before God through the death of Christ.

21. But I do not wish to hide from the dear reader, who stands in Christian resolution, how it usually goes with those who have such a firm resolution. Indeed, [it is] different with one than with another, according to how earnest and great his resolution is. For the spirit of God is not bound and it customarily uses many methods as He knows each [person] individually. It is just the same as when one who has been in battle can give an account of it and how it went with him [even though each account will be different].

22. If it so happens that such a heart comes thus before God with serious resolution and enters into repentance, it might go with it as with the Canaanite woman (Mark 7:24–30). If God does not listen, the heart remains without comfort. [A man's] sins and unworthiness still present themselves before his eyes as if he were worthless. His mind is as if dumb. The soul groans in the depths. The heart receives nothing, neither can it pour out its confession before God almost as if the heart and soul were locked up. The soul is eager, but the flesh holds it in captivity. The devil covers everything completely over and shows it again the road of vanity, and tickles it with fleshly lust, and

says in the mind, "Wait. First do this and that. Gather some money for yourself so that you do not need the world. Then live a pious life in penance. There is time enough."

23. O how many hundreds [of people] have perished in such a beginning and have returned once again into vanity. They are like little twigs broken off by the wind or parched by the heat.

24. Listen, dear soul. If you wish to be a conqueror of death and hell in your Savior Christ, and wish that your young shoot might be and grow as a tree in the kingdom of Christ, you must stand firm in your first earnest resolution, even if it costs you your first parental inheritance, as well as your body and soul. Either [be] an angel in God or a devil in Hell. If you want to be crowned, you must strive. You must gain victory in Christ, and not lie under the devil. Your resolution must remain firm. You must not prefer temporal honors and wealth to it.

25. If the spirit of the flesh says, "Wait, it is not yet fitting," the soul must say, "It is now my time and hour to return again to my fatherland out of which my father Adam led me. No creature shall hold me, and you, evil earthly body, you who have swallowed my pearl that God gave my father Adam in Paradise, will be extinguished in Christ's death, the will of your pleasure in vanity will be broken, and I will [enter] again the rose garden of my Redeemer Jesus Christ. As an evil dog you will be bound in the chain of my just resolution and therefore you will be as a fool before all men. Thus you will be obedient to my soul's first resolution. No one will free you from this chain except temporal death. In this may God and His power help me. Amen."

A Short Suggestion

How the poor soul shall come before God again, and how it is to strive for the noble, knightly crown; what kind of armor it must wear if it would strive against God's wrath, also against the devil, the world, and sin, against flesh and blood, against the stars and elements, and against all enemies.

26. Dear soul, for this [undertaking] earnestness is required. There must not simply be a repetition of such words. An earnest, resolute

will must pursue this or it will not be attained, for if the soul wishes to obtain Christ's conqueror's crown from the noble Virgin Sophia, [it] must court Her with great love-desire. It must pray for it to Her in Her holiest of Names and must come before Her in highly chaste humility, not as a lustful bull or wanton Venus. As long as it is such, it ought not to desire such [things], nor will it receive them. And although something may be received during this time, it is only a ray compared to such [things].

27. But a chaste mind may well attain to it, so that the soul in its noble image, which died in Adam, might be alive. [This is to be] understood in the heavenly corporeality, according to the inner ground, so that She sets a victory-crown on [it] which, if done, is again taken away from the soul and as a crown laid aside, as one crowns a king and afterwards the crown is secured. Thus it also happens to the soul since it is still surrounded with the house of sin, so that if it should fall again, its crown would not be dirtied. To the children who have known and experienced this it is said clearly enough. A godless (pig-man) is not worthy to know more about this.

Guide

How the soul ought to meet its dear lover when He knocks in the centrum *in the locked room of the soul.*

32. Dear soul, you must always be in earnest, without relenting. You will obtain the love of a kiss from the noble Sophia in the holy Name *Jesus* for She stands immediately before the soul's door and knocks and warns the sinner of [his] godless ways. If he desires Her love She is willing and kisses him with a beam of Her sweet love, by which the heart receives joy. But She does not immediately enter the marriage bed with the soul, that is, She does not immediately awaken the corrupted heavenly image that was lost in Paradise in it [the soul]. This is dangerous for man; since Adam and Lucifer fell, this may occur again, because man is still firmly bound in vanity.

33. There must be a true covenant in your pledge. If She is to crown you, you must be first tested. She takes Her ray of love beams from you again and sees if you will remain true. She allows you to cry and does not answer with a glimpse of Her love. If She is to

crown you, you must first have been judged: You must taste the sour beer that you have poured into yourself by your abominations. You must first come to the gates of Hell and show your victory in and for Her love in power in the face of the devil's attacks so that She will again look at you.

34. Christ was tempted in the wilderness. If you wish to clothe yourself in Him, you must follow His whole way from His incarnation to His ascension. Even though you cannot nor dare not do this as He did, you must nevertheless enter His way completely, and ever die to the soul's vanity, for in this way the Virgin Sophia weds Herself to the soul only by this characteristic that sprouts in the soul through Christ's death as a new growth that is [rooted] in heaven. The earthly body at this time does not grasp this because it must first die to vanity. But that heavenly image which was corrupted in Adam, the true woman's seed in which God became man and brought His living seed of heavenly being into it [human nature], grasps the noble pearl in the [same] way in which it came to Mary in the fulfillment of the covenant.

35. Therefore watch what you do. When you give your word, keep it. She wishes to crown you more than you want [to be crowned]. But you must stand firm when the tempter comes to you with the world's pleasure, beauty, and glory. The mind must cast these out and say, "I shall be a servant in the vineyard of Christ, not a lord. I am God's servant for all that I have and [I] ought to use it as His word teaches me. My heart grows foolish in the dust and continually ought to be humble."

36. In whatever position you are, humility must be at the top or you will not reach marriage with Her, although true humility is first born in marriage to Her, but the free will of your soul must stand as a knight, for if the devil cannot conquer the soul with vanity, so that it will not bite [at his lure], then he comes along with unworthiness and with all the sins in the book. Then perseverance counts.

37. Christ's merits must be placed first for the creature cannot otherwise conquer the devil. Here it goes badly with many as even their external reason thinks that the person is senseless and possessed by the devil. Thus fiercely the devil defends himself in many because he has a great robber's castle in them, but if he weakens he must leave it. Here the fight begins, for heaven and hell strive with each other.

38. If the soul remains firm here and conquers the devil in all his attacks, and pays no attention to temporal things for the love of the noble Sophia, the precious conqueror's crown will be given to it as a sign of victory. Then the Virgin [Sophia] will come to the soul. She has revealed Herself in the precious Name *Jesus* as Christ the serpent-treader, as the anointed of God. She kisses [the soul] completely inwardly with her sweet love and presses love into its desire as a sign of victory. Here Adam according to his heavenly part is resurrected from the dead in Christ. Of this I cannot write; there is no pen in the world with which to do it for this is the marriage of the lamb when the noble pearl is sown with great triumph, although it is first but small, like a mustard seed, as Christ says (Matthew 17:20).

39. When this marriage has taken place, the soul should see that it has promised the Virgin [Sophia] that the pearl tree will grow and increase. Then the devil will come quickly with his stormy weather with godless men who will scoff, mock, and shout out that it is madness. Then the man must enter Christ's way under the cross. Here for the first time it will be shown by demonstration that he who allows himself to be called a Christian must allow himself to be called a fool and a godless person; indeed his very best friends, who had earlier praised his fleshly lust, now become his enemies and, although they do not know why, they hate him. Therefore Christ covers His bride under the cross so that it may not be known in the world and the devil also does this so that these children of the world are hidden so that more such branches may not grow in the garden that he thinks he owns. This I write for the information of the Christian-minded reader, so that if similar things happen to him he knows what to do.

A Short Formula of Prayer

[to be used] when the noble Sophia kisses the soul with Her love and offers love to it.

42. O holiest and deepest Love of God in Christ Jesus, give me Your pearl, press it into my soul. Take my soul into Your arms.

O sweetest Love, I am unclean before You. Break my impurity by Your death. Lead my soul's hunger and thirst through Your death into Your resurrection, into Your triumph. Strike down my "I" in Your death. Take it captive and lead my hunger into Your hunger.

O highest Love, You have appeared in me. Remain in me. Embrace me in Yourself. Keep me in You so that I cannot bend from You. Fill my hunger with Your love. Feed my soul with heavenly being and give it as drink the blood of my Redeemer Jesus Christ. Let it drink from Your fountain.

O mighty Love, awaken in me my corrupted image that died in my father Adam in the heavenly kingdom through Your word in the woman's seed in Mary. Awake and move it, Lord.

O Life and Power of the Godhead, You have promised us: We will come to you and make our dwelling in you (John 14:23). O sweet Love, I lead my desire into the word of Your promise. You have promised indeed that Your Father will give the Holy Spirit to them who ask for it. Therefore I lead my soul's hunger into Your promise, and take Your word in my hunger. Increase my hunger for You in me, O You sweet Love; in Your power, strengthen me. Make me alive in You so that my spirit may taste Your sweetness. Believe through Your power in me, for without You I can do nothing.

O sweet Love, I pray to You through that love with which You overcame God's wrath and changed it into love and into the divine kingdom. Change also the wrath in my soul through this great love so that I may be obedient to You, and that my soul might love You eternally in it. Change my will into Yours; lead Your obedience into my obedience so that I shall be obedient unto You.

O great Love of Jesus Christ, I cry to You. Lead my soul's hunger into Your wounds from which You poured Your holy blood and extinguished the wrath in the soul. Into Your wounded side, out of which blood and water ran, I lead my hunger, and throw myself completely into it. Be mine and revive me in Your suffering, and do not let me leave You.

O my noble Vine, give sap to Your branch, so that I might sprout and grow with Your power and sap in Your essence. Beget true power in me through Your power.

O sweet Love, You are my light; illuminate my poor soul in its dark prison, in flesh and blood. Lead it continually on the right path. Break the devil's will and lead my body through the course of this world, through death's chamber, into Your death and peace so that on the Last Day it will be resurrected out of Your death into You and live with You eternally. Teach me what I ought to do in You. Be my will, knowledge, and activity and do not let me do anything without You. I give myself fully and completely to You. Amen.

A Prayer for Divine Action, Protection, and Guidance

How the mind in the life tree ought to act with and in God for Christ.

43. In You, O living Source, I lift up my soul's desire, and call with my desire into You through the life of my Savior Jesus Christ.

O You Life and Power of God, awaken Yourself in my soul's hunger. Ignite my soul's hunger with Your love-desire through the thirst of Jesus Christ that he had for us men on the cross, and draw out my weak power through mighty powers into Your Spirit. Be with Your power the working and willing in me. Bloom in me through the power of Jesus Christ so that I may bring forth praise as the proper fruits in Your kingdom and never allow my heart and desire to turn eternally from You.

But since, in this troubled valley, in this external earthly flesh and blood, I swim in vanity and my soul and noble image, [made] according to Your image, is surrounded on all sides by enemies as with the devil's desire against me, with the false desires of vanity in flesh and blood, as well as with the opposition of those godless men who do not know Your name; [since] I swim with my external life among the stars and in elements where my enemies within and without [lie in] wait for me, [including even] temporal death that is the destroyer of this vain life; therefore I fly to You, O holy Power of God, because You have revealed Yourself with love in grace in our humanity through the holy Name *Jesus,* and have given Him as a companion to us. Therefore I do pray to You, let His holy angels, who serve Him, wait on our souls, and place themselves about us and protect us from the fiery arrows of the evil one's desires, which he shoots daily at us by the curse of God's wrath that has been awakened in our earthly flesh. Let Your power hold back the opposition in the beams of the star in which the evil one with his desire enters to poison us in soul and flesh, and to lead us into false desire as well as into sickness and misery. With the holy

Name *Jesus* keep away these beams of wrath from our souls and spirits so that they do not disturb us and let Your holy and good angel be by us so that he drive off these poisonous beams from our bodies.

O great Love and sweet Power, *Jesus,* Fountain-source of divine sweetness, I call to You with my soul's desire from the eternally great Name *Jehovah.* My soul calls in that spirit from which it was breathed into the body, which formed it to the image of God, and in its thirst it desires in itself the sweet fountain-source *Jesus* [who is] from *Jehovah,* as refreshment in its fire-breath of God, which is its own self, so that its fire-breath may rise through the Fountain-source *Jesus* [who is] from *Jehovah,* the sweet love *Jesus* and the holy *Christ,* and may reveal in my corrupted image the heavenly, spiritual corporeality, and become man, so that the poor soul might again receive its dear bride into its arms and might rejoice with her forever.

O Emmanuel, you Marriage of God and man, into Your arms, into Your desire toward us and in us I give myself. I desire You. Wipe out Your Father's wrath with Your love and strengthen my weak image in me so that it may overcome and tame the vanity in flesh and blood, and serve You in holiness and righteousness.

O great, holiest Name and Power of God *Jehovah,* who has moved Yourself in our corrupted heavenly humanity by Your sweetest power *Jesus* in the promised fulfillment of the covenant made with our father Adam in the woman's seed of the Virgin Mary, You have led Your living being in Yourself, Your holy power, in the Virgin Wisdom of God, into our corrupted humanity, and have given us life, victory, and a new birth. I pray to You with all my powers, bring me forth in Your sweet power *Jesus* to a new and holy life. [In this way] I might be revealed in You and You in me, and Your Kingdom in me so that my soul's will and walk might be in heaven.

O great, incomprehensible God, who fills all, be my heaven in which my new birth in Christ Jesus might live. Let my spirit be the stringed instrument, music and joy of the Holy Spirit. Play on me in Your reborn image and lead my harmony into Your divine kingdom of joy, into the great praise of God, into the wonders of Your glory and majesty, into the community of the holy angelic harmony, and establish in me the holy city Zion in which we, as the children of

Christ, shall all live in one city that is Christ in us. I sink myself fully and completely into You. Do in me what You will. Amen.

A Prayer in and against Temptation under the Cross of Christ

In the time when all enemies storm against us, and when we in the spirit of Christ are persecuted, hated, slandered, and reproached as evildoers.

44. I, poor man full of anguish and sorrow, wander again on my pilgrim's path into my lost fatherland, and go through the thorns and thistles of this world again to You, O God my Father. On all sides I am torn by thorns, plagued and despised by enemies. They mock my soul and despise it as an evildoer who has become faithless to them. They despise my way to You and consider it foolish. They think I am senseless because I travel on this thorny way and do not take their hypocritical road with them.

O Lord Jesus Christ, I fly to You under Your cross. Ah dear Emmanuel, take me, and lead me to You through Your own pilgrim's path that You travelled in this world, through Your incarnation and Your wretchedness, through Your [experience of] scorn and mockery, and through Your anguish, suffering, and death. Conform me to Your image. Send Your good angel with me who will show me the way through this horrid, thorny waste of the world. Stand by me in my wretchedness. Comfort me with the comfort [with] which the angel in the garden comforted You when You prayed to the Father and sweated Your bloody sweat. Uphold me in my anguish and persecution, under the scorn of the devil and those false men who do not know You and who will not go on Your way. O great love of God, they do not know Your way and do this out of blindness, by the devil's deception. Have mercy on them and lead them from blindness to light so that they will learn to know themselves, how they lie captured in the devil's mire and slime in a dark valley firmly bound with three chains. O great God, have mercy on Adam and on his children. Redeem them in Christ, the new Adam.

I cry to You, O Christ, man and God, [I] who must wander on the pilgrim's path in this dark valley on all sides mocked, in anguish and held to be a false and godless man. Lord it is Your judgment on me that my sins and inherited vanity may be set up in this pilgrim's way and carried as a sign of the curse in which Your wrath might be lessened, and thus thereby it might take the eternal scorn from me. It is Your love-token, and You lead me by it into the mockery, anguish, suffering, and death of my Savior Jesus Christ so that in my Savior I might thus die to vanity and in His spirit, through the mockery, scorn, and death [which came to Him] my new life might sprout forth.

I pray to You, O Christ, patient Lamb of God, by all the anguish and mockery [toward You], by Your suffering and death, by the contempt of the cross beam when You were scorned in my place, give me patience in my way of the cross and lead me to You like a patient lamb into Your conquest. Let me live with and in You and convert my persecutors who, altogether unknowingly, with their scorn, offer up my vanity and inherited sins before Your wrath. They do not know what they are doing. They think that they are doing evil to me, but they do me good. They do before You what I ought to do. I ought to uncover and acknowledge my shame daily before You and sink myself with it into the death of Your son so that it might die in His death. But, since I am too weary, feeble, and weak, You use them in Your anger so that they might uncover my shame before Your wrath, which Your anger grasps and which sinks them into the death of my Savior.

O merciful God, my vain flesh cannot know how You intend good for me in that You allow my enemies to take my offensiveness from me and offer it to You. My earthly mind thinks that You thus plague me because of my sins and then I am in every way afraid, but Your spirit in my inner, new man tells me that this happens to me because of love, that You intend it as good for me when You let my enemies persecute me, so that it serves me the best, that they do the work in my stead and uncover my sins before You in Your wrath so that it might swallow them and so that they might not follow me into my fatherland. Because they are yet strong and fat they can do it better than I, since I am weak and weary in the will of vanity. You know this, O righteous God.

I pray in You, therefore, O righteous God, since You use them as my servants to do the best for me, although my earthly reason does not really know [that] You wish to bring them also to a knowledge of my way, and to send them also such servants, and to lead them sooner to the light as You have led me, so that they might know You and thank You.

O merciful God in Christ Jesus, I pray to You in my knowledge from out of the depths of the love for us poor men that You have revealed in me, according to [our] hidden human nature, call all those to You who are in You. Move Yourself once more in us in these last troubles, in which Your wrath has been enflamed in us. Withstand Your wrath in us so that it may not swallow us in body and soul.

O Dawn of the day of God, break forth completely. When You have come forth, reveal Your holy city Zion, the new Jerusalem, in us.

O great God, I still slumber and do not see the depth of Your power and might. Awaken me completely in You so that I might be alive in You. Break down the tree of Your wrath in us, and let Your love sprout up within us.

O Lord, I lie before Your face and pray to You: Do not punish us in Your wrath (Psalm 6:2). Are we not Your own purchased possession? Forgive all of us our sins and redeem us from the evil of Your anger and the devil's envy and lead us under Your cross in patience into our Paradise. Amen.

A Little Prayer, or Conversation

In the internal ground of man, between the poor wounded soul and the noble Virgin Sophia, as between the spirit of Christ in the new birth and the soul; how much joy there is in the heaven of the new, regenerated man; how graciously the noble Sophia presents Herself to Her bridegroom the soul when the soul enters repentance; and how the soul acts when the Virgin Sophia is revealed to it.

The gates of the paradisiacal rose garden, no one but the children of Christ who have experienced this may understand.

45. When Christ the cornerstone moves in the corrupted image of man in his deep conversion and repentance, the Virgin Sophia appears in the movement of Christ's spirit in the corrupted image in Her Virginal clothing before the soul. Before Her the soul is

frightened in its impurity so that all its sins are first awakened and before Her they are horrified and trembling. Then judgment comes over the sins of the soul so that it turns back in its unworthiness ashamed by its beautiful lover; it turns into itself and rejects itself as altogether unworthy to receive such a treasure. We who have tasted this heavenly treasure understand this but no one else does. But the noble Sophia draws Herself near to the soul's being and kisses it in a friendly manner and tinctures the dark fire of the soul with Her love beams and penetrates the soul with Her loving kiss. Then the soul leaps in its body for great joy in the power of this virginal love. It triumphs and praises the great God, by virtue of the noble Sophia.

I will now present a short introduction as to what happens when the bride takes the bridegroom to the heart. [It is presented] to the reader who may not yet have arrived at this place for his consideration, if he desires to travel after us and to tread the paths where one plays with Sophia. If this happens, as is described above, the soul rejoices in its body and says:

Soul:

46. O great God, now may my praise, thanks, strength, glory, and honor be to You in Your power and sweetness, because You have redeemed me from the instigator of anguish. O beautiful Love, my heart grasps You. Where have You been so long? I thought I was in hell, in God's anger. O gracious Love, remain with me. Be my joy and revival. Lead me in the right paths. I give myself unto Your love. Ah, before You I am dark. Make me light. O noble Love, give me but Your sweet pearl. Lay it in me.

O great God in Christ Jesus, now do I honor and praise You in Your truth, and in Your great might and majesty because You have forgiven me my sins and have filled me with Your power. I rejoice with You in my life. I praise You in Your castle, which no one can open but Your spirit in Your mercy. My bones rejoice in Your power; my heart plays in Your love. Eternal thanks be to You because You have redeemed me from hell and made death in me to be life. Now I discover Your promised truth, O sweet Love. Let me not bend from You again. Give unto me Your crown of pearls and stay with me. Be my possession so that I may eternally rejoice in You.

Then the Virgin Sophia Speaks to the Soul:

47. My noble bridegroom, my strength and might, be always welcome to me. How have you forgotten me so long that I, in great sorrow, had to stand before your door and knock? Did I not always cry to you, [and] call on you? But you turned your face from me; your ears had left my land. You could not see my light for you walked in the dark valley (Psalm 23:4). I was near to you and continually cried to you, but your sins held you captive in death, so that you did not know me. I came in deep humility to you, and called to you, but you were rich in the might of God's wrath and you could not see my humility. You had taken the devil as a lover, and he had defiled you and built up his robber's castle of vanity within you, and turned you completely from my love and faith, toward his hypocritical false kingdom in which you have done much sin and evil, and broken off your will from my love; you have broken my marriage, and have had a strange love affair, and lost me, your God-given bride, [and caused me] to stand, a crushed being, without the strength of your fire's might. Without your fire's might I have not been able to be happy, for you are my husband; by you my own brightness is revealed. You are able to reveal my hidden miracles in your fire-life, and lead them into majesty. Apart from me you are a dark house in which is only anguish and pain and an enemy's torment.

O noble bridegroom, keep your face before me and give me your fire-beams. Lead your desire into me, and ignite me. By my meekness, I shall then change your fire-beams into a white-light, and direct my love through your fire-beams into your fire's essence and I shall kiss you eternally.

O my bridegroom, how good it is for me in your marriage. Kiss me, then, with your desire in your strength and might. Then will I show you all my beauty and bring you joy in your fire-life and sweet love and bright light. All holy angels rejoice with us now that they see us married once more. Now, my dear beloved, remain faithful to me. Do not again turn your face from me. Work your miracles in my love, for which God awakened you.

The Soul Speaks Further to Its Noble Sophia
As to Itself in Its Own Regenerate Love-play:

48. Ah, my noble Pearl and Flame of my light opened in my anguished fire-life, how You changed me into Your joy. O beautiful Love, I broke my faith with You in my father Adam, and, by the fire's might I have changed myself into the pleasure and vanity of the external world. I took a foreign lover and I would have had to walk in a dark valley in a foreign love if You had not remained in great faith and come into the house of my misery through Your penetration and destruction of the wrath of God, hell and dark death, and had [not] brought Your meekness and love to my fire-life again.

O sweet Love, You have brought the waters of eternal life from out of God's fountain, and revived me in my great thirst. In You I see God's mercy that earlier my foreign love had hidden. In You I can be joyful. You changed my fire-anguish into great joy. Ah gracious Love, give me Your pearl so that I may remain in such joy forever.

Thereupon the Noble Sophia Replies
to the Soul Again and Says:

49. My dear lover and great treasure, your beginning gives me the greatest joy. Through the deep gates of God, through God's wrath, through hell and death I have broken into the house of your misery, and I have given you my love out of grace, and released you from the chains and bonds by which you were bound fast. I have kept my faith with you, but you beg me now for a serious thing, which I do not eagerly wish to risk with you. You want to own my pearl as your possession. My dear bridegroom, think how you previously lost it in Adam! Because of this you still stand in great danger, and wander in two dangerous kingdoms: In your fire-source you wander in that land where God calls Himself a strong jealous God and a consuming fire; in the other kingdom you wander in the external world in lust, in the vain and corrupted flesh and blood, where the world's pleasures with the assaults of the devil rush over you every hour. In your great joy you might bring earthiness again into my beauty and darken my

pearl for me. Moreover, you might also become proud like Lucifer when he had the pearl as his possession, and you might turn away from God's harmony. Then I would be robbed eternally of my lover.

I shall keep my pearl to myself and shall dwell in your corrupted humanity now again made alive in me in the heaven within you and preserve my pearl for Paradise, until you lay aside your earthiness. Then I will give it to you as a possession. But I will eagerly give you my presence and the sweet beams of the pearl, during the time of this earthly life. I shall dwell with the pearl in the inner choir, and be your faithful, dear bride. I do not marry your earthly flesh for I am a Queen of heaven and my kingdom is not of this world (John 18:36). Yet I shall not cast aside your outward life, but I shall often visit it with my love-beam, for your external humanity shall return. But I do not wish the vain beast of vanity. God in His intention did not create it so uncouth and earthly, but your desire grasped this bestial grossness in Adam through lust out of all the essence of awakened vanity, [and of] earthly characteristics, in which heat and cold, pain, enmity, and destruction stand.

Now my dear beloved bridegroom, give yourself to me in my will. I shall not abandon you in this earthly life in your danger. Even if God's wrath should soon come over you so that you are afraid and think that I have left you, I shall be with you and defend you because you do not know what your office is. You must work and beget in this time. You are a root of this tree from which branches are born, which must all be born in anguish. I press through your branches into the sap and bear fruit on your boughs, and you do not know it. The Highest One has ordered me to dwell with and in you.

Therefore, cover yourself in patience, and guard yourself from the pleasures of the flesh. Break their will and desire. Keep them in the reins like an evil horse, and I shall often visit you in your fiery essence, and give you my love-kiss, and crown you with a crown from Paradise as a sign of my love, with which you will have joy. But my pearl I will not give you at this time as your own. You must remain in resignation and hear what the Lord plays in your harmony. Moreover, you must give Him the sound and essence of your tone by my power, for now you are a messenger of His mouth, to make known His fame and honor. For this reason, I have bound myself to you again and crowned you with my warrior's victory crown that I obtained in the battle against the devil and death. But the pearl-crown with which I have crowned you I have now laid aside for you. You will not wear it anymore until you are pure before me.

The Soul Speaks Further to the Noble Sophia:

50. My beautiful and sweet Spouse, what ought I to say before You? Only let me be committed to You, for I cannot protect myself. If You do not wish to give me the pearl now, then let Your will be done. Give me however Your love-beams and lead me through this pilgrim's path. Awake and bring forth within me whatever You will do through me. I had wasted Your sweet love, and not kept my faith with You by which I fell into eternal punishment. Yet since You came to me out of love in my hellish anguish, and redeemed me from pain and took me again as a bridegroom, I shall now break my will for Your love and be obedient to You and wait for Your love. I now have enough, since I know that You are with me in all my need, and You do not abandon me. O gracious Love, I turn my fiery face to You. O beautiful crown, take me immediately into You and lead me out of my restlessness. I wish to be with You eternally and nevermore depart from You.

The Noble Sophia Answers the Soul Comfortingly, and Says:

51. My noble bridegroom, be comforted. I have engaged myself to you in my highest love, and in my faith [have I] bound myself to you. I shall be with you in all the days to the end of the world. I shall come to you and make my dwelling in you in your internal choir. You will drink from my fountain, for I am now yours and you are mine, and the enemy shall no longer separate us. Work in your fiery characteristic [and] I shall give my love-beams in your activities. We wish to build Christ's vineyard. You give the essence of fire; I shall give the essence of light and growth. You be fire; I shall be water. We shall bring about in this world what God has foreordained for us [to do]; we shall serve Him in His temple which we ourselves are. Amen.

To the Reader

52. Dear reader, do not treat this as an uncertain story. This is the true ground and contains the whole Holy Scripture, for in this book is the life of Jesus Christ clearly depicted, even as it is known by the author himself, for this was his way. He gives you the best that he has. May God give the increase. There is known to be a heavy judgment on the one who scorns this. Let him be warned.

Translated by Peter Erb

Angelus Silesius
(Johannes Scheffler)

Johannes Scheffler, known to posterity as Angelus Silesius, was born into a Lutheran family of means in Breslau, Silesia (now Wroclaw, Poland) in 1624, and died there in 1677. He distinguished himself early through his literary efforts, but decided on a career in medicine, going abroad to study in Strasbourg, Leiden, and Padua. While in Leiden he was exposed to the ideas of Jacob Boehme there being disseminated by his Silesian countrymen; while in Padua, he was immersed in a new and wholly Catholic environment. Once established as a court physician back in his homeland, Scheffler aroused the ire of the Lutheran establishment because of the mystical bent of his planned literary projects. Finding Roman Catholicism more sympathetic to his goals, he converted to it in 1653, taking the name Angelus Silesius at that time. In 1661 he was ordained a priest. His two major literary achievements were *The Holy Joy of the Soul* (1657) and *The Cherubinic Wanderer* (second and enlarged edition, 1675), the text excerpted here. A collection of pithy, often paradoxical epigrams, this celebrated work epitomizes German Baroque mysticism at its most form-conscious and elegant.

From The Cherubinic Wanderer

From Book One

Purity of Spirit will Endure

Pure as the finest gold, hard as the granite stone,
Wholly as crystal clear your spirit must become. (1)*

One Must Go beyond God

Where is my dwelling place? Where I can never stand.
Where is my final goal, toward which I should ascend?
It is beyond all place. What should my quest then be?
I must, transcending God, into a desert flee. (7)

God in Me and I in Him

God is the fire in me and I in Him the shine;
Are we not with each other most inwardly entwined? (11)

Love Forces God

If it was not God's wish to raise me above God
I should compel him thus, by force of sheerest love. (16)

The Spiritual Virgin

The Virgin I must be and bring God forth from me,
Should ever I be granted divine felicity. (23)

To Be Nothing and Want Nothing

O Man, as long as you exist, know, have, and cherish,
You have not been delivered, believe me, of your burden. (24)

*Numbers given in parentheses are those of the original epigrams in sequence.

One Cannot Grasp God

God is the purest naught, untouched by time and space;
The more you reach for Him, the more He will escape. (25)

One Abyss Calls the Other

The abyss that is my soul invokes unceasingly
The abyss that is my God. Which may the deeper be? (68)

God Blossoms in His Branches

If you are born of God, then in you God will green;
His Godhead is your sap, your beauty is in Him. (81)

The Godhead Brings Forth Growth

The Godhead is my sap; what in me greens and flowers
It is the Holy Ghost who all the growth empowers. (90)

Christ

Oh, what a marvel! Christ is both Shepherd and Lamb,
When God within my soul today is born a man. (101)

Spiritual Alchemy

Myself I am the metal, spirit the furnace fires,
Messiah is the dye that body and soul inspires. (103)

The Rose

The rose which here on earth is now perceived by me,
Has blossomed thus in God from all eternity. (108)

The Creatures

If creatures do subsist in God's eternal Son
How can they perish then, or ever naught become? (109)

The Godhead Is a Naught

The tender Godhead is a naught and more than naught;
Who nothing sees in all, believe me, he sees God. (111)

I Must Be Sun

Myself I must be sun, whose rays must paint the sea,
The vast and unhued ocean of all divinity. (115)

The Symbol of the Trinity

Mind, Spirit, and the Word, they teach you clear and free,
That you may apprehend how God is One, yet Three. (148)

Eternal Wisdom

Eternal wisdom goes where all her children dwell.
But why? How marvelous! A child she is as well. (165)

The Sweetest Revelry

Oh, sweetest revelry! God, has become my wine,
Meat, table, serving man, my music when I dine. (207)

I, like God, God like Me

God is that which He is; I am that which I am;
And if you know one well, you know both me and Him. (212)

The Silent Prayer

God far exceeds all words that we can here express
In silence He is heard, in silence worshiped best. (240)

The Tincture

The Holy Spirit smelts, the Father does consume,
The Son the tincture* is, which gilds and does transmute. (246)

This Is the Day of Salvation

Arise, the bridegroom comes! And none shall he possess,
But the beloved bride who stands in readiness. (260)

God Is Unfathomable

So rich the Godhead is in Its diversity
That It can never plumb Its own depth utterly. (263)

Creatures Are God's Echo

Nothing is without voice: God everywhere can hear
Arising from creation His praise and echo clear. (264)

---

*In esoteric alchemy, Christ was equated with the "Tincture," also known as the "Elixir" or the "Philosophers' Stone." See Introduction, p. xix.

One Thing Alone Does Not Always Satisfy

My friend, if all together we utter but one tone,
What music would that be, all sung in monotone? (267)

Diversity Is Pleasing

The more we let each voice sound forth with its own tone,
The more diverse will be the chant in unison. (268)

The Voice of God

Creatures are but the voice of the Eternal Word:
It sings and sounds its self, in sweetness and in dread. (270)

The End of God

That God shall have no end, I never will admit,
Behold, He seeks my soul, that He may rest in it. (277)

One Must Go beyond Thought

What Cherubim may know will never bring me peace
Outstrip I must all thought, the highest goal to reach. (284)

Without Why

The rose does have no why; it blossoms without reason,
Forgetful of itself, oblivious to our vision. (289)

The Saints' Reward

What is the saints' reward? What ours after death?
It is the lily flower of purest godliness. (292)

From Book Two

The Bride Is the Most Cherished

Say what you will, the bride is the most cherished child,
Whom one finds in God's womb and in His arms enshrined. (10)

The Greatest Security

Slumber my soul and sleep, in the wounds of your lover,
You will security and sweet repose discover. (11)

Proper Use Does Not Bring Loss

Man, if you say that things keep you from loving God,
Then you don't use the world in quite the way you ought. (34)

The Inexpressible

You think that you may utter the name of God in time?
It is not even uttered throughout eternity. (51)

God's Spiritual Temple

The portals of your city are wrought so pearl-fine,
A flash must be my spirit, your temple and your shrine (79)

Eternity

What is eternity? It is not This nor That,
Not Now, no Thing, no Naught; it is I know not what. (153)

What Is Sanctity?

True sanctity of spirit is like a glass of gold
Wholly polished and pure; observe what you behold (211)

The Seraphic Life

With love to walk and stand, love breathe and speak and sing
That is to spend your life as do the Seraphim (254)

The Five Spheres in God

Five spheres there are in God: serf, friend, son, bride, and spouse.
Who goes beyond becomes oblivious of those. (255)

From Book Three

God-Man

Reflect! God becomes me, entering earth's misery,
That I enter His realm and may become as He. (20)

The Spiritual Sulamite

God is my Solomon, I am His Sulamite;*
When I adhere to Him, He will in me delight. (78)

You Must Blossom Now

Awake, O wintry Christian! May greens before your gate.
If now you grow not verdant, death surely be your fate. (90)

The Secret Rose

The rose is like my soul, the thorn is carnal lust,
The spring is like God's grace, His wrath is cold and frost,
The blossoms are good works, the thorns contempt of flesh,
With virtue it is adorned, in heaven it seeks rest.
In the fullness of time, when spring it has become,
God's rose it will then be, the only chosen one. (91)

The Secret Kingdom

I am a mighty realm, my heart is the high throne,
The soul reigns as its Queen, the King is God's own Son. (131)

God Dwells in Calm

O Man, becalm your heart; God is not in great sound,
In tremblings of the earth,† or conflagrations found. (142)

The Wondrous Birth

The Virgin is a crystal, her Son celestial light;
Wholly she is pierced by Him and yet stays unimpaired. (242)

From Book Four

The Unknowable God

One knows not what God is. Not spirit and not light,
Not one, truth, unity, not what we call divine.
Not reason and not wisdom, not goodness, love, or will,

*The name of King Solomon's beloved in the Song of Songs.
†Cf. 1 Kings 19:11f.

No thing, no no-thing either, not being or concern.
He is what I or you, or any other creature
Has never come to know before we were created. (21)

On the Wounds of Christ

I look upon Christ's wounds as wide celestial gates
And know that I can enter through the five safest places.
How may I come straightway to stand close to my God?
I shall through feet and hands enter the heart of love. (46)

Virtue

Virtue, the wise man says, is its own best reward.
If he means here and now, I am not in accord. (90)

The Inscrutable Cause

God is all to Himself, His Heaven and His bliss.
Why are we then created? We cannot answer this. (126)

God's Wandering Canopy

The soul in which God dwells is (Oh, wondrous delight!)
A wandering canopy of the eternal light. (219)

From Book Five

The Distance to Heaven

Christian, do not believe that Heaven is so distant;
The path that leads to it takes nothing but an instant. (67)

One Discovers God in Leisure

God comes more readily if He finds you in leisure
Than if you spend yourself in strenuous endeavor. (195)

Equanimity

The Saint deems it the same: If God lets him lie ill,
He thanks Him just as much as he were sound and well. (227)

Three Kinds of Birth

The Virgin bears the Son of God externally,
I inwardly in spirit, the Father eternally. (249)

God's Birth Persists Forever

God does beget His Son: He does this timelessly,
And hence this birth persists throughout eternity. (251)

Translated by Maria Shrady

ACKNOWLEDGMENTS

Every reasonable effort has been made to locate the owners of rights to previously published works and the translations printed here. We gratefully acknowledge permission to reprint the following material:

Paulist Press for excerpts from *The Cherubinic Wanderer* by Angelus Silesius, translated by Maria Shrady with introduction and notes by Josef Schmidt; *Johannes Tauler: Sermons*, translated by Maria Shrady; *The Theologia Germanica of Martin Luther*, translated by Bengt Hoffman; *The Way of Christ* by Jakob Boehme, translated by Peter Erb.

HarperCollins Publishers for excerpts from *Meister Eckhart: A Modern Translation*, translated by Raymond Bernard Blakney. Copyright © 1941 by Harper & Row.

Constable Publishers for excerpts from *On the Election of Grace* by Jakob Boehme, translated by John Rolleston Earle. Copyright © Constable and Company, 1930.

THE GERMAN LIBRARY
in 100 Volumes

Friedrich Hölderlin
Hyperion and *Selected Poems*
Edited by Eric L. Santner

Philosophy of German Idealism
Edited by Ernst Behler

G. W. F. Hegel
*Encyclopedia of the Philosophical Sciences
in Outline and Critical Writings*
Edited by Ernst Behler

Heinrich von Kleist
Plays
Edited by Walter Hinderer
Foreword by E. L. Doctorow

E. T. A. Hoffmann
Tales
Edited by Victor Lange

Georg Büchner
Complete Works and Letters
Edited by Walter Hinderer and Henry J. Schmidt

German Fairy Tales
Edited by Helmut Brackert and Volkmar Sander
Foreword by Bruno Bettelheim

German Literary Fairy Tales
Edited by Frank G. Ryder and Robert M. Browning
Introduction by Gordon Birrell
Foreword by John Gardner

F. Grillparzer, J. H. Nestroy, F. Hebbel
Nineteenth Century German Plays
Edited by Egon Schwarz in collaboration with
Hannelore M. Spence

Heinrich Heine
Poetry and Prose
Edited by Jost Hermand and Robert C. Holub
Foreword by Alfred Kazin

Heinrich Heine
The Romantic School and other Essays
Edited by Jost Hermand and Robert C. Holub

Heinrich von Kleist and Jean Paul
German Romantic Novellas
Edited by Frank G. Ryder and Robert M. Browning
Foreword by John Simon

German Romantic Stories
Edited by Frank Ryder
Introduction by Gordon Birrell

German Poetry from 1750 to 1900
Edited by Robert M. Browning
Foreword by Michael Hamburger

Karl Marx, Friedrich Engels, August Bebel, and others
German Essays on Socialism in the Nineteenth Century
Edited by Frank Mecklenburg and Manfred Stassen

Gottfried Keller
Stories
Edited by Frank G. Ryder
Foreword by Max Frisch

Wilhelm Raabe
Novels
Edited by Volkmar Sander
Foreword by Joel Agee

Theodor Fontane
Short Novels and other Writings
Edited by Peter Demetz
Foreword by Peter Gay

Theodor Fontane
Delusions, Confusions and The Poggenpuhl Family
Edited by Peter Demetz
Foreword by J. P. Stern
Introduction by William L. Zwiebel

Wilhelm Busch and others
German Satirical Writings
Edited by Dieter P. Lotze and Volkmar Sander
Foreword by John Simon

Writings of German Composers
Edited by Jost Hermand and James Steakley

German Lieder
Edited by Philip Lieson Miller

Arthur Schnitzler
Plays and Stories
Edited by Egon Schwarz
Foreword by Stanley Elkin

Rainer Maria Rilke
Prose and Poetry
Edited by Egon Schwarz
Foreword by Howard Nemerov

Robert Musil
Selected Writings
Edited by Burton Pike
Foreword by Joel Agee

Essays on German Theater
Edited by Margaret Herzfeld-Sander
Foreword by Martin Esslin

German Novellas of Realism I and II
Edited by Jeffrey L. Sammons

Friedrich Dürrenmatt
Plays and Essays
Edited by Volkmar Sander
Foreword by Martin Esslin

Max Frisch
Novels, Plays, Essays
Edited by Rolf Kieser
Foreword by Peter Demetz

Gottfried Benn
Prose, Essays, Poems
Edited by Volkmar Sander
Foreword by E. B. Ashton
Introduction by Reinhard Paul Becker

German Essays on Art History
Edited by Gert Schiff

German Radio Plays
Edited by Everett Frost and Margaret Herzfeld-Sander

Hans Magnus Enzensberger
Critical Essays
Edited by Reinhold Grimm and Bruce Armstrong
Foreword by John Simon

All volumes available in hardcover and paperback editions at your bookstore or from the publisher. For more information on The German Library write to: The Continuum Publishing Company, 370 Lexington Avenue, New York, NY 10017.